Rethinking Foreign Investment for Sustainable Development

Rethinking Foreign Investment for Sustainable Development

Lessons from Latin America

Edited by
KEVIN P. GALLAGHER
DANIEL CHUDNOVSKY

Foreword by
JOSÉ ANTONIO OCAMPO

ANTHEM PRESS
LONDON · NEW YORK · DELHI

Anthem Press
An imprint of Wimbledon Publishing Company
www.anthempress.com

This edition first published in UK and USA 2009
by ANTHEM PRESS
75–76 Blackfriars Road, London SE1 8HA, UK
or PO Box 9779, London SW19 7ZG, UK
and
244 Madison Ave. #116, New York, NY 10016, USA

British Library Cataloguing in Publication Data
A catalogue record for this book is available from the British Library.

Library of Congress Cataloging-in-Publication Data

Rethinking foreign investment for sustainable development : lessons for Latin America/
edited by Kevin P. Gallagher & Daniel Chudnovsky; forward by José Antonio Ocampo.
p. cm.
ISBN-13: 978-1-84331-316-8 (hardcover : alk. paper)
ISBN-10: 1-84331-316-2 (hardcover : alk. paper)
ISBN-13: 978-1-84331-324-3 (e-book)
ISBN-10: 1-84331-324-3 (e-book)
1. Sustainable development—Latin America. 2. Investments, Foreign—Latin America.
3. Sustainable development—Environmental aspects—Latin America.
I. Gallagher, Kevin, 1968- II. Chudnovsky, Daniel.

HC130.E5R45 2009
338.98'07—dc22
2008046194

ISBN-13: 978 1 84331 316 8 (Hbk)
ISBN-10: 1 84331 316 2 (Hbk)

ISBN-13: 978 1 84331 324 3 (Ebk)
ISBN-10: 1 84331 324 3 (Ebk)

1 3 5 7 9 10 8 6 4 2

TABLE OF CONTENTS

LIST OF FIGURES

LIST OF TABLES

FOREWORD

This volume is a major contribution to a growing body of literature that questions the assumptions of market reforms undertaken in Latin America in recent decades, on the basis that market reforms did not deliver on their basic promise: rapid economic growth. Indeed, even when we take into account the recent period of exceptional conditions in international commodity and capital markets that has facilitated rapid growth in Latin America since 2004, the rate of GDP growth in the region has been 3.3 percent from 1990 to 2007 (and only 2.5 percent if the point of reference is 1980), far short of that achieved during the phase of import-substitution industrialization—or, as I prefer to call it, state-led industrialization—when Latin America grew at an average rate of 5.5 percent a year. Another set of criticisms relates, of course, to the disappointing social effects of market reforms. Again, a simple reflection of this fact is that only in 2005 did Latin America return to the poverty levels of 1980—i.e., the region experienced not a decade, but a quarter century lost in terms of poverty reduction.

The volume concentrates on one of the major aspects of the globalization and liberalization processes: the growing role played by multinational corporations (MNCs) and the opening up of the Latin American economies to foreign direct investment (FDI). Drawing on case studies from about half of the countries in the region, it explores the determinants of FDI, the role that it has played in advancing environmental sustainability, and some political economy issues associated with such investments. The editors are correct in claiming that the volume, for the first time, collects, synthesizes and analyzes in the English language the rich academic and policy discussions that have taken place in Latin America over the past two decades on these issues, and asks for a fundamental rethinking of the role of FDI in development.

I thus feel deeply honored to have been asked to write this forward. I am, furthermore, deeply moved by the fact that one of its editors and a dear friend, Daniel Chudnovsky, died shortly after this book was finished. I thus write this forward in his memory.

A Bit of History

The relations between FDI and development in Latin America have a long history, which has been the subject by heated economic and political debates. Latin America was very open to foreign investment since Independence, and all countries in the region actively promoted FDI in the nineteenth and early twentieth centuries, particularly in the exploitation of natural resources and the development of its infrastructure.

Later, largely as a result of the major slowdown of world economic growth and commodity prices in the interwar period, and the virtual collapse of the world economy in the 1930s and during the Second World War, development patterns became much more inward-oriented. Initially, such a reorientation was, therefore, more a result of external circumstances than of policy design. However, it turned gradually into an explicit development strategy, which was rationalized in the early postwar years by the United Nations Economic Commission for Latin America and the Caribbean (CEPAL, for its Spanish acronym).

Interestingly, although the state-led industrialization strategy that emerged took a mixed view on the opportunities that natural resource-based exports provided for development, such pessimism was initially *not* extended to foreign direct investment. Indeed, a policy of promoting investment by MNCs in new industrial activities became a central ingredient of state-led industrialization in Latin America. FDI was furthermore seen as a reliable source of private external financing in a world economy that offered, in the early postwar years, few opportunities of that sort. However, many countries in the region simultaneously took an increasingly hard line against the more traditional forms of foreign investment in natural resources and infrastructure, which were seen with skepticism in terms of development in the first instance, and the natural domain of the state in the case of infrastructure. The purchase by Perón of British investments in the Argentinean railroads was a landmark in this regard. Thus, during the early years of state-led industrialization, Latin America did not reject FDI, so long as it contributed to its industrialization.

The revalorization of the role of exports, particularly since the 1960s, was accompanied by a more mixed view of foreign direct investment. This was reflected in the limits placed on royalties and profit remittances, associated with the view that MNCs were getting excessive benefits from their investments in the region and the partial or full nationalization of foreign investment in natural resources and, in some case, other sectors. The nationalizations of the copper industry in Chile and of the oil industry in Venezuela in the early 1970s were some of the most important manifestations of this process, as the nationalization of the oil industry in Mexico in 1938 had been an earlier landmark.[1] But, contrary to the usual criticism that Latin American had underutilized the opportunities provided by FDI during its period of state-industrialization, the opposite is actually true, as reflected in the fact that in 1973–1981 Latin America received close to 70 per cent of all FDI flows to the developing world.[2]

Market Reforms and FDI

The liberalization process opened up the economies of the region to foreign direct investment, with very few exceptions. Foreign investment became intrinsically tied with the emerging patterns of integration into the world economy, which broadly followed two dominant patterns. A "Northern" regional pattern, shared by Mexico, several Central American and some Caribbean countries, is characterized by manufacturing exports with high content of imported inputs (in its extreme form, *maquila*), mainly geared towards the United States market. This pattern goes hand in hand with traditional agricultural exports and agricultural export diversification in Central America, as well as the growth of tourism in Mexico and the Caribbean. The "Southern" pattern, typical of South American countries, is characterized by a combination of extra-regional exports of commodities and natural-resource-intensive (and, in many cases, also capital-intensive) manufactures, and active intra-regional trade dominated by manufactures. In the case of Brazil, this has been mixed with some technology-intensive manufactures and services. There is also a third pattern of specialization, in Panama and several Caribbean economies, in which service exports (financial, tourism and transport services) predominate.

The "Northern" specialization pattern attracted MNCs actively involved in internationally integrated production systems, whereas in South America, investment has concentrated in services and natural resources. In the terminology of this volume, whereas the first pattern attracted more "efficiency-seeking" investments, the latter was more biased towards "natural resource-seeking" and "market-seeking" foreign investments. FDI has included large shares of acquisitions of existing assets, first through privatization and then through private buyouts. A corollary of this process was the rapid increase in participation of foreign firms in production and sales, at the expense of public-sector firms in the first half of the 1990s, and of both public and private firms in the second half.[3]

The liberalization process was also accompanied by the transformation of large domestic firms into foreign investors, mostly to other countries in the region, but in the case of a few large firms, into global players. This involved, interestingly, some firms that remained totally or partially state-owned. The Mexican and, with some lag, the Brazilian firms became the largest players in this game, but some Chilean and Colombian companies were also important in the regional arena.

A simple way to understand why this very active and, in a sense, successful process of export development and inward and outward investment did not generate rapid overall economic growth is that the multiplier effect and the technological externalities generated by these high-growth activities have been weak.[4] Indeed, in many cases the new dynamic activities became mere "enclaves" of globalized production networks with few links with the rest of the countries where they were located.

Slow growth was therefore matched by poor productivity performance. Productivity did increase in dynamic firms and sectors. However, contrary to the expectations of reformers, positive productivity shocks did not spread. The growing number of "world-class" firms, many of them subsidiaries of MNCs, was therefore accompanied by the growth of low-productivity informal-sector activities, which accounted for seven out of every ten new jobs created in Latin American urban areas over the 1990s and most of them during the "lost half-decade" of 1998–2003. This pattern was only reversed during the boom that started in 2004. This growing dualism in productive structures also reflects the fact that restructuring was not neutral in terms of its impact on different economic agents, and had therefore deep distributive effects.

The Contributions of This Volume

On this background, the authors of this volume analyze whether the promise of reformers that opening to FDI would become a source of dynamic growth has been fulfilled. Beyond directly boosting exports and economic activity, the hope was that MNCs would bring knowledge spillovers that would build the skill and technological capacities of local firms, as well as the diffusion of the best environmental practices in the world. The real prize in FDI was, in this sense, the potential for "spillovers" in the form of human capital formation, demonstration and competition effects, backward and forward linkages and improved environmental standards.

The authors first analyze the determinants of FDI into the region during the liberalization period. Interestingly, they find that some of the most significant determinants of FDI flows to the region in recent decades— market size and economic growth and, therefore, market access—were similar to the determinants of those investments during the period of state-led industrialization. A second determinant was more specific to the recent phase of development: export orientation. As pointed out previously, this factor affected not only the quantity but also the nature of investments into specific countries. Political and macroeconomic stability also played a role, as reflected in the latter case by the negative association between FDI and the level of inflation and/or the level of external debt of the receiving country.

Interestingly, however, the authors do not find strong evidence that trade and investment agreements have an independent effect on FDI flows in the region, putting into question the benefits of the boom of regional and bilateral trade and investment agreement (RBTIA) that has taken place in the region. At best, they argue, the impact of bilateral investment treaties (BITs) on FDI is small and secondary to the effects of other determinants, especially market size. They also find no evidence that Latin America's relatively weaker environmental regulations vis-à-vis those of industrial countries served as an independent determinant of FDI flows, indicating, in this sense, the region has not been a "pollution haven."

Most importantly, in my view, the authors find what they call "almost unanimous evidence that FDI resulted in very limited productivity spillovers for the region. Indeed, the boom of FDI in the 1990s coincided with a period in which domestic investment actually fell, suggesting, according to one of authors, that FDI could have actually "crowded out" domestic investment, by wiping out locally competing firms—a pattern that is in sharp contrast with the evidence for East Asia. The close analysis of microeconomic and sectoral data indicates, on the other hand, that foreign firms tend to have higher levels of productivity and higher wages, as well as positive effects on trade, but that they fall far short of generating "spillovers" and backward linkages and, as noted, may have even "crowded out" domestic investment. The use of tax incentives to attract FDI is another negative spillover. In terms of the hypothetical effect on macroeconomic stability, particularly of bringing capital flows that are less pro-cyclical, the evidence is also mixed; whereas FDI remained resilient to the recession that started in 1998, this was not true in the early 2000s and its performance over the past two decades has been, broadly speaking, pro-cyclical.

The chapters on FDI and the environment, although somewhat mixed in their conclusions, are, overall, positive in their evaluation of foreign investment. It is found that MNCs play a positive role in transferring clean technology, particularly environmental management systems to countries in the region, and in diffusing some good practices through the supply chain, including labeling schemes. Nonetheless, this seems strongly associated with the environmental standards set by consumer movements in the industrial world—and thus stronger in the case of exports to Europe. On the less positive side, the authors find that the transferred technologies and management practices fell short of best practice in several cases, and find no evidence that foreign firms are more apt to be in compliance with domestic environmental laws than domestic firms.

The volume ends with two chapters that focus on the changing political economy of FDI and natural resources in the region. The first, associated with the resurgence of the role of the public sector in the hydrocarbon sector in three left-leaning Andean countries, find that MNCs have generally decided to negotiate with new governments instead of making use of the rights to protection and arbitration they acquired during the liberalization phase through bilateral investment treaties. The second, dealing with the conflict between Argentina and Uruguay derived from the installation of large paper-pulp-producing plants in the banks of the frontier river, indicates that the conflict reflects less the true environmental nature of the problem than the weakness of the regional institutions for economic cooperation.

On the basis of this analysis, Gallagher, Chudnovsky and other authors of this volume draw three broad lessons, which I find very appealing. The first is that FDI has the potential to increase exports and competitiveness of firms while also generating technological and other spillovers, but in the absence of appropriate policies, it can also lock a nation into low-value-added assembly manufacturing, create "enclaves" where foreign firms operate on high-productivity islands devoid of spillovers, and even crowd out domestic investment. As a result, the capture of spillovers requires a proactive, coherent government industry policy that upgrades the capabilities of national firms and provides benchmarks for environmental protection. Finally, since the room to maneuver that international agreements provide to do so has been increasingly constrained by international agreements of global (WTO), regional or bilateral character, the authors claim that that those agreements should provide developing nations the "policy space" for active domestic policies necessary to foster development, including policies aimed at increasing the benefits from FDI.

A Broader Reading of These Results

This leads me to some considerations on the role of FDI in the process of global convergence or divergence of levels of development, which was analyzed in the United Nations report that I had the opportunity to coordinate, together with other colleagues.[5] The report argued that the specific strategies that countries follow to integrate their economies into the global markets for goods and services, and to attract foreign investment, largely determine the extent of the benefits those countries derive from enhanced trade and investment flows. Particularly important in this regard is whether production for the world market and by MNCs creates sufficient linkages with other domestic sectors and firms, so that these activities allow for a dynamic transformation of the economy. In this context, FDI, when properly managed and incorporated into a strategy aiming at the continuous upgrading of the country's technological capacities, can bring lasting benefits, but success in capturing certain investments (such as assembly tasks) may not lead to rapid or sustained growth if these activities have limited value added. They are also likely to be footloose.

A key determinant of whether or not such FDI will reduce global income inequalities is the establishment of the dynamic investment-export nexus that emerged in the success stories in East Asia and led to a steady diversification of production away from those activities requiring only natural resources and unskilled labour. A good deal depends, as Gallagher and Chudnovsky argue in this volume, on whether FDI brings increased technological and organizational spillovers to developing countries and crowds in local private investment. To date, the evidence does not support the claim that such a nexus exists in most parts of the developing world. Indeed, in many cases, very dynamic investment has been associated with very limited increases in domestic incomes and value added, not least because FDI cross-border linkages are many times strengthened at the expense of domestic ones. One of the reflections of this fact is that FDI and domestic capital formation have been moving in different directions in the 1990s; as FDI flows increased, domestic investment rates declined or stagnated in many parts of the developing word. This is consistent with the evidence that "crowding out" of domestic investment by FDI is more prevalent in the developing world that "crowding in," and is part of the broader conclusion that, on balance, the empirical evidence of positive spillover effects of FDI is inconclusive. This volume presents strong evidence that these results are valid for Latin America.

The report therefore concludes, as this volume does, that in order to profit from FDI, countries need to have the necessary absorptive capacity among domestic firms and institutions. Countries where an inflow of FDI has been paralleled by significant investments in building domestic capabilities (for example, Singapore and Ireland) have been the most successful in leveraging inward FDI. Conversely, when FDI is attracted in response to major tax incentives, or as a result of trade policy distortions (such as textile and clothing quotas), without a simultaneous buildup of local capabilities and without the creation of linkages between foreign affiliates and local firms, there is limited scope for long-term benefits from FDI. In this sense, *domestic* market integration—including creating the linkages between the activities of FDI with those of domestic firms—is at least as important as integration in international markets, and is indeed essential for the latter to succeed.

The successful post-war experiences of Eastern Asia and its integration into the global economy resulted from well-targeted trade and sectoral policies that constantly and consistently promoted the building up of technological capabilities. The space for these interventions is not absent but has been significantly reduced in recent decades. Therefore, policy space should not be reduced further and perhaps some of the current disciplines need to be reassessed in terms of their true value for development.

José Antonio Ocampo

ACKNOWLEDGEMENTS

Although this volume is listed as edited by Daniel Chudnovsky and myself, it is the product of The Working Group on Development and Environment in the Americas, founded in 2004, bringing together economists and political scientists from several countries in the Americas who have carried out empirical studies of the social and environmental impacts of economic liberalization. The goal of the Working Group Project is to contribute empirical research and policy analysis to the ongoing policy debates on national economic development strategies and international trade. The project also brings more prominently into US policy debates, the rich body of research carried out by Latin American experts, as well as their informed perspectives on trade and development policies.

Daniel Chudnovsky and I both participated in the first working group report and book on the environment in 2004. We subsequently went on to conduct original research on the impact of foreign investment in Latin America under the Washington Consensus. In 2005 Daniel and I started talking about putting together a similar effort on the impacts of foreign investment in the region. We put together the great group of economists exhibited in these pages, commissioned the chapters you will find here, and set out to identify the major themes across the chapters and to begin writing the introduction to the volume. Daniel fell suddenly ill in late 2006 and passed away in early 2007. This volume is in memoriam to him and dedicated to Daniel and his wonderful wife and daughter who survive him.

Daniel Chudnovsky earned his PhD in economics from Oxford University and was most recently Professor of International Business and Development Economics at the University of San Andrés and Director of the Centro de Investigaciones para la Transformación (CENIT) in Argentina. During his career, Daniel worked as Professor of Economic Development at the University of Buenos Aires, as an economist for the United Nations Conference on Trade and Development (UNCTAD) in Geneva, and as the Director of the Centro de Economía Internacional, in Argentina. He was loved and admired by scholars and policymakers across the globe.

One such scholar and policymaker is José Antonio Ocampo. Dr. Ocampo knew and collaborated with Daniel for close to thirty years. When Dr. Ocampo heard about this volume he quickly agreed to write the foreword in Daniel's honor. We thank José Antonio Ocampo for this very much.

This international collaboration was created by many people and organizations, in addition to members of the Working Group on Development and Environment in the Americas. We also thank the numerous foundations that provided support for the research that went into this report: the Ford Foundation, Rockefeller Brothers Fund, The Charles Stewart Mott Foundation, and the General Service Foundation.

Roberto Porzecanski, a pre-doctoral fellow at the Global Development and Environment Institute (GDAE) at Tufts University deserves special thanks. Roberto has faithfully served as the coordinator of this project, providing assistance on everything from background research and writing, to editing, translation and logistics. The project could not have been completed without his hard work and cheerful attitude.

Tej Sood and the wonderful staff at Anthem Press who have brought this project to completion are to be thanked as well.

Tufts University's Global Development and Environment Institute is where the working group project is 'housed' and deserves great thanks. This volume is part of a larger project between GDAE, CENIT, and Research and Information Systems for Developing Countries (RIS) in Delhi, India. Andrés López has succeeded Daniel as the Director of CENIT and now serves with me as the co-chair of these efforts along with Nagesh Kumar at RIS. I thank the both of them and Timothy Wise at GDAE for their commitment to this work and their friendship throughout.

I thank Boston University for providing a home for my teaching and research throughout this project. The creative thinking and discussions with my students and colleagues in the Department of International Relations that I encounter on a daily basis at Boston University are a constant inspiration. My work as a research fellow at the Frederick Pardee Center for the Study of the Longer-Range Future has also provided additional financial support and creative inspiration for this effort as well.

Finally, I thank my wife Kelly Sims Gallagher and son Theodore Sims Gallagher for the utmost joy, inspiration and love that fills my life.

Kevin P. Gallagher

AUTHOR BIOGRAPHIES

José Antonio Ocampo Professor of Professional Practice in International and Public Affairs, Colombia University. Prior to his appointment, Professor Ocampo served in a number of positions in the Government of Colombia— most notably as United Nations Under-Secretary-General for Economic and Social Affairs; Executive Secretary of the Economic Commission for Latin America and the Caribbean (ECLAC); Minister of Finance and Public Credit, Chairman of the Board of Banco del República (Central Bank of Colombia); Director, National Planning Department (Minister of Planning); Minister of Agriculture and Rural Development, Chairman of the Board of Banco Cafetero (Coffee Bank) and Caja de Crèdito Agraria, Industrial y Minera (Agrarian Bank) and Executive Director, FEDESARROLLO. Dr. Ocampo received his B.A. in Economics and Sociology from the University of Notre Dame and his Ph.D. in Economics from Yale University, 1976. He was a Professor in the Advanced Programme on Rethinking Development Economics at Cambridge University, a Professor of Economics at Universidad de los Andes, a Professor of Economic History at the National University of Colombia, as well as a Visiting Fellow at Yale and Oxford. He is the author of numerous books and articles on macroeconomics policy and theory, economic development, international trade and economic history. His recent publications include *Stability with Growth:Macroeconomics, Liberalization and Development*, with Joseph E. Stiglitz, Shari Spiegel, Ricardo French-Davis and Deepak Nayyar, (New York: Oxford University Press, 2006).

Manuel R. Agosin A specialist in International Economics and Macro-economics, he is currently Professor, Department of Economics, University of Chile, a post he has held since 1992. He also works on a regular basis for the Inter-American Development Bank as Consultant. Between 2001 and early 2006 he was Chief Economist for Central America, Dominican Republic, Haiti and Mexico at the Inter-American Development Bank in Washington, D.C. He holds a Ph.D. from Columbia University and a first degree from the University of Chile. He has been economic advisor to several Latin American governments and a consultant to the United Nations and international financial institutions. He has published several books in Spanish and English and is the author of numerous articles published in international journals.

Martina Chidiak An economist (from Argentina) with special interest and background in both Industrial and Environmental Economics. Graduated from the University of Buenos Aires, with further studies at University College London (MSc in Environmental and Resource Economics) and Ecole des Mines de Paris (Docteur, specialité Economie Industrielle). Research and consultancy experience mostly focused on Climate Change, Firms' Environmental Management, Public-Private Partnerships (Voluntary Agreements) and International Trade and Environment issues. Previous engagements as consultant to international organizations (such as ECLAC, GTZ and JICA) and government bodies (European Commission; ADEME, France; Environmental Secretariat, Argentina). Currently works as independent consultant. As of March 2007, Lecturer in Environmental Economics (University of Buenos Aires).

Daniel Chudnovsky Daniel Chudnovsky (1944–2007) was Director of the Centro de Investigaciones para la Transformación (CENIT) and Professor at the Universidad de San Andrés. He worked as an economist for UNCTAD in Geneva, Switzerland, and as the first Director of the Center for International Economics in Buenos Aires. He was Director of CENIT (Centro de Investigaciones para la Transformación) since its foundation. He directed several international research projects and was a consultant to ECLAC, UNCTAD, UNIDO, IADB, INTAL, the World Bank, IDRC, the Development Centre of the OECD and the UNDP. He was Full Professor at University of San Andrés, where he taught courses on Development Economics, International Business and Technological Innovation in undergraduate and postgraduate programs.

Andrés López Andrés López is currently the Director of the Centro de Investigaciones para la Transformación (CENIT), where he has been working since 1991. He has been consultant of various international institutions, such as ECLAC, UNCTAD, IADB, INTAL, IDRC, WIPO, JICA and UNPD. He is also Associate Professor at the University of Buenos Aires, where he teaches courses in undergraduate and postgraduate programs. Furthermore, he is Professor in graduate and postgraduate programs at the Universities of San Andrés and General Sarmiento and in FLACSO.

José Cordero José Antonio Cordero is Professor of Economics at the University of Costa Rica, where he was Director of the Economics Department from 2001 to 2005. He is presently Visiting Professor at Mount Holyoke College, Massachusetts, USA.

Eva Paus Eva Paus is Professor of Economics and the Carol Hoffmann Collins Director of the McCulloch Center for Global Initiatives at Mount Holyoke College, Massachusetts, USA. She has published widely on different aspects of globalization and development. Her most recent publications include *Global Capitalism Unbound: Winners and Losers from Offshore Outsourcing* (Palgrave Macmillan, 2007), and *Foreign Investment, Development, and Globalization. Can Costa Rica Become Ireland?* (Palgrave Macmillan 2005, University of Costa Rica Press, 2007). Her current research projects focus on the implications of the rise of China for the development prospects of (other) developing countries, the dilemma of policy space for proactive development policies under current international multilateral and bilateral trade agreements, and the role of foreign investment in the development of recent EU accession countries.

Nicola Borregaard Nicola Borregaard holds a PhD in Land Economy from Cambridge University, and a Master in Economics from The State University of New York at Albany. She has created the Environmental Economics Unit in the National Commission on Environment in Chile; was Executive Director of the Centro de Investigación y Planificación del Medio Ambiente, CIPMA; and one of the founders and Executive Director of Recursos e Investigación para el Desarrollo Sustentable (RIDES). Since 2004, she has worked as Advisor to the Chilean Minister of Economy, and in 2006 was appointed Director of the National Energy Efficiency Program. She is author of numerous publications in the area of environmental economics, and trade and environment.

Lucy Winchester Agricultural Economist (MA, Michigan State University, USA), currently freelance consultant in sustainable development in Chile and Latin America. Previously Expert to Sustainable Development and Human Settlements Division, Economic Commission for Latin America and the Caribbean, and Senior Researcher to SUR, Centre for Social Studies and Education (Chilean Independent Research and Training Centre). Specialist in evaluation of public policies and programs in social policy, urban and municipal development, and poverty. Consultant to United Nations Commission for Sustainble Development, UN-Habitat, Chilean Government, among others.

Leonardo Stanley Economist, School of Economic and Social Sciences, Universidad de Mar del Plata. Programa de Teoría Económica, Instituto de Desarrollo Económico y Social, Buenos Aires (1992–1993). MA in Science in Economics, Queen Mary & Westfield, London University, United Kingdom (1994–1995). Diplome d'Etudes Approfondies en Analyse Economique: Modélisation et Méthodes Quantitatives, Universidad de Evry Val-d'Essone,

France (1998–2000). Visiting Researcher in the Department of Economics, CEDES. Teaches at graduate and undergraduate levels in several universities and institutions.

Enrique Dussel Peters Enrique Dussel Peters, BA and MA studies in Political Science at the Free University of Berlin (1989) and PhD in Economics at the University of Notre Dame (1996). Since 1993 he works as a full time professor at the Graduate School of Economics at Universidad Autónoma Nacional de México (UNAM). He has taught more than 90 courses at the BA, MA and PhD level in Mexico and internationally, and participated in more than 260 national and international seminars and conferences. His research has concentrated on theory of industrial organization, economic development, political economy, as well as on the manufacturing sector, trade and regional specialization patters in Latin America and Mexico. He has collaborated and coordinated projects with Universidad National Autónoma de México (UNAM), Economic Commission for Latin America and the Caribbean (ECLAC), the International Labor Organization (ILO), Ford Foundation and the Inter-American Development Bank (IADB), among other institutions. He has received several research distinctions in 2000 and 2004.

Luciana Togeiro de Almeida Luciana Togeiro de Almeida is currently a Visiting Scholar at GDAE. She is a former President of the Brazilian Society for Ecological Economics (ECOECO) and current member of the ECOECO and ISEE boards. She holds a Doctorate in Economics from the Sao Paulo State University at Campinas and is Assistant Professor in the Department of Economics at the São Paulo State University at Araraquara, Brazil. She currently teaches Economics of the Environment, International Economics, Social and Economic Development, and International Trade and Sustainable Development. She is presently researching environmental issues in the WTO negotiations and in MERCOSUR. Her recent books include *Globalization and the Environment: Lessons from the Americas* (edited with Kevin P. Gallagher and Hernan Blanco), and she has published widely on trade and sustainable development issues in general. In addition, she has served as a consultant and advisor to the Brazilian Ministry of the Environment and to numerous environmental NGOs.

Celio Hiratuka Celio Hiratuka received his PhD. in economics from the State University of Campinas (UNICAMP), Brazil. His main fields of interest are international economics, technological change, industrial policy and development economics. He is currently Assistant Professor at the Institute of Economics of State University of Campinas and director of the Center of

Industrial and Technology Economics (NEIT) in the same University. His most recent works focus on the impacts of transnational corporations and foreign direct investment in the Brazilian economy. He is also member of the Mercosur Economic Research Network, a research institution that links twelve research centers with broad experience in the analysis of the MERCOSUR integration process.

Lyuba Zarsky Lyuba Zarsky is associate professor of international environmental policy at the Monterey Institute for International Studies, and Senior Research Fellow with GDAE's Globalization and Sustainable Development Program. She was formerly the Director of the Globalization and Governance Program at the Nautilus Institute for Security and Sustainability in Berkeley, California. She has written widely on global trade and investment, corporate accountability, and sustainable development, including the recent books, *Human Rights and the Environment: Conflicts and Norms in a Globalizing World*, and *Beyond Good Deeds: Case Studies and A New Policy Agenda for Corporate Accountability*. In addition, she has consulted with a number of international organizations, including the OECD Environment Directorate, the World Wide Fund for Nature, and the Asian Development Bank.

Kevin P. Gallagher Kevin P. Gallagher is Assistant Professor, Department of International Relations, Boston University. He is the author of *The Enclave Economy: Foreign Investment and Sustainable Development in Mexico's Silicon Valley* (with Lyuba Zarsky) and *Free Trade and the Environment: Mexico, NAFTA, and Beyond*, in addition to numerous reports, articles, and opinion pieces on trade policy, development and the environment. He has been the editor or co-editor for a number of books, including *Putting Development First: the Importance of Policy Space in the WTO and IFIs*, *International Trade and Sustainable Development* and others. Professor Gallagher is also a research associate at the Global Development and Environment Institute of the Fletcher School of Law and Diplomacy at Tufts University, an adjunct fellow at Research and Information System for Developing Countries in Delhi, India, and a member of the US-Mexico Futures Forum.

Roberto Porzecanski Roberto Porzecanski is a PhD Candidate at The Fletcher School of Law and Diplomacy and a PreDoctoral Fellow at the Global Development and Environment Institute, both at Tufts University.

Rethinking Foreign Investment for Sustainable Development

Chapter One

FDI AND SUSTAINABLE DEVELOPMENT IN THE AMERICAS

Kevin P. Gallagher, Daniel Chudnovsky and Roberto Porzecanski

Since the early 1980s nations in Latin America have been implementing a cluster of deep reforms to their economies. Referred to in the United States as the Washington Consensus and in Latin America as "neoliberalism," the reforms include a package of economic policies intended to promote economic development by opening national economies to global market forces. Over the last twenty-five years, governments throughout Latin America have reduced tariffs and other protectionist measures, eliminated barriers to foreign investment, restored "fiscal discipline" by reducing government spending and promoted the export sector of the economy (Williamson 1990).

Now, after 25 years of free-market reforms, many citizens in the hemisphere— and some governments—are questioning the wisdom of the Washington Consensus. Indeed, between October 2005 and December 2006, sixteen Latin American nations held either presidential or congressional elections. Nearly all of these contests have been referred to as referendum on the reforms. In many of the region's most significant economies—Argentina, Bolivia, Brazil, Chile, Uruguay, and Venezuela, candidates critical of the Washington Consensus prevailed. In other nations the outcome of the vote was so close that right-leaning governments at the very least have no mandate to deepen existing reforms.

This sea change in Latin American democracy has been portrayed in the Western press as an irrational resurgence by protectionists. However, a closer look at the record of the Washington Consensus shows that the concerns of citizens and governments can be justified. Indeed, the region has not experienced the economic growth that was promised would come as a result of the reforms. Economic growth has occurred at an annual rate of less than two percent between 1980 and 2005, compared to a rate of 5.5 percent between 1960 and 1980. Growth was faster during the 1990s than in the 1980s, but it still did not compare to the period previous to the reforms. Chile is the one exception, where growth rates almost doubled over the past twenty years compared to the 1960 to 1980 period. In addition, a debate has arisen over the extent to which Chile deviated significantly from Washington Consensus policies to achieve that growth.

The promise, among others, of following these policies is that FDI by multinational corporations will flow to your country and be a source of dynamic growth. Beyond boosting income and employment, the hope was that manufacturing FDI would bring knowledge spillovers that would build the skill and technological capacities of local firms, catalyzing broad-based economic growth, and environmental spillovers that would mitigate the domestic ecological impacts of industrial transformation.

This book evaluates the extent to which FDI fostered sustainable development in the Americas. Drawing on case studies from across the region—Argentina, Brazil, Bolivia, Chile, Costa Rica, Ecuador, Mexico, Uruguay, and Venezuela— the authors in this volume specifically look at how foreign investment during the reform period has affected economic growth, environmental policy and performance, and the countries' political economy. The authors have each authored numerous studies on the performance of FDI in their countries and region. Their chapters in this book synthesize that work and the work of others, most often for the first time in the English language. Hence, these chapters should not be seen as original research studies, but as synthesizing assessments of the situation in specific regions, written by leading in-country experts in the field. By and large, and consistent with the broader literature on the subject, the authors in this volume find that investment regime liberalization-led FDI has been a limited success at best in the Latin American case (for an exhaustive review of the literature, see Gallagher and Porzecanski (2007). In summary, we find that:

1. FDI was concentrated in a smaller handful of countries in the region.
2. FDI was attracted by traditional determinants, not whether a nation has a regional or bi-lateral trade and/or investment treaty (RBTIA) or if it can serve as a pollution haven for foreign firms.
3. When FDI did come, foreign firms tend to have higher levels of productivity and higher wages than were likely to increase trade in the region.
4. FDI fell far short of generating "spillovers" and backward linkages that help countries develop, and in many cases wiped out locally competing firms thereby "crowding out" domestic investment.

5. The environmental performance of foreign firms was mixed, in some cases leading to upgrading of environmental performance, and in others performing the same or worse than domestic counterparts.

It should be said up front that although this volume is highly critical of the performance of FDI under the Washington Consensus, the findings here should not be in any way be interpreted as recommending that FDI is not beneficial for sustainable development. Indeed, for economies to develop in a sustainable manner all forms of investment are crucial. The findings in this volume suggest that LAC (Latin America and the Caribbean) is simply not rising to the challenge to make FDI work for sustainable development. In order to rise to this challenge, the authors in this volume suggest three lessons for LAC and other developing countries seeking to successfully place FDI as part of a comprehensive development strategy:

1. FDI is not an end, but a means to sustainable development. A liberalization-led strategy will not automatically attract FDI nor generate economic growth in an environmentally sustainable manner when FDI does come.
2. FDI policy needs to be conducted in parallel with significant and targeted domestic policies that upgrade the capabilities of national firms and provide a benchmark of environmental protection.
3. International agreements, whether at the World Trade Organization (WTO) or at the level of RBTIAs, need to leave developing nations the "policy space" to pursue the domestic policies necessary to foster development through FDI.

This chapter is organized as follows: The first section provides an overview of FDI trends in LAC and the literature that examines the determinants of FDI in the region under the Washington Consensus. Section 2 outlines the theoretical framework regarding FDI and sustainable development and briefly reviews the literature on that subject. Section 3 consists of an outline of the volume as a whole and of an overview of the major findings. Finally, Section 4 suggests some policy recommendations to rectify the problems identified in the volume and suggests avenues for future research in this area.

FDI Trends and Determinants

LAC has been one of the largest recipients of FDI since the early 1990s. This section provides an overview of those trends and discusses the literature on the determinants of that FDI. By and large, the key factors, among others, that attracted FDI to LAC during the period were the ability to get market access to LAC markets, the ability to serve as an export platform to other markets, political and macroeconomic stability. Interestingly, the literature finds no relationship between whether a nation has signed a regional or bilateral trade or investment agreement (RBTIA) with an investing nation. What's more, there is no evidence that suggests that LAC is a "pollution haven," where foreign firms move to the region to avoid relatively stronger environmental standards in the developed world.

There is no question that the region experienced an unprecedented amount of FDI since the reform period began. For some countries it has been truly impressive. Figure 1.1 exhibits annual FDI flows to LAC from 1980 to 2006.

The 1990s was a period of unprecedented increases in the level of FDI in the world economy as a whole, reaching $1.6 trillion in the year 2000. However, the lion's share of that investment—70 percent of all FDI—stayed in developed countries. Of the FDI that did accrue to the developing world during the 1990s, almost 80 percent of it flowed to just 10 countries. Five of those countries (Brazil, Mexico, Argentina, Bermuda, and Chile) are in LAC. Even among the ten countries that benefited most heavily from FDI, the distribution was skewed; China, Brazil and Mexico received 58 percent of all FDI that flowed to the developing world in the 1990s (UNCTAD 2002).

Although the LAC region received a great deal of FDI, these flows were highly concentrated in just a handful of countries. Table 1.1 lists the top 31 nations that received the highest amount of annual FDI flows during the period 1990 to 2006. Brazil, Mexico, Argentina, Chile and Colombia top the list. Indeed, these nations received 81 percent of all FDI in the region. Investment in the top fifteen countries accounts for almost 97 percent of all FDI.

What factors led to the upsurge in FDI into the region (and the lack of flows in some countries)? The vast majority of studies on the determinants of FDI in LAC are econometric in nature. In other words, using FDI flows (or FDI/per capita) as a dependent variable, analysts statistically examine the extent to which other factors independently affect the level of such flows. There is unanimity among these studies that large and growing economies with low levels of inflation and debt (i.e., macroeconomic stability) are the key determinants of FDI in the region. There is also a consensus that weak environmental standards (in and of themselves) do not significantly attract FDI in the region. The jury is still out on the question of whether new treaties for trade and investment have independently led to attracting FDI. The following is an exhaustive guide the literature on these subjects.

In most cases, these studies have taken the form of cross-sectional analyses of total FDI flows for different groups of Latin American countries in the 1990s (and in some cases, longer periods). While each study has different model specifications, as they attempt to explain the relationship between FDI and one additional determinant, they generally share several core control

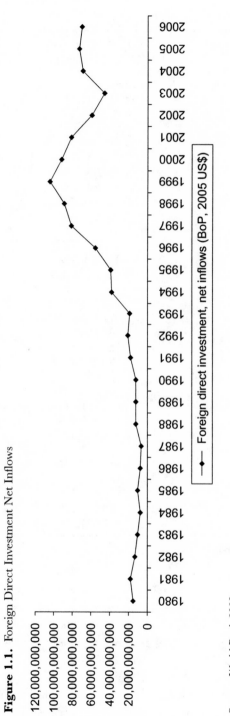

Figure 1.1. Foreign Direct Investment Net Inflows

Source: World Bank 2008.

Table 1.1. **LAC: FDI Flows (1990–2004)**

Country Name	FDI (2005 Dollars) 1990–2006 Average	FDI (%GDP) 1990–2006 Average
Brazil	15,918,081,738	2.07
Mexico	15,345,541,072	2.59
Argentina	6,904,619,703	2.44
Chile	4,684,568,103	5.22
Colombia	3,074,965,989	2.75
Venezuela, RB	2,514,557,609	2.42
Peru	1,959,664,580	2.92
Ecuador	845,882,051	3.27
Panama	750,750,953	5.69
Dominican Republic	693,710,040	3.44
Trinidad and Tobago	647,016,271	7.91
Costa Rica	581,044,058	3.43
Bolivia	441,730,562	4.77
Jamaica	426,842,948	4.95
Uruguay	306,589,718	1.70
El Salvador	242,168,502	1.61
Guatemala	214,590,538	0.98
Bahamas, The	187,956,776	2.27
Honduras	181,163,359	2.70
Nicaragua	179,007,893	4.20
Paraguay	138,721,341	1.53
Guyana	72,234,695	10.17
St. Lucia	70,481,894	9.53
St. Kitts and Nevis	62,630,610	17.49
Antigua and Barbuda	59,536,016	8.71
St. Vincent and the Grenadines	52,600,489	14.20
Grenada	49,227,536	11.48
Belize	39,322,869	4.20
Dominica	26,456,788	9.22
Barbados	19,923,295	0.79
Haiti	17,404,533	0.38

Source: World Bank 2008.

variables. These studies find FDI to be positively and significantly correlated with the market size of the receiving economy, and negatively but significantly correlated with the level of inflation and/or the level of external debt in the receiving country. Both variables are generally used to proxy macroeconomic stability (Nunnenkamp 2000; Arbelaez, Daniels, et al. 2002; Chudnovsky, Lopez, et al. 2002; Bengoa Calvo and Sanchez-Robles 2003; Bittencourt and Domingo 2004; Tuman and Emmert 2004; Gallagher and Birch 2005). These variables are found to be particularly important in the case of "market seeking" FDI—that is, FDI aimed at exploiting the domestic market (Chudnovsky and Lopez 2000). Agosin and Machado note, "in spite of the talk about the internationalization of production and the increasing global market orientation of MNEs [MNCs], looking at the broad picture, the size of domestic markets still seems to matter most to foreign investors" (Agosin and Machado 2006). In addition, the existence of resources (either natural of human) has also been generally found to be an important determinant of investment, particularly in the cases where FDI is "resource seeking" or "export oriented" (Chudnovsky and Lopez 2000).

In part because of the region's history and risk of expropriation (as mentioned above), it has been argued that the adoption of RBTIAs—which protect investors from, among other things, expropriation—should therefore be expected to promote foreign direct investment. In recent years, a literature has developed that attempts to test for the existence of a causal link between the adoption of investment treaties and an increase in the inflows of FDI. While most studies look at the issue at the developing country level, a recent study has focused on the case of Latin America. After conducting a cross-sectional data analysis for 133 countries between 1993 and 1995, UNCTAD finds that the impact of bilateral investment treaties (BITs) on FDI is small and secondary to the effects of other determinants, especially market size. UNCTAD's finding is shared by Hallward-Dreimeier, who looks at data from 20 OECD countries flowing to 31 developing countries from 1980 to 2000 (though unfortunately, it is unclear how many Latin American countries are included in the sample). Work by Tobin and Rose-Ackerman, who examine FDI for 63 countries (20 of which are from Latin America) from 1975 to 2000, also supports this conclusion (UNCTAD 1998; Hallward-Dreimeier 2003; Tobin and Rose-Ackerman 2004).

Some studies, however, have found a positive association between the adoption of BITs and foreign direct investment flows. Neumayer and Spess look at 119 developing countries (29 of which are in Latin America) between 1970 and 2001. They use as an independent variable the number of BITs a developing country has signed with OECD countries, weighted by the world share of outward FDI flow that the OECD country accounts for. They find that developing countries that sign more BITs with developed countries receive more FDI inflows (Neumayer and Spess 2005). This conclusion is shared by Egger and Pfaffermayr, who looking at the issue from the supply side; the authors examine a sample of 19 high-income-source countries and more than 50 host countries, 8 of which are from Latin America, and find that BITs exert a positive and significant effect on real stocks of outward FDI, with a lower bound of 15 percent (Egger and Pfaffermayr 2004). Finally, Salacuse and Sullivan look at 33 developing countries, eight of which are from Latin America, and find that the presence of a BIT with the United States has a large, positive and significant association with a country's overall FDI inflows. However, they find that this is not the case for BITs with other OECD countries (which have a weak positive, but not statistically significant, effect), nor for BITs with other developing countries (which have weak negative, but not statistically .significant, effect) (Salacuse and Sullivan 2005). As pointed out above, however, none of these studies focuses exclusively on Latin America.

The only study to have undertaken a region-specific study of this kind is that of Gallagher and Birch, who find very limited evidence that BITs in general attract additional FDI and strong evidence that an investment agreement with the United States will not lead to additional FDI (Gallagher and Birch 2005). This second finding is consistent with the conclusions of Tobin and Rose-Ackerman, but contradictory to that of Salacuse and Sullivan, although both studies conduct non-region specific analyses (Tobin and Rose-Ackerman 2004; Salacuse and Sullivan 2005).

There are also a significant number of studies that have focused on the impact that processes of regional integration might have had on FDI flows to Latin America. In a study conducted by panel data analysis that looks at bilateral FDI flows (not exclusively for Latin America, but with the aim of assessing the possible FDI impact of the FTAA), Daude, Levy Yeyati et al. argue that sharing membership in a regional integration agreement with a source country increases the likelihood of receiving FDI from that country by 27 percent, although these gains are very unlikely to be distributed evenly between members (Daude, Levy Yeyati et al. 2003). Aguilar and Vallejo, on the other hand, disagree with this finding, arguing that the FDI effects of a preferential trade agreement are ambiguous and depend on which effect (investment creation, investment diversion) prevails. They argue that the results obtained by Daude, Levy Yeyati et al. may be a consequence of the fact that these authors fail in their regressions to control for institutional and infrastructure quality. This critique is shared by Chudnovsky and Lopez and Bittecourt and Domingo (Chudnovsky and Lopez 2001; Aguilar and Vallejo 2002; Chudnovsky, Lopez et al. 2002; Bittencourt and Domingo 2004).

Another relationship that is often claimed in political discourse is that FDI is attracted to LAC and other developing areas because there are relatively weaker environmental standards in the region. This is the so-called "pollution haven hypothesis." Although there is a much smaller literature on this subject in LAC, the studies to date do not find such a relationship. Gallagher (2004) examined the extent to which the NAFTA encouraged US firms to migrate to Mexico in pursuit of weaker environmental standards and found no evidence. Gentry also examined this question, for LAC as a whole, and points out that the enforcement of environmental regulation will not deter foreign investment, as "non-environmental factors (access to resources, markets and labor) are the most important considerations for most foreign direct investors when deciding to invest" (Gentry 1998).

Table 1.2 exhibits these determinants more closely and groups the region into countries and sectors where FDI was generally "market-seeking" or establishing a presence in the region in order to access markets, or "efficiency-seeking" whereby the firm has established a presence in the region in order to export to other markets. Another category is added, that of "natural-resource-seeking," where firms move to gain access to natural resource and export them to other LAC and world markets.

Table 1.2. **FDI Strategies of TNCs in Latin America**

Corporate Strategy and Sector	Natural Resource Seeking	Market-Seeking	Efficiency-Seeking
Goods	**Petroleum and Gas** Andean Community Argentina Trinidad and Tobego	**Automotive** Mercosur	**Automotive** Mexico
	Mining Chile Argentina Andean Community	**Chemicals** Brazil	**Electronics** Mexico Caribbean basin
		Food Products Argentina Brazil Mexico	**Apparel** Mexico Caribbean basin Central America
		Tobacco Argentina Brazil Mexico	
Services	**Tourism** Mexico and Caribbean	**Finance** Mexico Chile Argentina Venezuela Colombia Peru Brazil	**Administrative Services** Costa Rica
		Telecom Brazil Argentina Chile Peru Venezuela	

(Continued)

Table 1.2. **Continued**

Corporate Strategy and Sector	Natural Resource Seeking	Market-Seeking	Efficiency-Seeking
		Retail trade Brazil Argentina Mexico	
		Electricity Colombia Brazil Chile Argentina	
		Gas distribution Argentina Colombia Chile Boliva	

Source: CEPAL 2004.

It should come as no surprise that Mexico and the Caribbean dominate the list of efficiency-seeking FDI because of their close proximity to the United States—the largest single market in the world. Hence the majority of FDI into the region is from the U.S. The majority of FDI to South American nations is from Europe and more in the form of market-seeking and natural-resource-based investment. Whereas manufacturing is a large part of FDI in Mexico and the Caribbean (as well as tourism), it is important to note that there has been a great deal of foreign investment into the services sector in South America; in financial services, telecommunications, retail and energy services. In terms of natural-resource-seeking FDI, the Andean region, Chile, Argentina, and Brazil have received a good deal of investment for petroleum and gas, and minerals.

FDI Spillovers: Theory and Evidence

The liberalization of foreign investment regimes has great promise for sustainable development, at least in theory. These potential benefits can come in three forms: First, liberalization can attract more FDI. FDI is seen as much less volatile than portfolio investment, whose volatility has plagued LAC with financial crises for the past 25 years. What's more, factories established in the region by foreign firms share the promise of generating much needed employment and tax revenue for the host nation. The real prize in FDI, however, is the potential for "spillovers."

Multinational corporations (MNCs) are considered to possess a "bundle of assets"—technology, technical and management expertise, links to global markets—that makes FDI more productive and more environmentally sustainable than domestic investment in developing countries. Because many of these special assets are a source of rents, MNCs work to keep them tightly in-house. Nonetheless, some knowledge "spills over" outside the firm.

Host-country knowledge spillovers from FDI can potentially be captured by:

1. MNC subsidiaries.
2. Other firms in the same industry as the MNC (horizontal spillovers).
3. Downstream suppliers to the MNC (vertical spillovers).
4. Firms in upstream market and other industries.

Except for MNC subsidiaries, whose access to knowledge is directly determined by their corporate parents, knowledge spillovers may occur in five ways:

1. *Human capital:* MNCs hire and train workers who can apply their technical and management knowledge in starting their own firms or in working for domestic firms in the same industry.
2. *Demonstration effects:* Domestic firms may adopt and produce technologies introduced by MNCs through imitation or reverse engineering. They may also adopt productivity-enhancing standards in relation to inputs, product quality, and environmental and labor management.
3. *Competition effects:* The presence of MNCs may exert pressure on domestic firms to adopt new technology or to utilize existing technology more efficiently.
4. *Backward linkages:* Domestic suppliers to MNCs may receive technical training to meet product specifications, and global quality and environmental standards. If MNCs purchase a substantial volume of inputs locally, and/or if they help their local suppliers find additional export markets, local suppliers may also capture economies of scale, thus increasing productivity and potentially 'crowding in' domestic investment.
5. *Forward linkages:* MNC-produced goods and services may enter into and increase the labor and resource efficiency of production processes of firms in upstream and other industries.

Table 1.3 outlines and deepens the contours of this promise in terms of efficiency-seeking and market-seeking FDI, but also outlines the potential costs of FDI if nations fail to deploy policies to foster FDI for sustainable development. FDI has the potential to increase exports and competitiveness of firms while also generating spillovers in the form of technology transfer, the training of domestic individuals and entrepreneurs that can lead to genuine

Table 1.3. **Possible Costs and Benefits of FDI in Latin America**

Corporate Strategy	Benefits	Possible Costs
Efficiency-seeking (export platform)	Increased exports of manufactures Improved international competitiveness Transfer and assimilation of foreign technology Training and human resources Creation and deepening of production linkages Local entrepreneurial development Conversion of platforms to manufacturing center	Low value-added trap Focus on static not dynamic local comparative advantages Dependence on imported components Lack of industrial agglomeration Crowding out local companies Race to the bottom in salaries, labor and environmental standards Race to the top in TNC incentives
Market seeking FDI	New local economic activities Increased local content Creation and deeping of production linkages Local entrepreneurial development Improvement of local services and national competitiveness	Internationally-competitive goods and services not achieved Crowding out of local companies Regulatory problems in services Investor-state disputes arising from international commitments on investment

Source: CEPAL 2004.

endogenous manufacturing clusters. However, without the proper policies in place, FDI can also lock a nation into low-value-added assembly manufacturing, create "enclaves" where foreign firms operate on high-productivity islands devoid of the spillovers and environmental benefits that generate sustainable economic growth and can even crowd out domestic investment.

Over the past thirty years, a large literature has emerged to determine empirically whether and in what circumstances FDI generates knowledge spillovers for industry upgrading (see, for example, Aitken and Harrison 1999; Blomstrom, Globerman et al. 1999; Amsden and Chu 2003; Lall and Urata 2003; Moran, Graham et al. 2005). Most statistical studies focus on *horizontal spillovers*—improved performance of domestic firms in the same industry as the MNCs. Using cross-sectional, industry-level data for a single year, early studies found that industries with a higher concentration of FDI were more productive (Caves 1974; Blomstrom 1983; Blomstrom and Wolff 1994).

As a whole, the evidence suggests that there is no assurance that FDI generates spillovers for industry upgrading. Central to the capture of spillovers is proactive, coherent government industry policy. In a review of 40 studies spanning both developed and developing countries, a World Bank paper found that only six of the 40 studies found evidence of positive spillovers (Görg and Greenaway 2004). *None* were in developing countries. Moreover, six of the 28 studies of developing and transition economies found evidence of *negative* spillovers.

Environmental Spillovers: Theory and Evidence

FDI potentially delivers three types of environmental spillovers for sustainable industrial development: *Clean technology transfer:* Transfer to MNC affiliates of production technologies which are less polluting and more input-efficient production than those used by domestic firms; *Technology leapfrogging:* Transfers of state-of-the-art production and pollution-control technologies; *Pollution halo:* Diffusion of best-practice environmental management techniques to domestic firms, including suppliers.

Evidence of environmental spillovers is mixed. The concept of technology leapfrogging is that, through transfer by MNCs of the least-polluting, state-of-the-art technology and management techniques, developing countries can move to the global production frontier. Besides upgrading industry, the reduction in the pollution intensity of production (and consumption) brings environmental benefits both locally and, in the case of global pollutants such as carbon emissions, globally. For example, Gallagher (2004) found that steel production in Mexico is "cleaner" per unit of output, in terms of criteria air pollutants, than in the US. The primary reason is that FDI, as well as domestic investment in new plants, deployed newer and more environmentally benign minimill technology rather than more traditional and dirtier blast furnaces.

Other studies have found that MNCs transferred technologies and management practices that fell well short of best practice. A recent study of FDI by US auto companies in China, based on extensive interviews with plant managers at Ford, GM and Jeep affiliates, found that US firms transferred outdated automotive pollution-control technologies (Sims and Gallagher 2006). Rosenthal (2002) found that, in explorations for oil and natural gas off Sakhalin Island, Exxon openly flaunted Russian law requiring environmental review and zero water discharge. Case studies of FDI in the petroleum industry, including in Nigeria, Ecuador, Azerbaijan and Kazahkstan, found that MNCs operated with "double standards"—environmental and human rights practices that would be fined or prosecuted in their home countries (Leighton 2002).

What about diffusion of good environmental practice to local firms? MNCs can require that suppliers meet company-set standards and provide training to enable them to do so. Another channel is the demonstration effect; that is, domestic firms copy foreign firms, or host-country governments adopt MNC standards as local regulations. A third channel is industry collaboration to promote better environmental management in developing countries through self-regulation.

A study of MNCs in the chemical industry in Latin America found that US companies played a leading role in diffusing the Responsible Care program to domestic companies in Mexico and Brazil (Garcia-Johnson 2000). Developed in the early 1980s in Canada by the chemical industry in response to the Bhopal disaster, the program aims to raise industry self-regulation beyond mandatory government standards in the areas of environmental impact, employee health and safety, facility security and product stewardship.

A volume of case studies in Latin America found evidence that better environmental management practices were diffused through FDI, including through supply chains (Gentry 1998). One example was the cooperation of the US company Chiquita Brands International in the Better Banana Project. Started by the Rainforest Alliance, the Project uses NGO monitors to certify that growers meet strict environmental and social standards in the areas of toxic chemical use, pollution, water and soil conservation and worker health and safety (Rainforest 2000; Responsibility undated).

In India's manufacturing sector, however, Ruud (2002) found no evidence that MNCs diffused better environmental management practices to local partners, suppliers or consumers. While MNC affiliates were cleaner then domestic firms, they apparently operate as "islands of environmental excellence in a sea of dirt" (Ruud 2002). He concludes that local norms and institutions are central in determining MNC practice and that "FDI inflows do not automatically create a general improvement in environmental performance" (Ruud 2002, 116).

Outline of The Book

This book evaluates the extent to which FDI fostered sustainable development in the Americas. Drawing on case studies from across the region—Argentina, Brazil, Bolivia, Chile, Costa Rica, Ecuador, Mexico, Uruguay and Venezuela— the authors in this volume specifically look at how foreign investment during the reform period had affected economic growth, environmental policy and performance and political economy. Consistent with the broader literature on the subject discussed above, the authors find that investment-regime, liberalization-led FDI has been a limited success at best in the Latin American case.

The volume is divided into two sections. The first group of chapters provides comprehensive country studies on the impacts of FDI on growth, productivity, wages, spillovers and the environment in Brazil, Mexico, Costa Rica and Argentina. The second group of chapters examines the political economy of environment and natural resources in Argentina-Uruguay, Brazil and Chile, in Mexico, and in Ecuador, Bolivia and Venezuela.

Table 1.4 summarizes the findings of the comprehensive country studies. When FDI did come, foreign firms tended to have higher levels of productivity and higher wages than were likely to increase trade in the region; FDI fell far short of generating "spillovers" and backward linkages that help countries develop, and in many cases wiped out locally competing firms, thereby "crowding out" domestic investment.

The first chapter is an overarching and comparative analysis on the relationship between FDI and domestic or total investment by Manuel Agosin. Agosin and others have been engaged in a literature of statistical research that examines the extent to which FDI has "crowded in" domestic investment. In other words, when foreign firms come to a host country, does the existence of spillovers, demonstration effects and the like also serve as a magnet for domestic investment that pushes up total investment and leads to broad economic growth. Agosin synthesizes that statistical work and finds that, by and large, FDI is either crowding out or having a neutral affect in LAC, but crowding in FDI in East Asia. The United Nations Commission for Trade and Development reports that the region will need investment levels to reach twenty-five percent of GDP each year in order to put the region back on a path toward growth and development. There is a long way to go in LAC.

Table 1.5 reports the raw data on FDI as a percent of GDP and Gross Fixed Capital Formation (or total investment) as a percent of GDP for East Asia and the Pacific (EAP), China alone, and LAC. With the exception of China, during the period 1960 to 1980, the two larger regions had relatively similar levels of both FDI and total investment. In addition, from

Table 1.4. **Impacts of FDI: LAC Country Studies**

Indicator	Brazil	Mexico	Costa Rica	Argentina
Growth	−	−	+	−
Productivity	+	+	n.a.	+
Wages	+	+	+	+
Job creation	−	−	+	n.a.
Spillovers	−	−	−	−
Trade	+	+	+	+
Innovation	+	−	−	mixed

Table 1.5. **FDI: Crowding Out Domestic Investment?**

		1960–1980	1980–2005	2000–2005
East Asia and Pacific				
	FDI/GDP	0.4	2.3	2.7
	GFCF/GDP	24.6	34.9	34.8
China	FDI/GDP	0.02	2.5	3.2
	GFCF/GDP	26.2	38.2	39.5
Latin America and the Caribbean				
	FDI/GDP	0.8	1.9	3.1
	GFCF/GDP	21.9	20.0	18.9

Source: World Bank, World Development Indicators 2007.

the 1960–1980 period to the 2000–2005 period, both regions have received increases in the level of FDI as a percent of GDP. Indeed, both EAP and LAC received a 2.3 percent increase in the ratio of FDI to GDP during this period. What is stark, however, is that in EAP, as FDI increased, the level of total investment also sharply increased—by 10.2 percent in the 2000 to 2005 period relative to 1960 to 1980. LAC, on the other hand, actually saw a decrease in total investment of three percent. LAC's paltry 18.9 percent total investment has been widely cited as a reason why the region has experienced such slow growth in per capita terms since the 1980s. The case of China really stands out in contrast to both regions. Indeed, China's example interestingly enters the discussion of many of the chapters in this volume.

The country studies go deeper into and confirm Agosin's aggregate level analysis, but with some interesting variations. The Brazil study that leads off the volume finds that MNCs tend to have higher productivity, higher levels of wages, and (contrary to the findings in other studies) tend to introduce higher levels of innovation than their domestic counterparts. However, it is concluded that the lack of spillovers and linkages and the significant losses to domestic firms have crowded out the ability of Brazil to tap the full potential of the FDI in the country. Brazil is indeed rethinking the role of FDI in its development strategy and has chosen not to sign any new RBTIAs that may restrict their policy space to foster FDI for development, and has fought hard in the WTO to see to it that such measures are not restricted in the WTO as well. However, Hiratuka in this volume argues that although Brazil has advocated forcefully to provide itself with the policy space for industrial policies that may help the domestic economy benefit more from foreign presence, the new industrial strategies of the government are yet to focus exclusively on FDI.

Table 1.6. Environmental Impacts of FDI: Four Country Studies

Indictator	Brazil	Mexico	Chile	Argentina
EMS/Tech transfer	+	+	+	+
Compliance	–	?	n.a.	–
Spillovers	–			
Export upgrade	+	–	+	n.a

The studies on Mexico, Costa Rica and Argentina come to conclusions similar to the Brazil case, with one exception. Each chapter traces the history of FDI trends and policies in each country and outlines how FDI has largely led to higher productivity and higher wage enclaves mostly divorced from the domestic economy in terms of linkages and spillovers; however, whereas in the Brazilian case foreign firms were more apt to introduce new innovations and products, in both Mexico and Argentina, FDI has been shown to have either no effect or a negative one on the amount of R&D and innovation. The Costa Rican case also highlights how the lack of taxation of MNCs (used as an incentive to attract firms) robs the nation of the revenue needed to put in place necessary domestic policies for development.

The second set of chapters in the volume examines the political economy of natural resources and the environment in relation to MNCs in the region. One set of papers on the forestry, electronics, petrochemicals, and pulp-and-paper sectors in Brazil, Chile and Mexico examines the extent to which FDI has generated environmental spillovers of the type outlined in the previous section. In these chapters the record is more mixed with respect to the environment. As shown in Table 1.5, and discussed in each of these chapters, there is ample evidence that when MNCs came to these countries, they brought with them environmental management systems (EMS), such as ISO 14001, which are certifications for basic levels of processes within firms with respect to the environment. However, the record is more mixed regarding the extent to which foreign firms were in actual compliance with host country environmental laws. In Brazil and Chile foreign firms were no more likely to be in compliance than domestic firms; in Argentina and Mexico it was hard to tell, but suspect, if MNCs were in compliance with domestic law or if MNCs were degrading the environment.

In both Brazil and Chile it was found that MNCs were more apt to change their production processes in an environmentally sound manner in response to market signals outside the country. In the case of Brazil, in the pulp-and-paper sector, when exports were heading toward Europe where consumers demand a certain level of environmental standards for products entering their markets, firms were likely to upgrade. In response to citizen-advocacy efforts in the US and elsewhere, there has been a movement for "fair trade certification" of forestry products under the auspices of the Forestry Stewardship Council. Here products that are harvested sustainably are labeled as such so environmentally minded consumers can purchase products produced in this manner. Such labeling schemes have led to an environmental upgrading of exports in Chilean and Brazilian forestry. In the Mexican electronics industry, however, it was found that foreign firms are not exporting high-technology products to meet strong standards in Europe, given that their chief export market, the United States, does not have such standards. Interestingly though, other subsidiaries of those same firms in Ireland and Hungary do produce to meet the standards because those two particular export platforms serve the European market.

This book ends with two chapters that focus specifically on the changing political economy of FDI and natural resources in the region. Stanley points out that in three Andean countries (Bolivia, Ecuador and Venezuela), we are witnessing a resurgence of the role of the public sector in the critical sector of hydrocarbons. In all three cases, Stanley argues, there were precisely the economic crises derived from the shortcomings of the Neoliberal model that led to political transformation (by any standard, a move to a more nationalist and left-leaning approach to policymaking) and also to the establishment of a new vision of FDI benefits and costs, especially in the strategic oil and gas sectors.

What is puzzling in these cases is that firms have decided to renegotiate with new governments instead of making use of the rights to protection and arbitration they acquired during the liberalization phase (through bilateral investment treaties). This may be a signal that firms are always driven by economic and not institutional considerations, and that, at this stage and given the prices of hydrocarbons, this may be the most economically rational strategy to pursue. However, argues Stanley, a firm's choices may rapidly change if the prices of hydrocarbons make tolerance of nationalization unacceptable. This could turn the strategies pursued by the governments of Bolivia, Ecuador and Venezuela, considered a short-term successes, into a longer-term failures and, as such, prove shortsighted.

Finally, Chidiak looks at the conflict between international environmental regulations and international agreements for the protection of foreign investment in the high-profile case of the conflict between Argentina and Uruguay stemming from the installation of a large paper-pulp producing plant on the banks of the border Uruguay River. Chidiak argues that this is a critical case because it embodies the fundamental tension that can exist between international environmental and foreign investment regulations, both at the regional and multilateral levels, as well as due to the continuing importance the pulp-and-paper industry is bound to have in the region in the future. Therefore, argues the author, the outcome of the Argentina-Uruguay conflict is likely to set an important precedent.

Chidiak's observations about the case are dire. She is skeptical about the true environmental nature of the conflict (arguing that the countries see this dispute as a matter of "national pride"), which undermines the capacity of governments to learn from this conflict in order to better address similar tensions between investment and environment that may arise in the future. Finally, Chidiak argues that the case has shown an alarming lack of regional cooperation and the weakness of existing institutions in the region designed, precisely, to deal with these sorts of issues.

Lessons for Policy and Research

Newly elected governments in Latin America are fundamentally questioning the merits of current FDI policy in the region. This volume shows that such a reevaluation is justified. The book critically assesses the rather extensive literature on the developmental impacts of FDI in LAC since the 1990s.

We find that only a handful of nations received the lion's share of FDI in the region. Indeed, just five countries—Brazil, Mexico, Argentina, Chile, and Colombia—received more than 80 percent of all the FDI in the region. The most significant determinants of FDI flows to the region were market size, economic growth rates, and export orientation. Interestingly, there is mixed, at best, evidence that trade or investment agreements have an independent effect on FDI flows in the region. Nor is there evidence that LAC's relatively weak environmental regulations served as an independent determinant of FDI flows.

We also find almost unanimous evidence that FDI resulted in very limited productivity spillovers for the region. Indeed, the chapter by Agosin finds that on the whole, FDI "crowded out" domestic investment in the region during the 1990s. The chapters on environmental spillovers are more mixed, however. It is found that MNCs are indeed transforming EMS to their developing-country counterparts and in some significant cases are taking part in labeling schemes that upgrade domestic facilities. On the other hand, it is not clear that foreign firms are more apt to be in compliance with domestic environmental laws than domestic firms.

Virtually all the governments mentioned in this volume are rethinking the role of foreign investment in their economies. While some are simply at the stage of starting to debate the issue (in Mexico, for example), others are going so far as to nationalize foreign firms. Yet, most other governments are looking for a more balanced approach. What this paper makes clear is that new policies are needed. Based on the research here, three broad lessons can be drawn out as principles for policymaking in this field:

1. ***FDI is not an end, but a means to sustainable development. Simply attracting FDI is not enough to generate economic growth in an environmentally sustainable manner.*** The volume shows that even in the nations that received the lion's share of FDI in the region—Brazil, Argentina, and Mexico—FDI fell short of generating spillovers and sustained economic growth. FDI needs to be part of a comprehensive development strategy aimed at raising the standard of living of a nation's population with minimal damage to the environment.

2. ***FDI policy needs to be conducted in parallel with significant and targeted domestic policies that upgrade the capabilities of national firms and provide a benchmark for environmental protection.*** The chapters in the volume outline numerous country-specific policies that are either being implemented or debated regarding ways in which LAC nations can overcome information and coordination externalities, access to credit problems, and competitiveness issues on the part of their domestic firms. Many of the chapters draw parallels or lessons from Asia, where nations have put in place targeted industrial policies to link domestic firms and foreign firms to the extent that the domestic firms develop into competitive exporters themselves.

3. ***International agreements, whether at the WTO or at the level of RBTIAs, need to leave developing nations the "policy space" to pursue the domestic policies necessary to foster development through FDI.*** Some of the chapters in this volume pinpoint how the emerging international regime of international investment rules is restricting the ability of developing nations to pursue some of the policy instruments that have been successful at channeling FDI for development in Asia and elsewhere. When acting collectively under the auspices of the WTO, developing nations have largely succeeded in blocking proposals that would further restrict such policy space. However, slower movement in global trade talks has led to a proliferation of RBTIAs between developed and developing countries where developing countries have much less bargaining power and end up exchanging policy space for market access.

For the first time in English, this volume collects, synthesizes, and analyzes the rich and broad academic and policy discussions that have been burgeoning in the Americas over the past twenty years. Collectively, the chapters in this volume show that there is a fundamental rethinking of the role of FDI in national development in Latin America and beyond, and suggest ways in which such a rethinking can be channeled into concrete policy.

Chapter Two

IS FOREIGN INVESTMENT ALWAYS GOOD FOR DEVELOPMENT?

Manuel R. Agosin

Summary

In this chapter, I explore the effects that FDI can have on domestic investment in recipient developing countries. An attempt is made to determine the circumstances under which FDI may be expected to induce additional investment from national firms, which is labeled as "crowding in" (CI). Under other circumstances, FDI may well displace investments that would have been made by domestic firms in the absence of the foreign investor, i.e., "crowding out" (CO) those investments. A third possibility is that FDI may translate into real investment on a one-to-one basis, a situation I label as "neutral effect." Recent findings suggest that FDI, over the period 1971 through 2000, has generally had neutral or CO effects on domestic investment. This means that a liberal policy toward FDI should be complemented with an effort to ensure that the recipient country attracts those investments that are more likely to maximize their investment rates.

Introduction

Foreign direct investment (FDI) is prized by developing countries for the bundle of assets that multinational enterprises (MNCs) deploy with their investments. Most of these assets are intangible and are particularly scarce in developing countries. They include technology, management skills, channels for marketing products internationally, product design, quality characteristics, brand names, etc. In evaluating the impact of FDI on development, however, a key question is whether MNCs crowd in (CI) domestic investment (as, for example, when their presence stimulates new downstream or upstream investment that would not have taken place in their absence) or whether they have the opposite crowding-out (CO) effect of displacing domestic G44 producers or pre-empting their investment opportunities.

This is a rather important issue. In most theoretical and empirical work, investment has been identified as a key determinant of economic growth. Thus, if FDI crowds out (CO) domestic investment or fails to contribute to capital formation, there would be good reasons to question its benefits for recipient developing countries. Moreover, given the scarcity of domestic entrepreneurship and the need to nurture existing entrepreneurial talent, a finding that MNCs displace domestic firms would also cast doubt on the favorable development effects of FDI. These are all the more important questions when one considers that FDI is far from being a marginal magnitude. As can be seen in Table 2.1, FDI as a share of total gross fixed capital formation is a significant magnitude in developing countries. In fact, it is more important in most developing regions than in developed countries.

The Issues

Investment by MNCs contributes directly to investment, because it is part of it. Indeed, domestic investment (I_d) plus investments undertaken by MNCs (I_f) ought to add up to total gross $I=I_d+I_f$ investment (I).

I_f is usually thought of as FDI. This formulation is, of course, an oversimplification, since FDI is not equivalent to new investments by foreign firms. FDI is a financial, balance-of-payments concept; on the other hand, investment is a real, national accounts variable. Much FDI never becomes investment in the real sense; mergers and acquisitions (M&As) are mere transfers of ownership of existing assets from domestic to foreign firms. In some countries, investments by MNCs could exceed FDI. This is the case of investments financed through borrowings on domestic capital markets. This phenomenon is more widespread in developed than in developing countries.

Table 2.1. **FDI Inflows as a Percentage of Gross Fixed-Capital Formation**

Region	2003	2004	2005
Developed Countries	6.4	6.3	8
Developing Countries	9.3	10.7	12.8
Africa	15.8	11.8	19.1
Asia	7.7	9.4	11.1
Latin America	13.5	15.9	16.8
Central and Eastern Europe	16.8	20.9	17

Source: UNCTAD 2006.

In the latter, borrowing costs on domestic financial markets are normally much higher than on international markets, and this usually discourages domestic borrowings by MNCs.

A crucial question as regards the development impact of FDI is the extent to which it affects investment by domestic firms (I_d). If it has no effect whatsoever, any increase in FDI ought to be reflected in a dollar-for-dollar increase in total investment. If FDI *crowds out* investment by domestic firms, the increase in total investment (I) ought to be *smaller* than the increase in FDI. Finally, if there is *crowding in*, I ought to increase by *more* than the increase in FDI.

The assessment of the effects of FDI on domestic and total investment is far from a trivial matter. Little can be said on an a priori basis. The effects of FDI on investment may well vary from country to country, depending on domestic policy, the kinds of FDI that a country receives and the strength of domestic enterprises.

It is possible, however, to specify conditions that are favorable to CI. In developing country settings, foreign investments that introduce goods and services that are new to the domestic economy, be they for the export or domestic market, are more likely to have favorable effects on capital formation than foreign investments in areas where domestic producers already exist. In the former case, the effects on capital formation will be positive because domestic producers do not have the knowledge required to undertake these activities and, therefore, foreign investors do not displace domestic investors.

This is precisely the spirit of Romer's (1993) important paper on the contribution of FDI to development. In Romer's paper, FDI is the driving force for the introduction of new goods to the economy and for the provision of human capital resources that are able to produce such goods.

If FDI enters the economy in sectors where there are competing domestic firms (or firms already producing for export markets), it may well preempt investment opportunities that were open to domestic entrepreneurs prior to the foreign investments. In other words, such FDI is likely to reduce domestic investments that would have been undertaken, if not immediately, at least in the future, by domestic producers.[1] The contribution to total capital formation of such FDI is likely to be less than the FDI flow itself.

This leads to a hypothesis linking the contribution of FDI to capital formation in the sector of the economy to which it goes. When the distribution of FDI by sector of the economy is substantially different from the distribution of the existing capital stock or of production, the contribution of FDI to capital formation will be more positive than when the distribution of FDI follows roughly the existing distribution of the capital stock by sector. In other words, *the relationship between FDI and domestic investment is likely to be complementary when investment is in an undeveloped sector of the economy* (owing to technological factors or to the lack of knowledge of foreign markets). On the other hand, *FDI is more likely to substitute for domestic investment when it takes place in sectors where there are plenty of domestic firms.* The same may occur where domestic firms already have access to the technology that the MNC brings to the country.

One can, of course, make an argument for exactly the opposite hypothesis. For instance, MNC investments in new activities may preempt investments by domestic firms that, with proper nurturing by government, could be in a position to enter the sector. This was the rationale for limiting foreign investments in certain high-technology sectors in South Korea and Taiwan. The bet in these cases was that domestic firms could in fact emerge, and it paid off (see Amsden 1989; Wade 1990). In most other cases in the developing world, however, the appearance of domestic producers in a new sector is unlikely or might take too long. Policies to foster entrepreneurship in new sectors can be very costly to the economy as a whole, if these sectors have technological requirements that run too far ahead of domestic capabilities. Besides, there are very few countries where governments can be as effective in nurturing technologically advanced domestic firms as the governments of South Korea or Taiwan were in the heyday of their industrialization drive. Examples of botched and costly intervention in favor of domestic firms in high-technology sectors abound in the developing world. One of the most disastrous was the Brazilian "informatics policy" of the early 1980s, which involved severe restrictions on FDI in information-technology sectors. These restrictions led to very little domestic investment, and the firms that were created were highly inefficient. The policy was abandoned well before the program was due to expire.

Also, it could be argued that the entry of an MNC into a sector where there exist several domestic firms may lead to investments by incumbent domestic firms in order to become more competitive. However, given the vast technological superiority of MNCs, their investments are more likely to displace domestic firms, and even cause their bankruptcy, than to induce domestic firms to invest.

Even where FDI does not displace domestic investment, foreign investments may not stimulate new downstream or upstream production and, therefore, may fail to exert strong CI effects on domestic investment. *Thus, the existence of backward or forward linkages from the establishment of foreign investors is a key consideration for determining the total impact of FDI on capital formation.*

It should be stressed, though, that linkages are a necessary but not sufficient factor for CI. In cases where foreign firms simply displace existing firms, the existence of linkages cannot prevent CO.

One may also hypothesize that the impact on investment is superior when FDI takes the form of a greenfield investment than when it is an M&A. This is ultimately an empirical matter. In studies on the impact of FDI on development in Latin America, sample surveys of MNC affiliates in Argentina and Chile revealed that, for the firms interviewed, the purchase of existing assets was a small component of the total investment. Postpurchase investments very often included modernization and rationalization of operations, and, above all, investments in technology (see Agosin 1996; Chudnovsky, López et al. 1996; Riveros, Vatter et al. 1996). These investments were particularly large in the privatizations of telecommunications and public utilities in Argentina in the early 1990s. Most of the acquisitions in Argentina and Chile during this period were made with the intention of running the firms so acquired and bringing them up to date technologically.

But M&As may not lead to any increase in the physical capital of a host country. In some cases, the acquisition of a domestic firm is almost akin to a portfolio investment, with the MNC doing nothing to improve the operation of the domestic company. This was the case of several acquisitions in Latin America in the 1990s, as those economies became desirable destinations of portfolio investments. Very recently, there has been a large number of such cases of FDI, all with doubtful impacts on capital formation. Many of the acquired companies are not in need of modernizing, since they operate with state-of-the-art technology. Nor is it likely that their purchase by a foreign company will be followed up by sequential investment that the acquired firms would not have made themselves. In such cases, FDI is *not* investment in the national accounts sense, and it does not lead to investments later.

In fact, large M&As, like large portfolio inflows, may have adverse macroeconomic externalities on the most interesting types of investments. When they are of a size that can no longer be considered marginal, M&As tend to appreciate the exchange rate and discourage investment for export markets (and, indeed, for the production of importables as well). In small countries, these investments constitute the engine of growth of the economy.

It is interesting that M&As are prohibited or heavily restricted in some of the most successful newly industrialized countries. Up until the late 1990s, Taiwan restricted foreign ownership of the equity of domestic companies in two ways: A single foreign person or entity could own no more than 15 percent of a domestic company, and all foreigners together were not allowed to own more than 30 percent in the equity of a domestic company. Until the financial crisis of 1997–1998, the Republic of Korea maintained similar restrictions. In order to assist in the restructuring of industry and to attract FDI, these restrictions have been dropped (Agosin 2001).

It is often argued that an acquisition will lead to capital formation indirectly, when those who have been bought out invest in new sectors of the economy. But the effect is likely to be weak, if it occurs at all. Most acquired firms are joint stock companies, and the shares purchased through a buyout are tendered by stockholders who are more likely to use the proceeds to purchase other financial assets (at home or even abroad) than to make real investments. Thus, the relationship between acquisitions of domestic firms by MNCs and real investment may be very tenuous indeed.

There are other macroeconomic externalities of MNC activities that could lead to CO. In many, if not most, developing countries, MNCs are not marginal. Therefore, their activities have macroeconomic effects. By raising domestic interest rates, the borrowing by MNCs on domestic financial markets may displace investment by domestic firms. Such borrowings may also worsen foreign exchange problems during times of balance-of-payments crises, as borrowing in domestic currency can be converted to foreign exchange and easily sent abroad by companies operating in global markets and having global financial connections.

To what extent this takes place in actual fact is an empirical question, and undoubtedly the situation will vary from country to country. But it may be critical in small countries negotiating with large firms. For example, in its foreign investment regulations, Chile, which has very liberal policies toward FDI, has retained the right to limit the access of foreign companies to the domestic banking system, if national conditions so warrant. The provision has never been invoked, but its very existence is a reminder that, for a small country, borrowing on domestic markets by MNC affiliates may, under certain circumstances, be problematic.

The Empirical Evidence on CI or CO

Undoubtedly, a part of FDI will become physical investment. It is very likely that this share will rise with the extent to which FDI is of the greenfield variety rather than M&As. As can be seen in Table 2.2, a significant proportion of FDI takes the form of acquisition of existing assets, which seems to validate the presumption that not all FDI becomes new capital investment. In the developing world, this share is particularly high in Latin America, where a significant share of FDI has gone into sectors that are particularly suited to M&As, such as telecommunications, energy, water and sanitation. In Asia, on the other hand, the share of M&As is low, because the regional FDI totals in recent years are very influenced by the enormous flows going to China, where M&As, by deliberate policy, are practically non-existent.

Table 2.2. **Mergers and Acquisitions, as a Percentage of FDI**

Region	2002	2003	2004
Developed Countries	58.9	55.3	83.1
Developing Countries	17.7	18.7	17.1
Africa	36.1	35.7	25.4
Asia	18.8	21.3	16.8
Latin America	44.4	25.8	37.4
Central and Eastern Europe	22.4	51.4	28.8

Source: UNCTAD 2006.

Moreover, even the part of FDI that is fresh investment may not add much to capital formation, if it crowds out investments that would have been carried out by domestic firms. In a recent paper, Agosin and Machado (2006) performed a series of econometric exercises to determine the extent to which FDI crowded in or crowded out domestic investment in three developing regions (Africa, Asia, and Latin America) over the period 1971–2000, and during each of the three decades of the period. The results suggest that, over the entire period, FDI displaced domestic investment in Latin America. In Africa and Asia, on the other hand, FDI increased overall investment one-to-one. In other words, there was no crowding in or crowding out, and foreign investment added to total investment one-to-one. If the three decades are taken separately, the results show CO in Latin America in the seventies and in Africa in the nineties. So, even in the case where FDI is of the greenfield variety, CI is not assured, because part of that investment could have been undertaken by domestic firms that are pre-empted by multinationals.

Why are multinationals able to preempt national firms? Basically, because of their superior technology, their access to human capital, their ability to penetrate their own domestic markets or their access to cheap financing. While these advantages are also the main reasons why their presence in host developing countries are sought after assiduously, the authorities of these countries must ask themselves the question of whether domestic firms could have built up some or all of these assets given a reasonable period of time. If the answer is negative, then multinational engagement can be seen in a positive light. However, if the answer is positive, then more selective policies for multinationals would seem in order.

Policy Implications

The main conclusion that emerges from this analysis is that positive impacts of FDI on domestic investment are not assured. In some cases, total investment may increase much less than FDI, or may even fail to rise when a country experiences an increase in FDI. Therefore, the assumption that underpins policy toward FDI in most developing countries—that a liberal policy toward MNCs is sufficient to ensure positive effects—fails to be upheld by the data. A recent paper (Agosin and Machado 2007) shows that the most far-reaching liberalizations of FDI regimes in the 1990s took place in Latin America, and that FDI regimes in Asia have remained the least liberal in the developing world.[2] Several Asian countries still practice screening of investment applications and grant differential incentives to different firms. As already noted, some types of investment have remained prohibited for most of the period under review. In Latin America, on the other hand, these practices have been eliminated in most countries. Nonetheless, liberalization during the nineties appears to have not changed the effects of FDI on investment as compared to the eighties.

In addition, the paper by Agosin and Machado (2007) shows that FDI liberalization, even after controlling other variables that may affect FDI, does not necessarily result in higher volumes of FDI. Liberalization appears to be a necessary, but not a sufficient, condition for attracting FDI. The host country's locational advantages seem to be a lot more important. An important aspect of those advantages is clearly the security of property rights. No amount of liberalization will attract FDI in the absence of legal assurance against expropriation or curtailment of investors' rights. In addition, the host country's assets, from the point of view of the investing multinationals, are also important, such as the availability of natural resources, good quality and low-cost labor, large domestic markets, etc.

Of course, FDI may be desirable for other reasons, which are not analyzed here in detail. While raising the investment rate is undoubtedly the most important one, there are other benefits that can be expected of FDI and multinationals in general. For example, the entrance of a multinational can increase competition and force national firms to modernize. Many developing-country markets are characterized by various degrees of imperfect competitions. A cozy coexistence of a few large firms may well be the norm. That coexistence can be broken by the entry of a large foreign firm, to the benefit of consumers. If the sector produces an input that is essential to the competitiveness of an upstream user sector, the entry of a multinational may lead to a spurt of growth and higher employment at higher wages.

Multinationals may also bring new technology, and they are courted by host countries precisely for this reason. But this need not always be the case. It is an empirical matter whether multinationals, in fact, introduce new technologies into host economies. Clearly, a policy toward FDI should keep in mind the technological contribution of multinationals. This will require discriminating between different investments on offer. But not all developing country bureaucracies are able to do so in an effective manner while avoiding being co-opted (or bribed) by the companies they are supposed to screen.

This analysis suggests that while there is considerable scope for active policies that discriminate in favor of foreign investments with positive effects on total investment, this is not an easy matter. This does not mean having to decide on each investment project or to practice cumbersome screening of investments, which will only work to discourage potential investors. But it does mean favoring some investments over others. Better to have greenfield investments than purchases of existing assets. Better to have investments that broaden a country's export portfolio, not just those that maintain the status quo. Better to have investments outside export-processing zones that use domestic inputs than investments inside export-processing zones that have no connection with the domestic economy other than using labor and paying for utilities. This may require complementing an open investment policy with a simple system of incentives for desired activities. And, of course, it also means discouraging the wrong type of investments. One such case in point is the use of income tax exemptions for firms located in export-processing zones.

Different countries clearly need different policy approaches. Selectivity toward investment, be it national or multinational, has yielded very positive results in some countries, notably the Asian exporters of manufactures. Other, lower-income countries have fared considerably worse with the same policies. The poorer the country and less developed its human resources, the more it should concentrate on fundamentals: good governance, ensuring that property rights are secure, good macroeconomic policies. Without the human resources and the social compact between business and government that is necessary for active industrial policies, it is better to eschew them. Many countries have attempted active industrial policies, of which FDI policies are an aspect, with disastrous results. Rent-seeking and policies that impede firms from taking advantage of existing comparative advantages have, in many cases, led to development disasters.

Does this mean that active policies toward FDI, and also toward domestic investment, are useless? Far from it. A large number of countries have been able to do very well with these policies. Such countries include not only the star performers of Asia, but also countries such as Finland and Ireland. These countries have been able to develop new comparative advantages through making winners, not just picking them. They have worked on the large variety of factors that make for success, such as coordinating private investment to ensure that all the pieces of the puzzle are there at the time they are needed.

Their use of incentives has been sparing and oriented to getting good value for money. Ireland, for example, gave startup grants to firms in selected sectors, against the promise that they would stay in the country at least for ten years. The grants paid for themselves in an average of four years in terms of the taxes collected from the firms. Some of the sectors chosen were information and telecommunication technologies, finance and pharmaceuticals. These firms had large backward and forward linkages and encouraged the emergence of strong clusters with lots of domestic and further foreign investment.

What the examples of Ireland, East Asia and Finland teach us is that active policies toward FDI must be framed by country visions, which orient development strategies, which in turn are the framework of policies. Not every country has arrived at the stage where this complex socio-economic-political process is possible to implement. It requires a social compact between business and government. For example, businesses do receive certain incentives, but as a *quid pro quo*, they are expected to perform. Also, the government bureaucracy is able to spot where development payoffs exist. While many countries are not there yet, many are. The crux is for the authorities to determine at what stage they are. Not an easy task.

Part One

COUNTRY ASSESSMENTS

Chapter Three

ISLANDS OF POSSIBILITY: MNCs AND ECONOMIC DEVELOPMENT IN BRAZIL

Celio Hiratuka

Introduction

Since the 1980s, the exhaustion of Brazil's postwar economic development model became manifest in severe macroeconomic disequilibriums and the inability to maintain earlier high, sustained rates of economic growth. The stagnation of investment and weak efforts at technical innovation translated into low levels of efficiency, productivity and technological modernization.

The 1990s saw a break with the statist postwar model in favor of reduced state economic intervention and a more comprehensive liberalization of both trade and capital flows. Among the economic policies adopted to this end, trade and financial liberalization and privatization of state-owned enterprises stand out. Proponents expected these policies to eliminate bottlenecks hindering the competitiveness of Brazilian industry and to hasten the convergence of Brazil's technology, managerial practices and levels of productivity to those of the "advanced" economies.

Some scholars and policymakers saw foreign corporations as the protagonists of this process.[1] They believed that most domestic private companies would not be able to survive or expand in a liberalizing, non-inflationary context without the subsidies they had enjoyed under the earlier model. Given the privatization process and the declining importance of state-owned companies, these analysts argued, economic modernization would be accomplished by affiliates of transnational corporations (MNCs). Under a liberalizing regime, these affiliates, mainly in the most capital and technology-intensive sectors, would have stronger incentives to invest in cost reduction and technology modernization, and to become more specialized and less vertically integrated, increasing their efficiency, productivity, and competitiveness in world markets.

Part of the knowledge accumulated by MNCs, according to this vision, would spill over to national firms, contributing indirectly to their modernization, and resulting in a more competitive economy, able to generate higher levels of income and employment in the long run.

During the 1990s, particularly in the second half of the decade, there was a boom in foreign direct investment flows to the Brazilian economy, which translated into an increase in the already large role of foreign corporations in the Brazilian productive structure. Despite some decline in FDI flows to Brazil in the first years of the twenty-first century, inflows remain high.

MNCs will probably continue to make important investments in Brazil and hold a prominent place in many sectors. Therefore, an assessment of these corporations' activities and the effects of government economic policy on them is crucial as a guide for future policymaking.

What have been the effects of the FDI boom and the growth of the foreign share of production in the Brazilian economy? Have the optimistic expectations of mentioned scholars and policymakers been fulfilled? If not, what have been the actual effects on foreign trade, productivity, employment and the technological capabilities of the Brazilian economy? What has been the impact of government economic policy in this process?

This chapter seeks to answer these questions based on a review of several studies on the topic. Besides this introduction, the chapter comprises three sections. The second section is a general characterization of recent FDI inflows, as well as of the growth of MNC affiliates' share in the Brazilian economy. In the third section, the impacts of FDI on productivity, trade flows, R&D expenditures and wage levels are analyzed. The last section comprises our final remarks and policy recommendations.

General Characteristics of the Recent FDI Boom in the Brazilian Economy

One of the basic characteristics of the Brazilian economy is a high level of internationalization, with foreign corporations playing a leading role in many sectors.

This is not a new phenomenon. FDI inflows and the MNCs' leading role in the most dynamic sectors have been key features of the Brazilian industrialization process from its beginnings. Especially from the early postwar years to the end of the 1970s, MNC affiliates, connected to public and private domestic companies by state planning, were fundamental to developing a diversified industrial structure, convergent with that of high-income countries at least in terms of the sectoral composition of output.

In the 1980s, however, the external debt crisis ended the Brazilian economy's long growth cycle. Brazil started to experience highly volatile GDP growth rates, as well as chronic inflation. FDI inflows stagnated at low levels, with MNC affiliates refraining from large-scale expansion projects.

The resumption of investment during the 1990s meant the return to more aggressive expansion strategies by MNC affiliates. Motivated by changes in economic policy and conditions—liberalization, privatization, and macroeconomic stability, followed by an increase in demand for consumer durables—MNCs began to expand their presence in the Brazilian economy again.

From approximately US$1.5 billion annually in the 1980s and early 1990s, FDI inflows increased to an average level of US$24 billion anually between 1995 and 2000. It's interesting to note that the inflows continued to grow through the year 2000, despite the Asian crisis of 1997, the Russian crisis of 1998, and even the Brazilian crisis of 1999. Starting in 2001, with a world economic slowdown considerably reducing trade and investment flows, FDI inflows to Brazil declined, reaching a low of US$10.1 billion in 2003. In 2004, the volume of FDI went up again, dipping slightly thereafter in 2005 (Figure 3.1).

Table 3.1 shows that Brazil's share in world FDI flows increased from less than 1 percent in 1990–1995 to 2.9 percent in 1996–2000, dropping to

Figure 3.1. Brazil – Inward Foreign Direct Investment – 1990–2005 – US $ millions

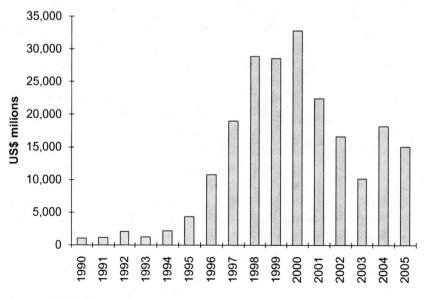

Source: UNCTAD 2005.

Table 3.1. **Brazilian Share in World and Regional FDI Inflows – %**

Period	1990–1995	1996–2000	2001–2005
Share in World FDI	0.9	2.9	2.3
Share in Developing FDI	2.8	11.9	7.3
Share in Latin America & Caribbean FDI	10.7	29.7	23.5

Source: UNCTAD 2005.

2.3 percent in 2001–2005. In the latter period, the Brazilian share of total inflows to developing countries was 7.3 percent, and represented 23.5 percent of total inflows to Latin American and Caribbean countries.

Important changes occurred in the sectoral composition of FDI inflows as well. Until 1995, the manufacturing sector accounted for almost 67 percent of all FDI stock in Brazil, whereas in the second half of the decade, the prevalence of the service sector was remarkable, with electricity, gas, water, postal services and telecommunications, financial services, and wholesale and retail trade attracting significant FDI flows. A large part of the investment in these sectors was associated with the privatization process. By 2000, the service sector's share in the FDI stock had increased to 64 percent and that of the manufacturing sector had dropped to 33.7 percent, though manufacturing industries such as food and beverages, automotive, chemicals, metallurgy, and telecommunications equipment continued to receive significant volumes of investment.

Between 2001 and 2006, the service sector continued to account for more than half of total inflows, although its share dropped compared to the previous period. The manufacturing sector, in turn, accounted for 38.5 percent of the total inflows during this period. Agriculture and mining also grew in importance, accounting for 7.1 percent of total FDI.

Another feature of recent FDI inflows to the Brazilian economy has been the importance of mergers and acquisitions. Figure 3.2 shows the value of international mergers and acquisitions, in which Brazil is the home country of the acquired company, as a percentage of the total value of FDI received. As we can see, the share peaked at a very high level at the height of the privatization process in the second half of the 1990s, but remained high even after the reduction in privatizations. Indeed, research on Brazil confirms the broader findings by Agosin in the previous chapter regarding the crowding out of domestic investment. The large share of FDI attributable to mergers and acquisitions shows that a substantial part of the investment inflows did not contribute to the development of new productive capacity (Laplane and Sarti 2002).

In fact, despite the high levels of FDI inflows, the Gross Fixed Capital Formation in the Brazilian economy stagnated during this period as a whole.

Table 3.2. Brazil – FDI Stocks and Flows by Industry

Economic Sector	Stock				Flows	
	1995		2000		2001–2006	
	US$ millions	%	US$ millions	%	US$ millions	%
Agriculture and mining	**925**	**2.2**	**2,401**	**2.3**	**8,249**	**7.1**
Manufacturing	**27,907**	**66.9**	**34,726**	**33.7**	**44,917**	**38.5**
Food and beverage	2,828	6.8	4,619	4.5	11,004	9.4
Chemicals	5,331	12.8	6,043	5.9	7,295	6.2
Automotive	4,838	11.6	6,351	6.2	6,335	5.4
Metallurgy	3,005	7.2	2,513	2.4	3,759	3.2
Electronic and telecom. equipment	785	1.9	2,169	2.1	3,023	2.6
Pulp and paper	1,634	3.9	1,573	1.5	2,642	2.3
Machinery	2,345	5.6	3,324	3.2	1,989	1.7
Electrical equipment	1,101	2.6	990	1	1,500	1.3
Rubber and plastic	1,539	3.7	1,782	1.7	1,402	1.2
Others	4,502	10.8	5,361	5.2	5,966	5.1
Services	**12,864**	**30.9**	**65,888**	**64**	**63,575**	**54.5**
Telecommunications	399	1	18,762	18.2	17,216	14.7
Electricity, water and gas	0	0	7,116	6.9	8,708	7.5
Finance services	1,638	3.9	10,671	04-Oct	7,916	6.8
Business services	4,953	11.9	11,019	10.7	7,248	6.2
Retail trade	669	1.6	3,893	3.8	5,353	4.6
Wholesale trade	2,132	5.1	5,918	5.7	3,773	3.2
Others	3,072	7.4	8,509	8.3	13,362	11.4
Total	**41,696**	**100**	**103,015**	**100**	**116,741**	**100**

Source: Central Bank of Brazil. Compiled by NEIT/IE/UNICAMP.

Figure 3.2. Brazil – Share of Mergers and Acquisitions in the Total FDI – %

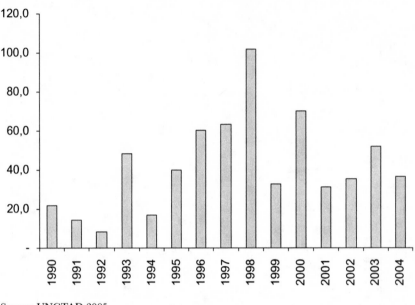

Source: UNCTAD 2005.

Table 3.3. **Importance of Foreign Majority-Owned Companies in the Brazilian Economy**

	1995	2000
Exports	31.20%	41.30%
Imports	31.40%	49.30%
Sales	14.40%	19.70%

Source: Brazilian Central Bank and IBGE National Accounts.

The high FDI inflows have meant an increase in the foreign share of the Brazilian economy. According to data from the census of foreign capital carried out in 1995 and 2000 by the Brazilian Central Bank, total sales of foreign-majority-owned companies reached 14.4 percent of Brazil's total output in 1995. In 2000, this ratio increased to 19.7 percent. Foreign corporations also increased their share of the country's foreign trade, reaching 41.3 percent of exports and 49.3 percent of imports.

The role of foreign capital is even stronger when we consider only large companies. Among the largest 500 private Brazilian companies, those under foreign control accounted for 41.2 percent of sales in 1989. This share increased to 49.9 percent in 1997 and, by 2003, reached 51.7 percent.

These data demonstrate the advance in the process of internationalization of the Brazilian economy. In the next section, we assess the effects of this process.

Impacts of Foreign Direct Investment and MNC Activity on The Brazilian Economy

The increases in FDI inflows and in the foreign share in the Brazilian productive structure inaugurated a series of studies assessing their impacts. This section aims at synthesizing the main results of those studies, organizing the discussion around four major questions. The first concerns the impacts on productivity. The second addresses the effects on foreign-trade flows. The third deals with the influence of foreign corporations on technology development and innovation by Brazilian companies, and the fourth details impacts on wages.

Impacts on Productivity

As we highlighted in Section 1, some scholars and policymakers expected the expansion of foreign corporations to improve the competitiveness of the Brazilian economy. In view of MNCs' greater technological capacity, it was expected that MNC affiliates would directly boost productivity levels. Besides the direct effect associated to an expansion in the presence of MNCs, indirect effects would appear if national companies absorbed part of the production and organization techniques adopted by their G81 foreign counterparts. According to the literature, these spillovers would occur due to both the "competition effect"—when national companies, facing competition from foreign corporations, have to modernize their production and management activities— and the "demonstration effect" – when national companies emulate the more advanced techniques of their foreign competitors.

According to data from the Brazilian Annual Industry Survey of 2003, MNCs are, on average, much larger than domestic companies.[2] Table 3.4 shows that foreign firms have an average size 4.5 times larger than that of national firms, based on number of people employed. When measured by gross revenue, the foreign firms are 11.4 times larger and, in terms of Value Added, 9.6 times larger. Foreign corporations are, on average, 4.3 times more productive than national companies.

Although in fact, MNCs are, on average, more productive than national companies, Gonçalves (2003) shows, based on a sample of 22,000 companies, that there is no evidence of faster productivity growth in the foreign companies than in their domestic counterparts. Using data from 1997 to 2000, he points out that national companies actually exhibit greater productivity growth.

Table 3.4. **Brazil – Characteristics of Transnational and National Companies in 2003 Average Values**

Averages	National	Transnational	MNC/NC
People Employed	128.0	577.0	4.5
Gross Revenue (R$ millions)	22.1	252.3	11.4
Value Added (R$ millions)	8.7	83.4	9.6
Productivity (Value Added/ People Employed) R$	32,501.0	138,323.0	4.3

Source: SECEX, BACEN, PIA, and RAIS. Extracted from Hiratuka and Dias (2007).

Moreover, comparing the 40 industries with the highest rates of productivity growth and the 40 industries with the highest rates of increase in the foreign share of total value added, only 14 industries were on both lists.

In the same study, Gonçalves sought to check, empirically, the existence of productivity spillovers from foreign to national companies. In a panel econometric model at firm level, the author tested whether the expansion of the foreign presence in a certain sector affected the productivity of the national companies in the same sector, controlling for other factors that could affect the productivity of the latter, such as size and sector of activity.

In a first general model, there was no evidence of spillovers, either positive or negative. In a second test, the national companies were classified into three groups according to the original gap in productivity relative to foreign corporations in the same sector, to check if companies with different levels of productivity would differ in their capacity to absorb potential spillovers. In addition, these sectors were classified according to their FDI strategy (market-seeking, resource-seeking or efficiency-seeking) to determine if investment directed toward export had a higher potential to generate spillovers.

Contrary to expectations, the national companies with a narrower productivity gap were negatively affected (that is, the increase in foreign share meant a lower increase in domestic productivity). For companies with a wider gap, the effect was positive. Regarding FDI strategies, market-seeking investments had negative impacts, whereas the others were not statistically significant. According to Gonçalves, these results show that for the largest national companies that compete directly with foreign companies in the domestic market, the positive spillovers associated with demonstration and competition effects were surpassed by the negative effects related to loss of scale and the shift to activities with a lower value-added potential.

In sum, the increased foreign presence did not have a dynamizing effect on productivity for the industrial structure as a whole. The indirect positive impacts were seized by a group of less productive companies that compete less directly with the foreign corporations, probably in market niches. For higher-productivity companies that compete directly with foreign firms in the domestic market, the evidence points to a negative impact, due to a shift to lower-productivity activities and to decline in scale.

Impacts on Foreign Trade

Several studies have analyzed the trade performance of foreign corporations and compared it to the trade patterns of national companies, using different databases and methodologies.

In general, these studies have demonstrated that foreign corporations have a greater orientation than national companies, although this difference is higher for imports than for exports.

Mesquita Moreira (1999), for example, analyzing 1997 data on the business income tax (IRPJ) for about 26,000 companies, confirms that for a given sector and company size, foreign corporations' exports were, on average, 179 percent higher than those of domestic companies, while imports were 316 percent higher on average.

De Negri (2004), investigating microdata from about 54,000 companies from 1996 to 2000, also confirms a difference in the trade behavior of national and foreign companies, based on a panel analysis. Again, the difference in favor of foreign corporations was much higher for imports than for exports. The results showed that foreign companies exported, on average, 70 percent more than domestic companies, and imported 290 percent more, even controlling for other factors, such as sector, size and level of labor education.

These results demonstrate that although foreign corporations do have a greater orientation than national companies, their contribution to positive trade balances has been small, precisely because of their higher level of imports. If it is true that one of the advantages of MNCs over domestic companies is MNCs' well-established trade networks, these advantages were used mainly to increase import flows.

Laplane, Sarti et al. (2001) show that a large proportion of foreign investment in Brazil is aimed at exploring growth opportunities in the domestic or, at the broadest, regional (Latin American) market. Investments intending to use Brazil as an export platform for markets beyond Latin America were rare.

Trade liberalization, combined with exchange-rate appreciation during most of the 1990s, meant a large increase in imports with no corresponding increase in exports, as the data in Figure 3.3 confirm. These data were compiled from two data sets. The first concerns foreign companies' propensities to export (exports/sales) and to import (imports/sales). Foreign companies in the Census of Foreign Capitals in 2000, had an average propensity to export of 14.3 percent and a propensity to import of 13.6 percent. Based on these ratios, the sectors were classified into four groups. The first group consists of sectors with a propensity to export above the average and a propensity to import below the average. The second includes sectors with a propensity to export below the average and a propensity to import above the average. The third group comprises sectors with propensities to export and to import below the respective averages. The fourth has both propensities above the respective averages. The second set of data relates to the volume of investment received in each group of sectors between 1996 and 2005. In Figure 3.3, the bubble size represents the volume of investment.

As Figure 3.3 illustrates, almost half of total investment was directed to sectors in Group 3, with a low degree of trade integration, in terms of either exports or imports. This group largely comprises service industries, which were oriented toward the domestic market and, for that reason, had little impact on trade flows. Group 2, with a high propensity to import and a low propensity to export, accounted for 31 percent of the accumulated flows between 1996 and 2005. This suggests that these industries prioritized the

Figure 3.3. Propensity to Export and Import of MNC Affiliates in Brazil – 2000

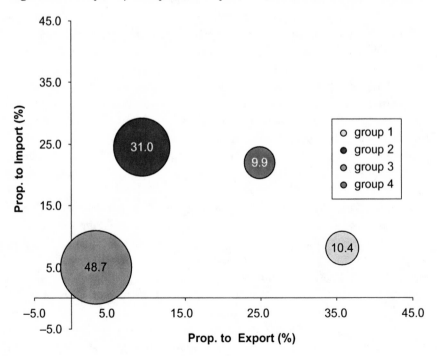

Source: Central Bank of Brazil. Compiled by NEIT/IE/UNICAMP.

domestic market, but with a high volume of imported inputs and components. The key industries within this group are chemicals, information technology products and telecommunications equipment. Group 1, characterized by a high propensity to export and a low propensity to import, accounted for 10.4 percent of the total investment. In general, these are sectors in which resource-seeking strategies predominate, as in mining. Finally, Group 4, with a high propensity to both export and import, includes sectors such as automobiles, as well as machinery and equipment.

Hiratuka and De Negri (2004) explain asymmetry in trade flows and in the propensities to import and export of foreign affiliates. They demonstrate, through panel econometric techniques, that affiliates established in Brazil receive most of their imports from their parent MNCs' home countries, while their main export destination is the regional market. Affiliates tend to import from their home countries products, inputs, and components that are highly technology-intensive, which results in significant differences between exports and imports flows, not only in value, but also in terms of technological profile.

Affiliates in Brazil tend to bring, from their headquarters or from other affiliates, technologically sophisticated inputs and final products, aiming to supply the domestic market and, in some cases, MERCOSUR and ALADI. Few affiliates in Brazil receive global mandates to produce and develop products in the most important stages of the corporate value chain. This finding is reinforced by studies assessing the position of Brazilian affiliates in the global distribution of MNCs' innovation activities, as we will analyze in Section 3.3.

Lastly, Hiratuka and Dias (2007) try to find evidence of spillover effects in exports from foreign affiliates to domestic companies in the period 1997–2003. An econometric test was carried out to check whether the presence foreign corporations, for whom the cost to enter the international market is lower, is associated with an increase in the exports of domestic companies in the same sector.

The results reveal that a higher foreign presence has a negative, albeit small, effect on the probability that national firms in the same sector will export. This may be attributable to the same crowding-out effect observed in the analysis of productivity. The effect is not significant, however, for the value of exports of firms that are already exporting. That is, the expansion of foreign corporations reduced the probabilities that non-exporting firms in the same sector would export, although it had no effect on the value of exports of national firms that were already exporting.

These studies indicate that the impacts on trade flows were limited, mainly when compared with existing expectations about the role of foreign corporations on the international competitiveness of the Brazilian economy.

This is explained by the fact that most of the foreign investment in Brazil targets the domestic market. However, in an environment of trade liberalization and exchange appreciation, as during most of the period under study, MNC affiliates also increased their imports, primarily of highly technology-intensive inputs.

Impacts on Innovation Activities

FDI may affect innovation and R&D expenditures in host economies. According to UNCTAD (2005), MNCs have been adopting strategies to decentralize R&D activities, to both reduce their associated costs and monitor technology advancements generated outside the home country. Although the internationalization of technology activities occurs primarily among high-income countries, this decentralization has reached developing countries as well.

In the Brazilian case, MNCs tend to introduce innovation more rapidly than domestic companies, even controlling for their sectoral distribution. According to Araújo (2004), 67.9 percent of foreign companies in Brazil introduced innovations from 1998 to 2000, compared to 30.6 percent of domestic industrial companies.

Although less innovative on average, domestic companies devote a larger part of their revenues to internal R&D expenditures (0.73 percent of total sales for domestic firms compared to 0.61 percent for foreign firms in 2000 (Araújo 2004)). Foreign corporations, instead, rely on methods developed at their headquarters or by other affiliates. Of all foreign corporations that introduced innovations, 68 percent stated that they had used, as a source of information, another firm, located abroad, in the same corporate group.

According to Araújo (2004), the higher average in R&D expenditures as a percentage of total sales for domestic companies is robust, even controlling for factors such as sector of activity and labor skills. This study also suggests that domestic companies tend to spend more on R&D when foreign corporations in the same sector also have high R&D expenditures. This may be due to the competition effect, and represent a positive spillover from the presence of MNC affiliates. However, the data structure in *cross section* makes it difficult to establish a relation of causality, since it is also possible that foreign corporations spend more in R&D precisely to be able to compete with their domestic counterparts.

In any case, the fact that the average R&D expenditures as a percentage of sales for foreign corporations is lower than for domestic companies shows that MNC affiliates' contribution to technology development in the Brazilian industry could be stronger than it is.

Hiratuka (2006) shows, based on data from US multinationals, that R&D expenditures outside the United States have been increasing even for affiliates in developing countries, although this trend is driven by affiliates in Asia. Latin America and Brazil are losing share in the total of R&D expenditures made abroad by US MNCs.

Table 3.5 shows that, in 2004, MNC affiliates in Brazil made R&D expenditures equaling 0.5 percent of total sales, more than the average for developing countries, but below the average for affiliates established in developing Asian countries, especially China, Taiwan, India, South Korea and Malaysia.

In the same table, it is also interesting to compare each country's share of total US MNC affiliates' R&D expenditures to its share of total USMNC affiliates' sales. Whereas Latin American countries are invariably more important as markets than as centers for R&D, the Asian countries' sales

Table 3.5. **Majority-Owned Foreign Affiliates of US Parent Companies – R&D Expenditures and Share of Selected Developing Countries in R&D Expenditures Abroad – 2004**

	R&D Expenditures/ Sales	Share in Total Sales	Share in R&D Expenditures	Share in R&D Expenditures/ Share in Sales
Affiliates' total	0.8	100	100	1
Developed countries	0.9	71.2	86.3	1.2
Developing countries	0.4	28.8	13.7	0.5
Latin America	0.2	11	3.2	0.3
Argentina	0.1	0.7	0.1	0.1
Brazil	0.5	2.2	1.2	0.6
Chile	0.1	0.3	0	0.1
Venezuela	0.1	0.4	0.1	0.1
Mexico*	0.3	3.9	1.3	0.3
Asia	0.7	12.6	9.8	0.8
China	1	1.9	2.3	1.2
Hong Kong	0.3	1.9	0.8	0.4
India	1.2	0.4	0.6	1.5
Korea, Republic of	1	0.8	0.9	1.1
Malaysia	0.9	1.1	1.1	1
Philippines	0.4	0.4	0.2	0.5
Singapore	0.6	3.8	2.6	0.7
Taiwan	1.2	1	1.3	1.4
Thailand	0.1	0.9	0.1	0.2

* 2002 data.
Source: BEA. Compiled by the author.

shares are not so different from their R&D shares. Some of them even stand out for having higher R&D shares than sales shares. Brazil's R&D share is only 60 percent of its sales share. Therefore, in 2004, Brazil was still more important than China as a location of production and sales for US corporations, but was less important as a location of technology activities.

These data show that MNC affiliates in Brazil, although making higher R&D expenditures relative to sales than affiliates in other Latin American countries, could contribute more to Brazilian innovation, just as they do in some Asian countries. However, it is worth remembering that industry and technology policies in Brazil may explain this difference compared to Asian countries, as we will detail in Section 4.

Impacts on Wages

This last part of Section 3 examines the influence of foreign corporations on wage levels in Brazil. The characteristics of people employed by domestic companies are quite different from those of people employed by foreign companies. According to Hiratuka and Fracalanza (2006), white-collar workers in foreign corporations earn, on average, three times more per hour than those in domestic companies, their number of years of study is 30 percent greater, and their average employment tenure is 70 percent longer. As for blue-collar workers, the differences are similar, although of a slightly lesser magnitude.

Econometric studies by Arbache and De Negri (2004) and by Bahia and Arbache (2005) find wage premiums for employees of foreign corporations of 38.3 percent and 21.7 percent for 1996-1998 and 2000, respectively. Although these studies confirm that foreign corporations pay higher wages, the effects of their growing presence in Brazil was not closely analyzed.

Table 3.6. **Brazil – Differences in Labor Characteristics and Wages Between Domestic and MNC Affiliates – 2002**

	NC	MNC	MNC/NC
White-collars			
Hourly wage (R$)	3.4	10.3	3.0
Years of study	8.6	11.0	1.3
Employment time (months)	37.0	62.6	1.7
Blue-collars			
Hourly wage (R$)	2.8	6.7	2.4
Years of study	6.9	8.7	1.2
Employment time (months)	39.0	65.5	1.7

Source: BACEN, PIA, and RAIS. Extracted from Hiratuka and Fracalanza (2006).

Hiratuka and Fracalanza (2006) assess, using a panel model with data on domestic industrial companies in Brazil from 1997 to 2002, to what extent the expansion of the foreign presence resulted in positive effects on the wages of both white and blue-collar workers, controlling for other factors that could affect pay, such as employment tenure and level of education. For blue-collar workers, the result was not significant, whereas for white-collar workers it was positive, although with a very low coefficient. Therefore, there is evidence that growth in the foreign presence had a positive, albeit small, impact on the wages paid to non-production workers in domestic companies of the same sector.

In the same study, the authors also used the propensity-score-matching technique, combined with a difference-in-difference model to check if companies acquired by foreign corporations started to pay higher wages. Basically, this technique consisted of analyzing the evolution of wages in a group of companies that had come under foreign control and comparing it with a control group made up of companies with similar characteristics, but which remained national. The statistical test showed no significant differences between the two groups; that is, ownership change did not cause wage levels of acquired corporations to change relative to domestic companies, for either blue- or white-collar workers.

Therefore, although the acquisition of national companies did not translate into an increase in wage levels in the acquired firms, foreign direct investment had a positive effect on the wages of white-collar workers in national companies of the same sector, in spite of not having a significant effect on the wages of the blue-collar workers.

Final Remarks and Policy Recommendation

The data analyzed in this chapter demonstrate that MNC affiliates operating in Brazil differ in several characteristics from the averages of domestic companies. In general, they have higher productivity and a more qualified labor force; they also pay higher wages, are more innovative and have a higher degree of trade integration.

These differences, which reveal ownership advantages accumulated by global corporations, have led many authors to predict that the expansion of these corporations in Brazil would contribute to faster and more sustained economic growth.

These expectations were reinforced by the fact that the new boom in FDI occurred at the same time as a set of economic reforms to create a more open environment, removing mechanisms of state intervention that dated back to the period of import substitution.

One of the most important reforms during the liberalizing period of the 1990s was precisely the gradual elimination of restrictions to the activity and movement of foreign capital, either in financial flows or in FDI flows.

Article 171 of the Brazilian Constitution of 1988 establishes the legal distinction between a domestic company and a foreign-owned company. Thus, it permits policies favoring domestic companies relative to foreign companies, such as selective fiscal incentives or access to financing, as well as legal mechanisms establishing special performance requirements for foreign companies. Moreover, the Constitution gives the state the power to control the movement of capital in accordance with the national interest, as well as establishing state monopolies in the extraction of radioactive minerals, oil and gas, and telecommunications services. Foreign capital was limited in several sectors, such as exploitation of mineral and water resources, and newspapers, radio and television.

From the beginning of the 1990s, the restrictions on foreign capital started to be eliminated. In 1991 changes in the Information Technology Law, in force since 1984, repealed the prohibition on foreign companies entering the sector. In 1993 the revision of the Constitution eliminated the distinction between domestic and foreign companies. Later, several constitutional amendments gradually eliminated the restrictions on capital movements.

These changes in the regulation of foreign capital occurred at the same time as the elimination of sector-specific industrial and technology policies. From that point on, "horizontal" policies affecting all sectors uniformly predominated, with only rare exceptions. The government policy toward foreign capital was basically to create a "freer" environment for MNC investment and activity.

It was expected by the policymakers that growth in the foreign presence, in a liberalized environment, would result in the transfer of the superior characteristics of MNCs to Brazilian industry as a whole. However, the findings analyzed in this paper show that the actual consequences fell far short of these optimistic expectations.

From a microeconomic perspective, the studies reviewed in this paper demonstrate that, despite the fact that foreign affiliates show higher levels of productivity, foreign trade integration, innovation and wages than domestic companies, their influence over the latter and was very limited and, in some cases, even had negative spillover effects, as in productivity and access to foreign markets.

Why were these effects so limited, especially when other developing countries were able to take advantage of FDI to spur economic development? In countries such as China, Malaysia and Singapore, the impacts of foreign investment on industrial and technology development and on the competitive insertion in foreign markets were far greater than those seen in Latin America, particularly in Brazil (UNCTAD 2002; Lall 2003).

One of the common traits among the countries that demonstrated this ability was the adoption of active industrial and technology policies (e.g., technical and higher education, support for basic research, financing and incentives to R&D activities) to establish important locational advantages, especially for activities with high technology content. Selective investment policies, structured to channel investment to strategic sectors, also increased the technology content of activities carried out by foreign affiliates and their degree of complementarity and integration with local companies and institutions.

As previously emphasized, the Brazilian government did not adopt a selective sectoral policy or a focus on more technology-intensive activities, but a horizontal policy whose main aim was to remove the existing restrictions on FDI and on the activities of foreign corporations.

MNC affiliates responded to this policy, seeking to increase efficiency, but with limited impact on the competitiveness of the rest of the economy. First, the possibility of relying on imported inputs and capital goods meant the replacement of local suppliers with foreign ones, reducing the productive links between MNC affiliates and domestic companies. Second, it also meant a decline in MNCs' technology efforts, previously directed toward adapting products to the local market.

More recently, the Brazilian government has been revisiting its industrial policy. In 2004 it launched the Industrial, Technology, and Foreign Trade Policy (Política Industrial, Tecnológica e de Comércio Exterior-PITCE). The PITCE includes a series of horizontal and sectoral measures. Among the horizontal measures, those turned to industrial modernization and technology innovation support stand out. An example is the new Innovation Law, which establishes a new regulatory framework for relationships among universities, research institutes and private companies, and, at the same time, make the concession of subventions to research activities easier.

Four sectors were deemed strategic (capital goods, pharmaceuticals, software and semiconductors) and three others "carriers of the future" (nanotechnology, biotechnology and renewable energies), and each given specific financing and support programs for scientific and technology development.

Although resuming a government policy directed to industry and technology development is laudable, its results are still just beginning. First, it has been necessary to create mechanisms to coordinate the ministries and agencies implementing this policy, including the Ministries of Treasury, Planning, Development, Industry and Commerce, Science and Technology, the Funding Agency for Studies and Projects (Financiadora de Estudos e Projetos-FINEP) and the National Bank of Economic and Social Development

(Banco Nacional de Desenvolvimento Econômico e Social-BNDES). Second, macroeconomic variables, especially fiscal restriction and high interest rates, are limiting the availability of resources for various programs and making it difficult for companies to make investment decisions, especially when these decisions are related to R&D and innovation. However, under more favorable macroeconomic conditions, the results of this new industrial policy would probably generate stronger results.

Even so, the new Brazilian industrial policy has the weakness of failing to acknowledge explicitly that, in some sectors, MNCs affiliates play a key role. In these sectors, the possibilities of competitive development depend on affiliates' ability to win from their headquarters—in competition with affiliates based in other countries—new projects for capacity expansion and technology development. The industrial policy could act in this direction, while trying to ensure spillover effects to other companies.

In Brazil, the vast presence of large MNC affiliates that are world leaders in their sectors, with intense worldwide innovation activity, remains an untapped source of skill and knowledge. The challenge for the future is to devise a foreign investment policy coupled with industrial, technology and foreign-trade policies. This requires recognizing the important role of foreign corporations in the Brazilian economy, understanding their role in different sectors, and, through well-chosen policies, fostering connections between these corporations and the local companies that will contribute to a more competitive economy with a greater growth capacity.

Chapter Four

FOREIGN INVESTMENT: THE POLARIZATION OF THE MEXICAN ECONOMY

Enrique Dussel Peters[1]

In the 1990s Mexico was one of the world's most successful countries in attracting FDI. This chapter examines the extent of this process and its effects on the Mexican economy. I provide an overview of Mexican FDI since the early 1990s, identify the factors that led to FDI inflows, and describe the effects of FDI in terms of output, employment, trade and R&D expenditures, among other variables. Specifically, I analyze these effects using newly available data on the industry level. Finally, I make several policy proposals aimed at improving both the quantity and quality of FDI in the future.

The chapter is divided into four sections. The first briefly outlines theories of FDI and development, including an overview of the literature on the impacts of FDI in Mexico. The second section highlights the main trends in Mexican FDI since the 1990s from an aggregate perspective, as well as some major sectoral tendencies. The third section analyzes the effects of FDI in Mexico's manufacturing sector at the industry level, considering more than 25 variables. The final section outlines the main conclusions and presents various policy proposals.

Brief Conceptual Background

The debate on the determinants of FDI and its effects is still unsettled. The current process of globalization—the opening of national economies, the growing role played by multinational corporations and the increasing transfer of segments of the production chain outside these corporations' home countries—has promoted the growth of global FDI flows (UNCTAD 2006).

Flows of capital and FDI have an increasing impact on national economies. Dunning's "eclectic" approach (Dunning 1993, Dunning 1998, Dunning 2005; Dunning 2006) has done a great deal to explain the reasons for FDI, the factors affecting FDI flows and the effects of FDI, but some issues still need further exploration.

The existing FDI literature points to such varied factors affecting FDI flows as the size and dynamism of host-country markets, the costs of production and distribution (in particular, labor costs and tax levels), geographic location, the macroeconomic environment of the host country and its level of commercial openness and capacity to attract FDI for specific purposes.[2] On the other hand, Sanjaya Lall and Michael Mortimore have made a significant contribution to the literature by classifying the aims of multinational corporations undertaking FDI into three broad categories: efficiency-seeking, market-seeking and natural-resource-seeking.

Findings on the causes and effects of FDI depend a great deal on the level of analysis undertaken, whether micro, meso, macro or regional. Studies done at different levels of analysis have arrived at differing, and even contradictory, empirical results. On the one hand, various studies using different methodologies have found positive associations between FDI and exports, GDP, wages and employment. However, others have found no positive associations between FDI and aggregate investment, investment in analyzed firms, imports or trade balances (Dussel Peters, Paliza et al. 2003, 293–298).

The variety of findings owes not only to the study of different countries and sectors, but also the use of different methodologies, levels of aggregation and periods of analysis that do not permit meaningful comparisons. Almost all existing studies and conceptual approaches focus on the intra-sectoral effects of FDI while inter-sectoral effects—which could be much more important, but for which information is lacking—have not received much attention.

The overall effect of FDI in Mexico has been limited. While FDI in Mexico is high in terms of percentages of GDP and employment, and there is a strong positive association between FDI and exports, much of this is based on "temporary" imports processed for reexport. The spillover effects of FDI—in terms of productivity, technology transfer and investment in R&D—may be positive or negative, depending on the level of aggregation of the analysis. Most FDI, however, involves only limited linkages with the rest of the Mexican economy, both in manufacturing as a whole and in specific regions.

Recent debates on competitiveness, territorial endogeneity and the international integration of specific products and processes, in this case through FDI (Bair and Dussel Peters 2006), highlight three aspects of the current globalization process:

Global Commodity Chains and Its Segments

Gary Gereffi, Jennifer Bair and Miguel Korzeniewicz, among others, have highlighted the enormous importance of the international insertion of firms in global commodity chains and in specific segments of these chains (Gereffi and Korzeniewicz 1994, Bair and Dussel Peters 2006). Global commodity chains are composed of various segments with very different characteristics: In the textile-apparel chain, for example, the research and development segments have much higher value added than the manufacturing segments (and the assembly segment in particular). Even though authors like Hirschman (1958) examined global commodity chains long ago, their methodology emphasized the development of international linkages, rather than the differing characteristics of various value-chain segments. A purely macroeconomic perspective—of structural adjustment, for example—does not explain the specific conditions and challenges of different chains, much less the conditions under which particular firms or countries "upgrade" from one segment to another within a specific chain (Rodrik 2006). In the Harmonized Tariff System (HTS), there are around 17,000 items registered (at the ten-digit level) for foreign trade. Their characteristics vary dramatically in terms of the firms, their size, the technology used, financing, employment, quality, training requirements, learning capacity and upgrading, commercial conditions, etc. If the analysis of FDI does not disaggregate at the product and process level, any specific proposals may be trivial and lack any content.

Systemic Competitiveness and Collective Efficiency

Since the 1990s, in an open critique of Michael Porter and of the competitiveness vision proposed by the Organization for Economic Cooperation and Development (OECD), a series of authors have pointed out the importance of integrating micro, meso and macro analyses of competitiveness (Messner and Meyer-Stamer 1994; Esser 1999). An exclusive emphasis on any of these analytic levels, they argue, fails to recognize the complexity of socioeconomic processes in time and space. These authors have highlighted the mesoeconomic level of competitiveness (the relationship between firms) and the role of institutions (Meyer-Stamer 2005), the control of specific value chains and their segments and the characteristics of particular global commodity chains (Humphrey 2004). These authors show the importance of integration between firms in fostering learning, innovation and collective efficiency.[3]

Territorial Endogeneity

Even though the previously mentioned studies are useful in counteracting the dominance of microeconomic and macroeconomic approaches, they generally fail to address territorial variations in forms of global integration. In the alternative approach of "territorial endogeneity," it is not firms, but territories or regions, that are the analytic starting point (Vázquez Barquero 2005; Bair and Dussel Peters 2006). This kind of analysis emphasizes how different territories are integrated into global commodity chains (from a "glocal"—global and local—perspective).[4]

In the last few decades, some segments of manufacturing value chains, particularly from industrialized countries, have been transferred to less-developed countries. This process is likely to continue and even to deepen in the services sector, which is much more significant than manufacturing, in terms of GDP and employment, in the countries of origin (Lall 2005; Sturgeon 2006). In the coming years, the repercussions of the "globalization of services" on receiving countries may be much more significant than the results, over the last few decades, of changes in the industrial organization of manufacturing.

Recent research on FDI at the international level calls attention to three issues First, recent scholarship has pointed out, with particular attention to the case of China (Rodrik 2006), that the most successful countries in terms of GDP growth and development broadly understood, have followed heterodox policies (Rodrik 2004).[5] However, it also highlights macroeconomic stability, integration to the world market, the protection of private property rights, and social cohesion and social stability as the principal factors in economic growth (Fernández-Arias and Hausmann 2000).[6] This kind of analysis suggests the need for bigger empirical studies, a certain skepticism (as implied by Dunning's eclectic theory of FDI) about sweeping theories on economic growth and openness to a diversity of heterodox policies (Hausmann, Rodrik et al. 2004).

Second, traditional authors like Dunning (2006) argue that in the current context of globalization, the potential for technological development, new networks within and between firms and new learning experiences have increased substantially. In this view, institutions and their quality, through incentive structures, property rights, etc., and the diverse types of FDI—market–, efficiency–, resource– or strategic asset-seeking—are critical to understanding the conditions and effects of FDI.[7]

Third, the origins and destinations of FDI in specific sub-national regions or territories has scarcely been studied. This is largely due to statistical and methodological issues, especially the lack of information about specific firms.

Background on the Relevance of FDI for the Mexican Economy

A series of analyses have described the growing significance of FDI in the Mexican economy since the liberalization at the end of the 1980s (Angel and Treviño 1993; Dussel Peters 2000; Dussel Peters, Paliza et al. 2003; Gallagher 2004; Ibarra and Moreno-Brid 2004). These studies have highlighted FDI both as one of the main means of financing the trade deficit—along with oil revenue, remittances and the surplus generated by the *maquila* industries—and as a source of potential modernization and integration into world markets.

Murillo Romo (2001) has made a particularly detailed analysis on the effects of FDI in Mexico. Including a general view of spillover effects and linkages, as well as several sectoral studies (e.g., for the chemical, fiber and pharmaceutical industries), the research concludes that FDI has generated a modern sector with high levels of productivity, but has also displaced Mexican firms. It still has not been proved that domestic firms absorb new technologies and processes as a result of FDI. In the case of Mexico, then, Romo Murillo argues that it is necessary not only to determine how to attract FDI, but also to understand in more detail what will be the likely results for the country's economy.[8]

The strategic importance of FDI has already been established for the public sector and, in accord with the liberalization strategy in place since 1988, on the macroeconomic level (Sojo Garza-Aldape 2005). In the period 1998–2004, FDI represented more than 100 percent of the country's current account deficit. Advocates of liberalization consider it important to Mexico's integration into world markets and the modernization of its productive base. Mexican policymakers since the 1980s have considered a favorable macroeconomic environment a prerequisite for attracting FDI.

Main Trends in FDI in Mexico

Currently, FDI is regulated by the Foreign Investment Law of 1993 (*Ley de Inversiones Extranjeras*, or LIE) (DOF 1993). The LIE incorporated changes made over the years to the law of 1973 as well as investment provisions of the North American Free Trade Agreement (NAFTA) (Dussel Peters 2000). It also simplified the procedures of the National Committee on Foreign Investment (CNIE), leaving only four criteria for evaluating investment petitions.

Without attempting to analyze in detail the regulation on FDI up to 2007, three issues stand out in regard to the current legal framework on FDI:[9]

1. Since the beginning of the 1990s there has been persistent controversy about the opening, either totally or partially, of the petroleum and electricity sectors

to private and foreign capital. There still is not, however, a proposal agreed to by all political parties on the advantages or disadvantages of foreign participation in these industries. This will certainly remain an important issue in political and legislative debates in the future.

2. Another important debate in the last few years has revolved around "neutral investment." The concept of neutral investment, which means investment by Mexican firms or in trusteeship, granting only beneficiary rights to its foreign investors (or, at most, limited corporate rights), was adopted for the first time in the Foreign Investment Law of 1993. This kind of investment is directed mainly at sectors reserved for Mexicans, and requires authorization by the Ministry of the Economy and registration at the Foreign Investment National Registry (RNIE). Neutral investment is not counted when determining the share of foreign investment in the total capital of Mexican firms nor in the statistics published by the RNIE. For several years there have been reform initiatives aimed at making this kind of investment more transparent.

3. Although the Foreign Investment Law has not been directly modified since the 1990s, the Mexican government has adopted some measures—particularly in the arena of trade policy—to promote FDI. It has signed several free-trade agreements and agreements for the reciprocal promotion and protection of foreign investment. Although most of these agreements were signed in the 1990s, since then Mexico has signed a free-trade agreement with Uruguay (2004) and entered into an economic association with Japan (2005). In addition to Mexico's joining the Organization for Economic Cooperation and Development (OECD) in 1994 and the coming into force of NAFTA in the same year, the country has also undertaken some sectoral competitiveness programs and entered into the International Agreement on Information Technology (ITA-Plus) to attract foreign investment.

Against this background, what have been the most important trends on FDI in Mexico? Mexico has lost importance as a host of FDI at the global level (UNCTAD 2006). From accounting for about 3.6 percent of global FDI in 1990–1995, it declined to only 2.0 percent in 2007. On the other hand, FDI has a high degree of importance in the Mexican economy. Although national and international statistics show different absolute values—due to methodological issues (Dussel Peters, Galindo Paliza et al. 2007)—the overall picture is clear (UNCTAD 2006). Worldwide, FDI has grown with respect to gross formation of fixed capital (GFFC) from 4.1 percent in 1990–1995 to more than 10 percent since. For Mexico, the ratio was significantly higher than the world average (14 percent for the entire period 1990–2005). While FDI in Mexico declined relative to GDP and GFFC over the period 1994–2005 (see Figure 4.1),

Figure 4.1. Mexico: FDI/GDP and Gross Formation of Fixed Capital (1994–2005)

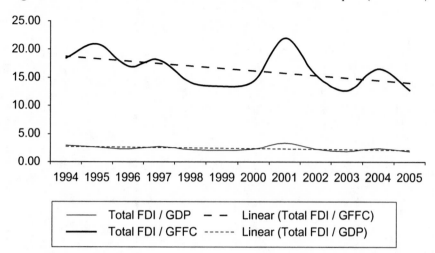

Source: Dussel Peters, *et al.* (2007).

the averages for FDI/GDP and FDI/GFFC were 2.35 percent and 15.63 percent, respectively.

Table 4.1 shows the main aggregate characteristics for FDI in Mexico between 1994 and 2006, in particular:

1. The composition of FDI in Mexico has changed substantially over this period: Until 1998, more than 50 percent of FDI (in 1997, 73.8 percent) was "new investment." Since then, new investment has fallen below 40 percent of total FDI in some years. The flipside has been the growth in reinvestment of dividends and, more importantly, in intra-firm transfers. For the latter, the average annual growth rate was 4.2 percent between 1994 and 2005, compared to −0.3 percent for new investments.
2. Within the "new investment" category, some important changes are also observable: investment in new fixed assets has declined steadily compared with mergers and acquisitions. The issue of greatest relevance regarding FDI in new fixed assets—using new investments as a proxy—has been constantly decreasing for the period.

Imports of fixed assets by *maquiladoras* with FDI have gone through several cycles: between 1994 and 2000 they grew at an average annual rate of 22.2 percent; for 2001–2005, at a much lower annual rate of 4.5 percent, though with a significant recovery since 2004. These figures are intimately liked with the conditions of the export *maquila* industry and the state of the US economy.

Table 4.1. **FDI in Mexico (1994–2006)**

	1994	1995	1996	1997	1998	1999	2000	2001	2002	2003	2004	2005	2006 Jan.–Sep.[d]		Accum. 1994–2006[b]	
													Value	Share %	Value	Share %
New Investments	*9,752*	*7,008*	*6,431*	*10,465*	*6,263*	*6,203*	*8,106*	*20,516*	*11,385*	*6,012*	*13,328*	*9,463*	*5,106*	*36.2*	*120,038*	*57.1*
New Investments	7,405	6,309	6,042	5,198	5,257	6,059	4,221	6,271	7,669	5,848	8,458	6,975	4,686	33.2	80,399	38.2
Notified to RNIE	7,405	6,309	6,042	5,198	5,257	6,059	4,221	6,271	7,669	5,848	8,458	6,975	1,436	10.2	77,149	36.7
Estimated[c]												0	3,250	23.0	3,250	1.5
Mergers and Acquisitions	2,347	699	389	5,268	1,006	144	3,884	14,245	3,716	163	4,870	2,488	419	3.0	39,639	18.8
Notified to RNIE	2,347	699	389	5,268	1,006	144	3,884	14,245	3,716	163	4,870	2,488	419	3.0	39,639	18.8
Estimated[c]												0	0	0.0	0	0.0
Reinvestment of profits	*2,367*	*1,572*	*2,590*	*2,150*	*2,864*	*2,333*	*3,850*	*3,854*	*2,440*	*2,067*	*2,330*	*3,460*	*3,048*	*21.6*	*34,923*	*16.6*
Notified to RNIE						2,333	3,850	3,854	2,440	2,067	2,330	3,460	3,048	21.6	23,381	11.1
Estimated[c]	2,367	1,572	2,590	2,150	2,864										11,542	5.5
Intra-firm Transfers	*2,039*	*–250*	*–350*	*–116*	*1,179*	*2,390*	*2,834*	*886*	*3,476*	*5,308*	*4,150*	*3,190*	*3,688*	*26.1*	*28,422*	*13.5*
Notified to RNIE						2,390	2,834	886	3,476	5,308	4,150	3,190	3,688	26.1	25,921	12.3
Estimated[c]	2,039	–250	–350	–116	1,179										2,501	1.2
Imports of fixed assets made by maquiladora	*895*	*1,366*	*1,417*	*1,680*	*2,111*	*2,778*	*2,983*	*2,172*	*2,044*	*1,961*	*2,475*	*2,822*	*2,274*	*16.1*	*26,976*	*12.8*
TOTAL	**15,052**	**9,696**	**10,087**	**14,180**	**12,416**	**13,704**	**17,773**	**27,429**	**19,344**	**15,348**	**22,283**	**18,934**	**14,114**	**100.0**	**210,359**	**100.0**

Source: Authors' elaboration based on Secretaria de Economia.

a Figures notified by September 30th, 2006.

b From January 1st, 1994 to September 30th, 2006.

c Estimation of Executed FDI not yet notified to RNIE.

d Includes estimation of executed FDI not notified to RNIE.

e In accordance with international practices, the sum of partial percentages may differ from the corresponding totals or sub-totals because the rounding is done automatically by the spreadsheet.

Note: The figures given in this paper are not comparable –and, therefore it is not valid to sum them up– with the statistics on FDI published by the Secretaría de Economía for years previous to 1994, due to the methodologies used Before 1994 annual FDI was integrated with the figures notified to the RNIE every year (without taking into consideration the lag with respect to the dates where the investments were actually made), in addition to the amounts involved in the authorized pr

In the figures obtained with the new methodology are integrated with the amounts notified to the RNIE that effectively materialized each year, an estimation of the amounts not yet notified to the RNIE and the value of imports of fixed assets.

The manufacturing sector (which includes *maquiladoras*) accounted for 49 percent of executed FDI between 1994 and 2005, constituting the most important sector.[10] The financial services sector, which ranks second in this category, increased its share of executed FDI substantially as a result of the sale of national banks between 2000 and 2002, although this tendency is likely to diminish. The third-ranked sector, accounting for 10.8 percent of executed FDI between 1994 and 2005, is commerce, with an average annual growth rate (AAGR) of 6.7 percent for the period.[11]

For both agriculture and for mining, FDI has been minimal, totaling only $455 million and $1,285 million, respectively, for the whole period, with average annual growth rates of 11.3 percent and 16.4 percent, respectively. The electricity and water sectors, surprisingly, have been the most dynamic for the period, with an AAGR of 25.9 percent between 1994 and 2005.

At the aggregate level, FDI is highly concentrated by place of origin and destination. The United States and the European Union together accounted for 87.4 percent of incoming FDI between 1994 and 2006 (see Figure 4.2). While the US share has been relatively stable, the EU's grew from less than 20 percent until 2002 to levels steadily higher than 30 percent since. In particular, Holland, Spain and Germany have increased their investments in Mexico. In contrast, the US remains dominant in *maquila industry for export* (MIE), with close to 90 percent of total FDI. The shares of the EU and Japan were 4.4 percent and 2 percent, respectively, between 1994 and 2006.

Executed FDI has been located mainly in the Federal District (DF). The DF accounted for 57.5 percent of FDI during the period 1994–2006, though with its share declining since the 1990s and falling below 50 percent since 2005. Nuevo León, Estado de México, Jalisco, Chihuahua and Baja California have increasingly attracted executed FDI.

Finally, the top 500 and 1000 companies by FDI in Mexico accounted for an enormous percentage of total FDI during 1999–2005:[12]

1. The 500 and 1000 most important companies account for a very high proportion of total FDI (64.9 percent and 74.7 percent, respectively). This concentration is increasing, as the average annual growth rates in FDI by the 500 and 1000 most important companies (4.9 percent and 4.8 percent, respectively) are much higher than for overall FDI (3.8 percent). In future studies, a detailed analysis of this group of companies would cover a very large share of total FDI and would render unnecessary a study of the more than 30,000 companies registered with the RNIE in 1994–2005.
2. For all the major FDI categories except MIE (in which the 1000 most important companies account for 62.9 percent during 1999–2005) the share of the 1000 top companies is more than 70 percent, reaching 82.98 percent for reinvestment of profits (see Figure 4.3).

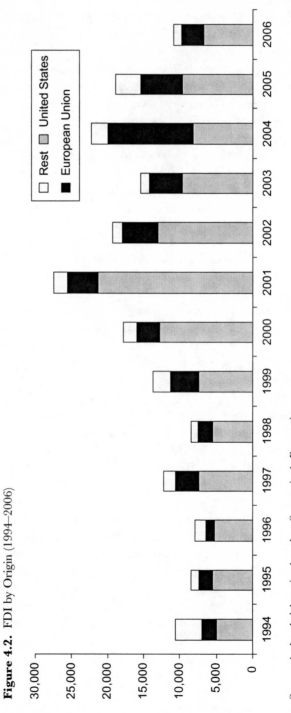

Figure 4.2. FDI by Origin (1994–2006)

Source: Authors' elaboration based on Secretaría de Economía.

Figure 4.3. Participation of the 500 and 1000 Most Important Companies in Respective Variables (1999–2005)

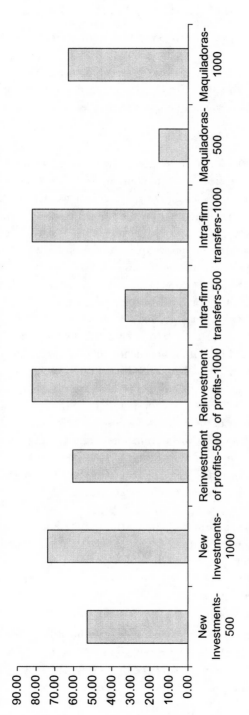

Source: Authors' elaboration based on Secretaria de Economia.

Effects of FDI at the Industry Level in Manufacturing

Newly available data for the 653 industries in Mexico's manufacturing sector make possible a much more detailed analysis. Looking at the characteristics of the 20 most important industries—ten with growing shares of FDI between 1994 and 2005 and ten with declining shares—the results are surprising. Table 4.2 shows substantial changes in the destinations of FDI by industry, including:

1. The ten industries that have grown the most, in terms of FDI, increased their total share from 8.73 percent in 1994 to 48.58 percent in 2005. Meanwhile, the ten whose shares declined went from a total share of 45.18 percent to a share of only 7.08 percent over the same period. In a relatively short period, these 20 industries—out of 653—have been responsible for most of the sectoral changes in FDI.

2. Among the industries whose shares of FDI have grown the most, several are particularly noteworthy: The auto and truck parts and accessories industry accounted for 9.97 percent of total FDI in 2005; food retail, highly linked with a small group of large retail companies, increased from 0.04 percent of FDI to 6.39 percent between 1994 and 2005; two industries linked to real estate, meanwhile, accounted for 8.07 percent of executed FDI in 2005. FDI to the ten FDI-growth industries grew at an average annual rate of 21.3 percent during the period 1994–2005 (compared to 3.8 percent for total executed FDI).

3. On the other hand, the industries whose shares of total FDI fell during the years 1994–2005 were linked to sectors such as petroleum retail, telephone services, pharmaceutical products, multiple banking, steel products manufacturing, and restaurants and bars. Although the causes of the decline in their shares vary, in several cases we observe FDI in the form of acquisitions of existing firms (often in quasi-monopolistic industries), followed by declines in FDI thereafter. For these industries, the AAGR of FDI was 12.3 percent during 1994–2005. After FDI inflows of more than $1,100 million in 1994, the steel-products manufacturing industry disappeared from the FDI register. Inflows fell constantly—even registering some negative figures—after 2002.

Building on previous efforts to analyze FDI at the industry level (Dussel Peters, Galindo Paliza, et al. 2007), we develop a typology of the most important industries in the manufacturing sector during 1994–2005. Using detailed information from the National Institute of Statistics, Geography and Informatics (INEGI) and the Ministry of the Economy for the 205 existing industries in manufacturing (of which we analyzed 197 due to missing data for the others), we developed selection criteria for the ten and twenty most important industries by FDI share during 1994–2005.[13] We describe the characteristics of not only the most important industries, but also the other 177.

Several characteristics of the ten and twenty most important manufacturing industries are noteworthy, in contrast to both the rest of the manufacturing sector and the characteristics highlighted by previous research. At the industry level, three types of activities stand out by their weight in FDI: the automotive and auto parts chain; the electronics chain (including parts and accessories, telecommunications product repair, television sets and sound equipment, etc.); and industries linked to the manufacturing of alcoholic (beer) and non-alcoholic beverages, cigarettes, pharmaceuticals, cosmetics, perfumes, plastics and home products, among others. There are some industries with negative FDI flows for the whole period, while 98 industries (half of the manufacturing universe studied) had, as share of FDI, flows less than 0.1 percent of the total during 1994–2005.

The results of the typology shown in Table 4.3 characterize the performance of the most important manufacturing industries for 1994–2005. It is particularly worth noting that:

1. The ten and twenty most important industries have a growing share of manufacturing FDI, of 48.93 percent to 66.77 percent for 1994–2003, respectively. The remaining 177 industries represent only a third of total FDI for the period and are declining in importance.
2. The executed FDI in manufacturing has substantially increased as a percentage of gross fixed-capital formation, from 90.07 percent in 1994 to 160 percent in 2003. This trend is much more dramatic for the ten and twenty most important industries, for which the equivalent figure was over 300 percent in 2002 and 2003. In other words, in manufacturing, and particularly in the most important industries, FDI has been much more important than domestic investment.
3. FDI as share of total output (by value) decreased over the period, both for the manufacturing sector as a whole and for the ten and twenty most important industries; for the latter it declined from 9.69 percent in 1994 to 7.41 percent in 2003.
4. As manufacturing employment has declined since 2000, total FDI per employee has increased from less than $10,000 in the mid-1990s to more than $13,000 in the twenty most important industries. The differences between manufacturing as a whole and the ten and twenty most important industries are significant (see Figure 4.4).

Table 4.2. FDI by Economic Classes

	Millions of Dollars													Participation				AAGR 1994–2005
	1994	1995	1996	1997	1998	1999	2000	2001	2002	2003	2004	2005	1994–2005	1994	2000	2005	2005–1994	
10 Classes with the greatest increase in participation (1994–2005)																		
1 Manufacturing of parts and accessories for cars and trucks	299	343	364	407	391	680	824	1,112	805	883	890	1,601	8,598	2.80	4.64	9.97	4.91	16.5
2 Retail of food products in supermarkets and convenience stores	4	45	113	1,632	320	263	1,108	978	433	578	613	1,026	7,112	0.04	6.23	6.39	4.06	64.9
3 Other professional, technical, and specialized services non mentioned before	96	61	50	47	113	664	1,073	575	309	438	50	1,140	4,617	0.90	6.04	7.10	2.64	25.2
4 Trusteeship of real estate located in the restricted zone	0	0	2	6	11	17	45	97	242	250	322	630	1,623	0.00	0.25	3.92	0.93	92.8
5 Manufacturing assembly and repair of information processing machines	31	31	117	73	224	220	279	275	190	145	235	584	2,403	0.29	1.57	3.64	1.37	30.7
6 Preparation and mix of animal food	3	2	17	−6	4	26	56	52	11	26	−3	514	703	0.03	0.32	3.20	0.40	57.8
7 Manufacturing of air conditioning, refrigeration and heating equipment	15	43	18	36	36	63	34	58	70	268	104	478	1,223	0.14	0.19	2.98	0.70	37.0
8 Manufacturing of products not elsewhere classified	85	72	118	194	290	474	1,203	458	497	333	340	541	4,605	0.80	6.77	3.37	2.63	18.3
9 Other telecommunication services	168	435	156	262	123	245	401	718	−8	157	30	623	3,309	1.58	2.26	3.88	1.89	12.6
10 Services of purchase, sale and management of real estate (real estate agencies).	229	68	18	70	61	181	303	155	169	63	138	666	2,120	2.14	1.70	4.15	1.21	10.2
Subtotal	931	1,101	971	2,721	1,574	2,833	5,325	4,478	2,718	3,140	2,719	7,801	36,313	8.73	29.96	48.58	20.73	21.3
Rest	9,733	7,273	6,876	9,419	6,797	10,863	12,449	22,664	16,321	11,999	16,204	8,259	138,859	91.27	70.04	51.42	79.27	−1.5

10 Classes with the greatest decrease in participation (1994–2005)

644 Petroleum and tractoline retail	121	54	49	0	0	0	0	0	0	0	0	0	224	1.14	0.00	0.00	0.13	—
645 Phone Services	496	289	263	90	256	16	−2,524	1,934	695	1,467	1,159	517	4,657	4.65	−14.20	3.22	2.66	0.4
646 Building of industrial plants	169	23	5	2	15	−23	11	−3	45	27	34	24	328	1.58	0.06	0.15	0.19	−16.4
647 Manufacturing of pharmaceutical products	157	119	158	165	198	294	58	−710	788	120	329	−23	1,653	1.47	0.33	−0.14	0.94	−183.9
648 Beer and Malt industry	510	0	0	605	561	77	36	27	58	310	343	419	2,947	4.78	0.20	2.61	1.68	−1.8
649 Manufacturing of snacks and corn products not elsewhere classified	425	0	2	0	−148	77	202	−676	177	1,060	1	2	1,123	3.99	1.13	0.01	0.64	−37.7
650 Manufacturing and assembly of cars and trucks	558	517	236	558	25	1,380	460	115	339	153	1,182	89	5,614	5.24	2.59	0.55	3.20	−15.4
651 Multiple Banking	654	276	129	312	58	33	1,610	12,466	3,100	947	4,485	197	24,266	6.13	9.06	1.22	13.85	−10.3
652 Restaurant and Bar Services	605	18	3	19	35	107	51	29	80	26	108	−72	1,011	5.68	0.29	−0.45	0.58	−182.4
653 Manufacturing of other steel products	1,123	95	315	30	33	21	32	17	31	9	23	−15	1,715	10.53	0.18	−0.09	0.98	−167.6
Subtotal	4,818	1,390	1,159	1,782	1,033	1,983	−63	13,200	5,314	4,120	7,664	1,137	43,537	45.18	−0.36	7.08	24.85	−12.3
Rest	5,846	6,984	6,688	10,358	7,338	11,714	17,837	13,942	13,726	11,019	11,260	14,923	131,635	54.82	100.36	92.92	75.15	8.9
TOTAL	10,664	8,375	7,848	12,140	8,370	13,697	17,773	27,142	19,040	15,139	18,923	16,060	175,171	100.00	100.00	100.00	100.00	3.8

Source: Authors' elaboration based on Secretaría de Economía (Dirección General de Inversión Extranjera). Data coverage up to April 2nd 2006.

Table 4.3. **Typology of Manufacturing Economic Classes by Participation in Total FDI (1994–2005)**

		TOTAL ECONOMIC CLASSES	100.00
		MOST IMPORTANT 10	
1	384126	Manufacturing of other parts and accessories for cars and trucks.	11.72
2	384110	Manufacturing and assembly of cars and trucks.	7.65
3	313050	Manufacturing of sodas and other non-alcoholic beverages.	4.82
4	314002	Manufacturing of cigarettes.	4.71
5	383109	Manufacturing of electric material and accessories.	4.35
6	313040	Beer and malt industry.	4.02
7	382302	Manufacturing, assembly and repair of data processing machines.	3.28
8	383202	Manufacturing of parts and repair of communication equipment.	3.07
9	352221	Manufacturing of perfumes, cosmetics and similar products.	3.07
10	383103	Manufacturing of accessories for automotive electrical systems.	3.01
		11–20 MOST IMPORTANT	
11	352100	Manufacturing of pharmaceutical products.	2.25
12	312129	Manufacturing of food products for human consumption.	1.87
13	383206	Manufacturing of components and repair for radios, television receivers and audio equipment.	1.87
14	352222	Manufacturing of soaps, detergent and toothpaste.	1.86
15	383101	Manufacturing, assembly and repair of electric motors and equipments for the generation, transformation and use of electric, solar or geothermic energy.	1.80
16	383204	Manufacturing and assembly of radios, television receivers and audio equipment.	1.71
17	382206	Manufacturing of equipment and machines for air conditioning, refrigeration and heating.	1.67
18	383304	Manufacturing and assembly of small domestic goods.	1.62
19	356012	Manufacturing of other plastic products not elsewhere classified.	1.61
20	312127	Manufacturing of snacks and corn products not elsewhere classified.	1.53
		REST	32.49

Source: Authors' elaboration based on data directly provided by INEGI.

Figure 4.4. Executed FDI in Manufacturing by Employee (1994–2003 Average)

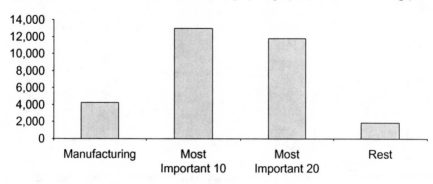

Source: Authors' elaboration based on INEGI and SE.

5. Job creation was negative for manufacturing as a whole, the ten and twenty most important industries, and the remaining manufacturing industries. Employment in manufacturing, and particularly in the ten and twenty most important industries, increased until 1999, but has declined since 2000. The share of the ten and twenty most important classes in total manufacturing employment has been quite steady, with the twenty most important industries averaging 23.66 percent of total manufacturing employment for 1994–2003.

6. Wages in the ten and twenty most important industries are significantly higher than the average in manufacturing (see Figure 4.5), with the differences remaining constant over the period 1994–2003. Figure 4.5 shows that the gap between productivity and wages has increased significantly for the ten and twenty most important industries, but has decreased for the rest of the 177 manufacturing industries. Productivity gains in the most important industries have not been redistributed in terms of wage growth, while the rest of the industries in manufacturing have shown, during 1994–2003, unsustainable rates of wage growth above their rates of productivity growth.

7. Figure 4.5 shows huge differences in productivity between different industries. In 2003, productivity in the ten and twenty most important industries exceeded that in manufacturing as a whole by 84.53 percent and 59.91 percent, respectively. Productivity in the other 177 manufacturing industries was 20 percent below the manufacturing average. There is a clear positive association, then, of FDI with productivity levels and growth rates, although without job creation.

8. The typology establishes a clear positive association between the industries with the greatest weight in executed FDI and foreign trade (both exports

Figure 4.5. Wages by Employment and Productivity (1994–2003)

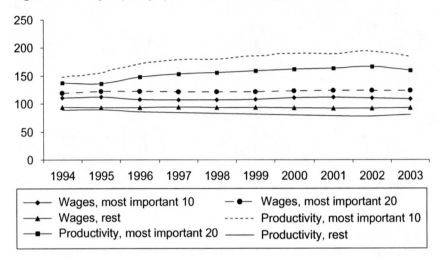

Source: Authors' elaboration based on Secretaria de Economía.

and imports). Although the most important industries' share of total sales increased – from 31.14 percent in 1994 to 39 percent in 2003—the increase in their share of foreign trade stands out. These industries increased their exports as a function of total output (by value) from 25.16 percent in 1994 to 43.55 percent in 2003 and decreased their imports as a function of total output from 27.29 percent to 27.08 percent. Both exports and imports (as a share of total output) are about 50 percent lower for the rest of the manufacturing sector. The twenty most important industries now have a significant trade surplus relative to total output, going from a deficit in 1994 to a surplus of 16.47 percent in 2003. The trade surplus relative to output was only 2.89 percent for the rest of the industries in the manufacturing sector in 2003.

9. One of the most surprising results of this typology is that FDI is not positively associated with research and development (R&D) expenditures. The twenty most important industries in terms of executed FDI actually exhibit a clear declining trend in R&D expenditures over the period, from 0.39 percent of output value in 1994 to 0.07 percent in 2002. The latter was well bellow the equivalent figure for the remaining industries, which was 0.14 percent in 2002. These figures are particularly important as indicators of the potential for technological upgrading and spillovers through FDI.

10. The weighted tariff rate in manufacturing with respect to imports has fallen significantly, from 7.24 percent in 1994 to 0.69 percent in 2002

(see Table 4.4). This trend has been stronger for the most important industries in terms of FDI than for the rest of the manufacturing sector, although the differences are small; while the weighted tariff rate for the twenty most important industries was 0.53 percent in 2002, it was 0.90 percent for the remaining manufacturing industries.

Preliminary Conclusions and Proposals

This chapter has examined a new approach to the analysis of growth and competitiveness with an emphasis on systemic competitiveness and territorial endogeneity. While recognizing the importance of trade liberalization and macroeconomic stability, these are not sufficient for long-run sustained economic growth. It is indispensable to consider new "glocal" forms of organization and the integration of territories and regions into specific products and processes. It is these segments of value chains that determine the characteristics of territorial endogeneity, technological diffusion and learning, and potential for growth. The potential of FDI to contribute to technological diffusion and upgrading of activities also depends on specific global commodity chains, the conditions for systemic competitiveness, and the degree of territorial endogeneity.

Current research on the origins and destinations of FDI is insufficient; for Mexico there are, so far, no studies at all on the issue. Methodological and statistical challenges likely explain the lack of such research, despite its importance for understanding the role of FDI in achieving the main aims of the liberalization, both in terms of the balance of payments and of the modernization of manufacturing.

The second section addressed the main characteristics and effects of FDI in the Mexican economy. FDI flows have remained relatively constant during the period 1994–2006, diminishing as a share of GDP and gross fixed-capital formation. The "new investments" category of FDI has diminished substantially, while the shares of mergers and acquisitions, intra-firm transfers, and reinvestment of dividends have increased. At the sectoral level, manufacturing accounted for 49 percent of total FDI, although the services sector, particularly the financial sector, has significantly increased its share since 2000. This section also highlighted the enormous weight of the 500 and 1,000 most important companies in terms of FDI during 1994–2005, suggesting that future studies may focus on this group of companies rather than studying all 30,000 companies that reported their activities to the RNIE in 1994–2005.

The twenty most important industries in terms of FDI exhibit a lack of job creation, a growing gap between productivity and wages, a growing trade

Table 4.4. **Typology Based on Most Important Manufacturing Economic Classes (by Participation in Total FDI During 1994–2005)**

	1994	1995	1996	1997	1998	1999	2000	2001	2002	2003	1994–2003
FDI (millions of dollars)	4,625	4,298	3,977	6,638	4,291	7,904	7,835	4,342	7,523	5,749	57,182
10 Most Important Classes, by FDI participation	2,086	1,785	1,253	4,310	1,671	3,851	3,483	2,904	3,908	2,335	27,587
20 Most Important Classes, by FDI participation	3,362	2,675	2,160	5,138	2,256	4,921	4,937	2,411	5,561	4,227	37,646
Rest, by FDI participation	1,263	1,623	1,817	1,500	2,035	2,983	2,898	1,931	1,963	1,523	19,336
FDI (1994 = 100)	100.00	92.92	85.98	143.52	92.77	170.88	169.39	93.87	162.65	124.30	—
10 Most Important Classes, by FDI participation	100.00	83.95	62.74	200.19	81.99	182.63	155.57	85.19	200.79	103.95	—
20 Most Important Classes, by FDI participation	100.00	89.27	81.41	171.70	93.71	172.38	180.91	75.62	181.79	134.61	—
Rest, by FDI participation	100.00	99.53	94.26	92.49	91.09	168.14	148.54	126.91	128.01	105.64	—
FDI (total = 100)	100.00	100.00	100.00	100.00	100.00	100.00	100.00	100.00	100.00	100.00	100.00
10 Most Important Classes, by FDI participation	48.12	43.48	35.12	67.13	42.53	51.44	44.20	43.68	59.41	40.25	48.93
20 Most Important Classes, by FDI participation	64.42	61.89	60.99	77.07	65.07	64.99	68.80	51.89	72.00	69.76	66.77
Rest, by FDI participation	35.58	38.11	39.01	22.93	34.93	35.01	31.20	48.11	28.00	30.24	33.23
FDI/Gross Fixed Capital Formation	90.07	111.87	75.43	123.93	74.48	138.33	126.81	71.16	139.84	160.34	111.74
10 Most Important Classes, by FDI participation	237.08	182.42	112.59	340.92	141.52	323.41	221.97	192.59	303.50	267.79	235.31
20 Most Important Classes, by FDI participation	269.12	222.91	152.37	317.12	138.29	293.73	236.58	118.89	325.83	369.79	239.71
Rest, by FDI participation	32.51	61.45	47.14	40.15	49.28	73.86	70.83	47.40	53.43	62.34	55.31
FDI/Production Value	4.15	4.99	3.79	5.40	3.40	5.61	4.92	2.79	4.78	3.93	4.35
10 Most Important Classes, by FDI participation	8.21	8.90	4.59	12.97	4.68	9.21	6.96	5.88	7.87	5.52	7.22
20 Most Important Classes, by FDI participation	9.69	10.16	6.21	12.10	4.93	9.18	7.74	3.76	8.51	7.41	7.53
Rest, by FDI participation	1.65	2.72	2.59	1.86	2.52	3.42	3.04	2.11	2.13	1.71	2.40
FDI/Employment (dollars by worker)	3,401	3,434	3,096	4,891	3,049	5,551	5,420	3,137	5,715	4,585	4,241
10 Most Important Classes, by FDI participation	9,983	9,496	6,437	21,072	7,606	16,847	14,586	12,556	18,274	11,881	12,982
20 Most Important Classes, by FDI participation	10,959	9,497	7,511	16,806	6,886	14,401	13,825	6,907	16,977	13,819	11,799
Rest, by FDI participation	1,200	1,673	1,823	1,427	1,885	2,756	2,662	1,866	1,985	1,606	1,898
Gross Fixed Capital Formation (total = 100)	100.00	100.00	100.00	100.00	100.00	100.00	100.00	100.00	100.00	100.00	100.00
10 Most Important Classes, by FDI participation	17.13	25.47	21.11	23.60	20.50	20.84	25.40	24.71	23.94	24.32	23.00
20 Most Important Classes, by FDI participation	24.33	31.23	26.88	30.25	28.32	29.32	33.78	33.24	31.72	31.87	30.60
Rest, by FDI participation	75.67	68.77	73.12	69.75	71.68	70.68	66.22	66.76	68.28	68.13	69.40

Employment (1994 = 100)	100.00	92.05	94.47	99.80	103.50	104.70	106.31	101.77	96.80	92.22	—
10 Most Important Classes, by FDI participation	100.00	89.96	93.19	97.91	105.18	109.41	114.30	110.68	102.37	94.06	—
20 Most Important Classes, by FDI participation	100.00	91.80	93.72	99.66	106.81	111.39	116.40	113.79	106.77	99.70	—
Rest, by FDI participation	100.00	92.12	94.69	99.84	102.53	102.75	103.37	98.27	93.90	90.04	—
Employment (total = 100)	100.00	100.00	100.00	100.00	100.00	100.00	100.00	100.00	100.00	100.00	100.00
10 Most Important Classes, by FDI participation	15.36	15.02	15.16	15.07	15.61	16.06	16.52	16.71	16.25	15.67	15.76
20 Most Important Classes, by FDI participation	22.56	22.50	22.38	22.53	23.28	24.00	24.70	25.22	24.88	24.39	23.66
Rest, by FDI participation	77.44	77.50	77.62	77.47	76.72	76.00	75.30	74.78	75.12	75.61	76.34
Wages (total = 100)	100.00	100.00	100.00	100.00	100.00	100.00	100.00	100.00	100.00	100.00	100.00
10 Most Important Classes, by FDI participation	17.02	16.87	16.31	16.10	16.67	17.24	18.27	18.58	17.85	16.96	17.39
20 Most Important Classes, by FDI participation	26.88	27.42	27.34	27.34	28.20	29.18	30.28	31.12	30.71	30.21	29.45
Rest, by FDI participation	73.12	72.58	72.66	72.66	71.80	70.82	69.72	68.88	69.29	69.79	70.55
Wages/Employment Level (pesos)	37,486	44,898	54,568	64,435	75,762	91,615	106,966	119,664	127,454	134,707	85,931
10 Most Important Classes, by FDI participation	41,535	50,455	58,732	68,818	80,865	98,347	118,329	133,054	140,031	145,784	94,850
20 Most Important Classes, by FDI participation	44,665	54,726	66,662	78,202	91,749	111,400	131,109	147,637	157,320	166,860	106,951
Rest, by FDI participation	35,395	42,046	51,081	60,432	70,910	85,367	99,047	110,228	117,561	124,335	79,416
Wages/Employed Population (total = 100)	100.00	100.00	100.00	100.00	100.00	100.00	100.00	100.00	100.00	100.00	100.00
10 Most Important Classes, by FDI participation	110.80	112.38	107.63	106.80	106.74	107.35	110.62	111.19	109.87	108.22	110.38
20 Most Important Classes, by FDI participation	119.15	121.89	122.16	121.36	121.10	121.60	122.57	123.38	123.43	123.87	124.46
Rest, by FDI participation	94.42	93.65	93.61	93.79	93.60	93.18	92.60	92.11	92.24	92.30	92.42
Production Value (total = 100)	100.00	100.00	100.00	100.00	100.00	100.00	100.00	100.00	100.00	100.00	100.00
10 Most Important Classes, by FDI participation	22.81	23.29	26.02	27.03	28.26	29.70	31.46	31.74	31.54	28.91	29.16
20 Most Important Classes, by FDI participation	31.14	30.59	33.16	34.56	36.24	38.08	40.07	41.22	41.50	39.00	37.91
Rest, by FDI participation	68.86	69.41	66.84	65.44	63.76	61.92	59.93	58.78	58.50	61.00	62.09
Productivity (Production Value/Employed Population) (total = 100)	100.00	100.00	100.00	100.00	100.00	100.00	100.00	100.00	100.00	100.00	100.00
10 Most Important Classes, by FDI participation	148.46	155.11	171.71	179.34	181.01	184.96	190.46	189.95	194.13	184.51	185.04
20 Most Important Classes, by FDI participation	138.02	135.96	148.14	153.39	155.64	158.66	162.24	163.42	166.78	159.91	160.22
Rest, by FDI participation	88.92	89.56	86.12	84.48	83.11	81.48	79.58	78.61	77.88	80.67	81.34
Sales (total = 100)	100.00	100.00	100.00	100.00	100.00	100.00	100.00	100.00	100.00	100.00	100.00
10 Most Important Classes, by FDI participation	22.81	23.29	26.02	27.03	28.26	29.70	31.46	31.74	31.54	28.91	29.16
20 Most Important Classes, by FDI participation	31.14	30.59	33.16	34.56	36.24	38.08	40.07	41.22	41.50	39.00	37.91
Rest, by FDI participation	68.86	69.41	66.84	65.44	63.76	61.92	59.93	58.78	58.50	61.00	62.09

(Continued)

Table 4.4. Continued

	1994	1995	1996	1997	1998	1999	2000	2001	2002	2003	1994–2003
Exports (total = 100)	100.00	100.00	100.00	100.00	100.00	100.00	100.00	100.00	100.00	100.00	100.00
10 Most Important Classes, by FDI participation	43.69	44.68	52.89	53.42	54.79	57.36	60.05	61.41	60.09	57.14	56.80
20 Most Important Classes, by FDI participation	47.81	47.90	55.99	56.71	58.14	61.29	63.72	65.75	64.31	61.51	60.64
Rest, by FDI participation	52.19	52.10	44.01	43.29	41.86	38.71	36.28	34.25	35.69	38.49	39.36
Exports/Production Value (percentage)	16.39	28.69	29.90	29.00	29.15	29.23	29.73	29.58	28.68	27.61	28.60
10 Most Important Classes, by FDI participation	31.38	55.03	60.76	57.30	56.51	56.45	56.74	57.23	54.64	54.56	55.71
20 Most Important Classes, by FDI participation	25.16	44.92	50.48	47.59	46.78	47.04	47.26	47.18	44.44	43.55	45.75
Rest, by FDI participation	12.42	21.53	19.68	19.18	19.14	18.27	18.00	17.23	17.49	17.42	18.13
Imports (total = 100)	100.00	100.00	100.00	100.00	100.00	100.00	100.00	100.00	100.00	100.00	100.00
10 Most Important Classes, by FDI participation	40.72	43.16	49.22	50.23	49.65	50.67	51.60	50.41	48.82	45.04	48.91
20 Most Important Classes, by FDI participation	48.49	50.08	55.62	56.88	56.47	57.74	58.64	58.56	57.49	54.37	56.52
Rest, by FDI participation	51.51	49.92	44.38	43.12	43.53	42.26	41.36	41.44	42.51	45.63	43.48
Imports/Production Value (percentage)	17.53	20.17	22.10	22.22	22.31	21.85	21.94	21.57	20.67	19.42	22.80
10 Most Important Classes, by FDI participation	31.29	37.38	41.79	41.29	39.19	37.28	35.99	34.26	31.99	30.25	35.49
20 Most Important Classes, by FDI participation	27.29	33.02	37.07	36.58	34.77	33.13	32.11	30.64	28.63	27.08	35.70
Rest, by FDI participation	13.11	14.51	14.67	14.64	15.23	14.91	15.15	15.21	15.02	14.53	15.49
Trade Balance/Production Value (percentage)	−1.14	8.51	7.80	6.78	6.85	7.38	7.78	8.01	8.01	8.19	7.41
10 Most Important Classes, by FDI participation	0.09	17.66	18.97	16.01	17.32	19.17	20.75	22.97	22.65	24.31	20.16
20 Most Important Classes, by FDI participation	−2.13	11.90	13.41	11.01	12.01	13.91	15.15	16.54	15.81	16.47	14.15
Rest, by FDI participation	−0.69	7.02	5.01	4.54	3.91	3.36	2.85	2.02	2.48	2.89	3.29
Expenditures in Research and Technological Development, total (total = 100)	100.00	100.00	100.00	100.00	100.00	100.00	100.00	100.00	100.00	n.d.	100.00
10 Most Important Classes, by FDI participation	18.60	19.90	37.66	41.65	41.17	41.64	28.14	25.02	17.35	n.d.	31.23
20 Most Important Classes, by FDI participation	32.33	25.97	46.83	52.65	55.40	54.85	42.78	42.97	40.41	n.d.	45.31
Rest, by FDI participation	67.67	74.03	53.17	47.35	44.60	45.15	57.22	57.03	59.59	n.d.	54.69

Expenditures in Research and Technological Development, total/Production Value (percentage)	0.48	0.25	0.21	0.19	0.24	0.21	0.15	0.14	0.14	n.d.	0.17
10 Most Important Classes, by FDI participation	0.39	0.21	0.31	0.29	0.35	0.30	0.13	0.11	0.07	n.d.	0.18
20 Most Important Classes, by FDI participation	0.50	0.21	0.30	0.29	0.37	0.31	0.16	0.15	0.13	n.d.	0.20
Rest, by FDI participation	0.47	0.27	0.17	0.14	0.17	0.15	0.14	0.14	0.14	n.d.	0.15
Expenditures in Research and Technological Development, Productive Process (total = 100)	100.00	100.00	100.00	100.00	100.00	100.00	100.00	100.00	100.00	100.00	100.00
10 Most Important Classes, by FDI participation	18.53	20.26	42.57	45.67	45.54	46.47	31.12	21.28	18.74	12.97	34.17
20 Most Important Classes, by FDI participation	34.50	26.71	51.39	57.11	59.74	60.01	47.17	43.96	46.79	15.79	49.63
Rest, by FDI participation	65.50	73.29	48.61	42.89	40.26	39.99	52.83	56.04	53.21	84.21	50.37
Expenditures in Research and Technological Development, Environmental Monitoring (total = 100)	100.00	100.00	100.00	100.00	100.00	100.00	100.00	100.00	100.00	100.00	100.00
10 Most Important Classes, by FDI participation	18.81	18.48	14.19	17.59	11.20	7.79	13.99	35.56	12.32	n.d.	17.65
20 Most Important Classes, by FDI participation	24.82	23.12	24.98	25.96	25.67	18.71	21.98	40.17	17.29	n.d.	25.43
Rest, by FDI participation	75.18	76.88	75.02	74.04	74.33	81.29	78.02	59.83	82.71	n.d.	74.57
Maquila Services, total (total = 100)	100.00	100.00	100.00	100.00	100.00	100.00	100.00	100.00	100.00	100.00	100.00
10 Most Important Classes, by FDI participation	9.48	15.09	14.68	10.93	13.41	17.19	12.13	13.40	15.33	12.97	13.71
20 Most Important Classes, by FDI participation	12.45	17.80	18.45	14.40	17.58	20.67	14.69	16.27	18.22	15.79	16.86
Rest, by FDI participation	87.55	82.20	81.55	85.60	82.42	79.33	85.31	83.73	81.78	84.21	83.14
Maquila Services/Production Value (percentage)	1.19	1.10	1.11	1.09	1.08	1.10	1.02	1.05	1.02	1.00	1.06
10 Most Important Classes, by FDI participation	0.50	0.71	0.63	0.44	0.51	0.64	0.39	0.44	0.49	0.45	0.50
20 Most Important Classes, by FDI participation	0.48	0.64	0.62	0.45	0.53	0.60	0.37	0.42	0.45	0.40	0.47
Rest, by FDI participation	1.52	1.30	1.35	1.43	1.40	1.42	1.45	1.50	1.42	1.38	1.42
Tariff Rate, Weighted by Imports (with M of tariff archives)	7.24	2.81	1.98	1.85	0.58	0.70	2.11	0.69	n.d.	n.d.	1.59
10 Most Important Classes, by FDI participation	4.85	1.17	0.58	0.60	0.17	0.22	0.87	0.26	n.d.	n.d.	0.62
20 Most Important Classes, by FDI participation	6.93	2.21	1.26	1.28	0.41	0.57	1.78	0.53	n.d.	n.d.	1.22
Rest, by FDI participation	7.53	3.42	2.90	2.62	0.79	0.89	2.58	0.90	n.d.	n.d.	2.07
Tariff Rate, Weighted by Imports (simple average tariff archives)	8.81	7.27	6.62	6.87	5.51	5.88	6.73	7.16	n.d.	n.d.	6.86
10 Most Important Classes, by FDI participation	10.20	7.03	7.94	7.31	4.09	7.51	7.09	8.32	n.d.	n.d.	7.44
20 Most Important Classes, by FDI participation	9.80	6.97	7.32	7.16	5.07	7.36	7.42	7.90	n.d.	n.d.	7.38
Rest, by FDI participation	8.68	7.31	6.53	6.84	5.56	5.70	6.65	7.07	n.d.	n.d.	6.79

Source: Author's elaboration based on data directly provided by INEGI.

surplus and a lack of R&D expenditures. In keeping with the findings of previous studies (Dussel Peters 2000; Dussel Peters, Galindo Paliza et al. 2007), FDI may have actually exacerbated Mexico's socioeconomic and territorial polarization since the implementatipon of the liberalization strategy in 1988.

FDI flows to Mexico offer potential that has yet to be sufficiently exploited. A new long-term strategy is needed to promote and attract FDI that will transfer knowledge, technology and value-added to Mexico. Similarly, the attraction of strategic and high-quality FDI requires a dynamic perspective. Segments of value chains that are currently of interest to Mexico may not be a few years down the road. It is crucial to manage a steady upgrading to more desirable (more knowledge-intensive and higher value-added) segments of global value chains. It is critical to have a strong institution in charge of this process.

FDI can clearly allow for development—in terms of technology, employment, wages and overall learning processes—but only if it is part of a larger socioeconomic strategy. In Mexico there have been no regional or sectoral policies, accompanying FDI flows, to promote technological development, training, support for particular products and processes, etc. The new government's National Development Plan for 2007–2012, PEF (Poder Ejecutivo Federal 2007), clearly reflects this failing; it views macroeconomic stabilization as the sole basis for competitiveness, while ignoring trade, industrial, regional and sectoral policies, as Mexico's governments have since the end of the 1980s. Mexico requires a commitment from the public sector—at the municipal, regional and national levels—to policies that will promote such a development process.

A major question is: Is it possible to implement policies to improve the performance of FDI in Mexico in the context of NAFTA? NAFTA has decreased the options for its three members in terms of national policies (e.g., trade policies, industrial policies, etc.). This is particularly worrisome for Mexico, the least developed nation in the region and the one with the most acute socioeconomic and territorial polarization. Nevertheless, the three countries are able to implement local policies to enhance FDI and this is probably, in Mexico's current situation, its best option.

Reforms in the FDI law are necessary to promote a long-term perspective and improve the quality of FDI and its links with the rest of the country's productive structure. It is indispensable—as suggested by the experiences of countries as diverse as Ireland, the United Kingdom and the People's Republic of China—to establish an institution for the strategic promotion of FDI, and not only the management of licenses and registration of FDI, as is currently done by the RNIE and the SE.

It is necessary to evaluate in much greater detail the effects of FDI by sector and industry, as well by geographic origins and final destinations. Although this work has already begun (Dussel Peters, Galindo Paliza et al. 2007), much more research into the effects of FDI at the macro, meso, and micro levels in Mexico is still required. Last but not least, it is important not to overvalue the potential of FDI; for Mexico, although there are positive associations between FDI in manufacturing and foreign trade, productivity and wages, among other important variables, it is also clear that the aggregate impact of FDI on the economy is relatively small. Hence, even a coherent and long-term strategy on FDI cannot substitute for a long-term national development strategy. FDI will not resolve the structural socioeconomic problems of entire countries, much less of countries as large and complex as Mexico.

Finally, there are a number of more specific issues Mexico should address in a future reform of FDI policy. Among the most important is the liberalization of FDI in sectors such as petrochemicals and electricity. So far, there has not been sufficient analysis of the potential effects of FDI on these sectors, especially its likely fiscal impact. Over the last decade, Petróleos Mexicanos (PEMEX), the state-owned oil company, has accounted for 30–40 percent of public sector income. A rapid process of privatization would have dramatic fiscal impacts in Mexico. The concept of "neutral FDI" lacks transparency and should be abolished, as it allows hidden FDI in sectors, such as telecommunications and air transportation, in which foreigners are barred by Mexican law from ownership of more than 49 percent of any enterprise. The liberalization of these sectors, allowing foreign ownership of majority interests, should be considered. Finally, FDI-promotion policies should guide investment in terms of places of origin and final destination. Japanese FDI in Mexico, for example, has been concentrated in a few states and sectors. Promotion efforts should concentrate according to these specialization patterns. Otherwise, and as discussed throughout the chapter, FDI will continue to deepen Mexico's overall polarization process since the end of the 1980s and be unable to increase potential endogeneity processes.

Chapter Five

A MISSED OPPORTUNITY: FOREIGN INVESTMENT AND SUSTAINABLE DEVELOPMENT IN ARGENTINA

Daniel Chudnovsky and Andrés López

FDI has played a major role in Argentina's economic transformation. During the 1990s, a period of deep structural reforms largely based on the neoliberal "Washington Consensus," Argentina was one of the main destinations for FDI among "emerging markets." MNCs were already a major presence in the Argentine economy. With the surge in FDI during this period, the role of MNCs reached unprecedented levels. In 2003 more than 80 percent of the value-added generated by the 500 leading Argentine firms belonged to MNC affiliates.

In the view of the reformers, FDI was to play a significant role in the needed restructuring of Argentina's economy. At the macroeconomic level, FDI was to help finance current-account deficits. Since MNCs often follow long-term investment strategies and, once installed in a host country, have large sunk costs, the reformers believed FDI would be less volatile than portfolio investment and other types of international financial flows. Last but not least, FDI was supposed to contribute to investment, and therefore to economic growth and increased employment, not only directly, but also indirectly; that is, by fostering investments by local firms competing with, serving as suppliers to, or making purchases from MNCs (so-called "crowding in" effects discussed by Agosin in the Chapter Two).

At the microeconomic level, foreign firms engaging in FDI usually have ownership advantages (Dunning 1993) over local firms in the host markets where they invest. These ownership advantages may include, among others, greater access to state-of-the-art technologies—and, therefore, to the development of new products and processes of production—as well as to superior organizational, productive, managerial and/or marketing (including brands) capabilities.

Foreign firms' advantages should be reflected in their productivity records and their introduction of new products and processes of production in the countries where they invest. Unless a MNC invests only to serve the internal market where the affiliate is located, those advantages should also be reflected in MNC affiliates' export performance. MNCs' international production and trade systems should foster the export performance of their affiliates, since affiliates may act as suppliers of products or components to the parent company or other affiliates and as recipients of inputs and products from them.

MNCs could also transfer environmentally friendly technology to developing economies and may find it advantageous to comply (even in their overseas establishments) with home-based regulations that tend to be stricter than those of the host country. It is often more cost-effective to establish a single set of practices and standards instead of scaling back environmental investments at overseas facilities. In addition, the greater level of scrutiny that MNCs are exposed to and the prospect of liability for failing to meet the appropriate level of standards tend to drive these firms to adjust their operations to higher requirements than those imposed by local regulations (see Chudnovsky and López 2002).

FDI could also have indirect effects (i.e., spillovers) on host countries, mainly through the impact of MNCs' presence on domestic firms' performance. The indirect effects of FDI can be very significant, since domestic firms are the bulk of the business sector in almost all countries.

This chapter synthesizes the work to date that examines the extent to which these promises were fulfilled in Argentina. the first section presents an account of the role of FDI under the agro-export (1860–1930) and - import substitution (1930–1990) models in Argentina. The second section focuses on the structural reforms period of the 1990s, describing the evolution of key economic and social variables as well as the nature of FDI inflows during that period. The third section deals with the Convertibility crisis and its effects, reviewing the main changes in FDI trends during this period. The fourth section describes the available evidence of FDI impacts in Argentina, including key economic, social and environmental variables. The main conclusions and policy recommendations are laid out in the fifth, and final, section.

Main Historical Trends

Foreign investment has played a key role in the Argentine economy since the beginning of the country's modern history. During the period of the so-called agro-export model (1860–1930), under which primary-product exports drove a powerful economic expansion, FDI was one of the main channels of technology transfer (along with immigrants, who were the bulk of industrial entrepreneurs, and capital goods' imports) (Barbero 2003).

FDI was important in several areas, including: (1) export-related activities (e.g., railroads, meat-packing), (2) sectors where demand was growing due to urbanization and economic modernization (e.g., public utilities, banking) and (3) industries aimed at meeting booming domestic demand (e.g., food and beverages, chemicals). British investment was particularly important (between 1880 and 1913, British investment in Argentina increased twentyfold (Romero 2002), but FDI from the United States had a growing presence throughout this period as well (especially in industrial sectors).

The Great Depression of the 1930s led to the end of the agro-export model and to the beginning of the import-substitution industrialization (ISI) process. FDI shrank sharply, due first to the economic crisis (and the disruption of the world's trade and capital flows) and then to the Second World War. The Peronist regime (1945–1955) mostly did not welcome FDI, although General Perón tried to attract foreign investment in areas such as oil and automobiles during the last years of his government.

The big FDI boom was to take place under the *desarrollista* (developmentalist) government of President Frondizi (1958–1962), who launched an ambitious industrialization program aimed at "deepening" import substitution by promoting foreign investment in the intermediate, consumption durables and capital goods industries. Law 14780 on FDI and Law 14781 on industrial promotion were the main pillars of the effort to attract FDI to these sectors.[1]

MNCs were key participants in this stage of the ISI process. Between 1958 and 1963, some 200 foreign companies made greenfield investments in the country. By the early 1970s, MNCs' share in industrial production had reached 33 percent (Kosacoff and Bezchinsky 1993).

Though many MNCs brought secondhand machinery to Argentina, they also transferred modern product and process technologies, quality-control techniques, and subcontracting practices to their subsidiaries. This, together with the MNCs' use of more capital-intensive techniques and their propensity to locate in capital-intensive sectors, ensured higher labor productivity in MNC affiliates than in than local firms (Sourrouille, Kosacoff et al. 1985).

The massive arrival of MNCs had a substantial impact on Argentine industry. Many MNCs created engineering departments and supplier development programs. They trained their labor force, introduced their personnel to the technological and entrepreneurial culture of their parent companies and diffused the use of quality norms as part of the routine industrial practices. In some cases, they even played a role in the transfer of engineering services within the corporation to affiliates operating in similar environments (Katz 1999).

Even though MNCs did not invest in Argentina with the explicit intention of developing a local technological capacity—and, in fact, their expenditures in R&D were usually low—in practice, they often contributed to this development. MNC affiliates often had to develop new methods to apply product and processes technologies developed in their respective parent companies under the varying circumstances of different host countries (Cimoli and Katz 2003).

As MNCs invested in Argentina primarily with the aim of supplying the domestic market, exports played a marginal role in their activities.[2] They often used product and process technologies which fell well short of international practices and operated plants with strong diseconomies of scale. However, a technological learning process took place in many affiliates, contributing over time to increased export flows, which were mostly, but not exclusively, destined for other Latin American countries (Katz and Ablin 1977).

The large MNC presence in the Argentine economy led to increasing concerns—on the part of intellectuals, politicians, and public opinion—about their market power (concerns which, in fact, had begun with the dominance by MNCs of the meatpacking industry in the first decades of the century). Hence, it is no wonder that the different governments of the turbulent late 1960s to mid-1970s aimed at restricting and controlling MNCs' activities.

This trend was dramatically reversed when a military dictatorship took office in 1976. As part of a package of pro-market reforms, the dictatorship passed a new foreign investment law.[3] In spite of this legal change, FDI flows were not significant during the military government and, in fact, some large MNCs, especially in the automobile sector, closed their subsidiaries or scaled down their operations in those years.

The volatile and stagnating macroeconomic conditions of the 1980s did not attract much new FDI, although some MNC investment took place in the second half of the decade under external debt-equity swap programs. In any case, from 1976 to 1990, MNC affiliates reduced their presence in Argentina's economy, while some large domestic conglomerates emerged as the new "economic elite."

The FDI Boom of the 1990s

The Convertibility regime and the structural reforms: from boom to bane

After coming into office in 1989, the administration of Carlos Menem made several unsuccessful attempts to stabilize an economy suffering from hyperinflation. The renewed inflationary episodes of 1990 and the resignation of two Ministers of the Economy led the way to the appointment of Cavallo as Minister of the Economy in early 1991.

Cavallo launched a currency-board scheme (the so-called Convertibility Law) in order to stop inflation. The adoption of the currency board went hand-in-hand with a complete deregulation of international capital flows.

Convertibility was part of a far-reaching program of structural reforms that had been cautiously initiated during the late 1980s. By the early 1990s, Argentina was ahead of other Latin American countries in privatization of state enterprises, market deregulation, trade and financial liberalization, central-bank independence and social-security reforms.

As a result of structural reforms and price stabilization, the Argentine economy entered into a stabilization and growth period that lasted until 1998 (interrupted only by the recession in 1995, due to the so-called "Tequila effect." Between 1991 and 1998, GDP grew at an annual average rate of 5.9 percent. From the levels reached in 1989 and 1990 (index number 100 in 1990), the consumer price index dropped to 84 in 1991 and 17 in 1992. One-digit inflation rates were registered by 1993 and 1994, and there was practically no inflation during the rest of the 1990s.

Total factor productivity (TFP) increased at an annual average of 3.2 percent between 1991 and 1998. In fact, TFP was the main source of growth, since both the size of the capital stock and aggregate employment increased at relatively low rates (Maia and Kweitel 2003). However, productivity performance was heterogeneous, both in terms of sectors and firms.

On the basis of information from both large firms and small and medium enterprises (SMEs), a study by FIEL (2002) shows that, while TFP grew for firms in non-tradable sectors, the opposite occurred with firms in tradable activities. In fact, although value added in the manufacturing industry increased by 19 percent between 1991 and 2000, the share of industry in Argentina's GDP fell steadily during that decade, from 18.5 percent in the early 1990s, to 17 percent in 1998, to less than 16 percent in 2001. The services sector, including privatized utilities, gained the share lost by industry.

Within the industrial sector, when comparing 1993 and 2000, the "winning" sectors—i.e., those with the highest growth rates—were food and beverages, petroleum refining, chemicals, rubber and plastics, and, to a lesser extent, metals and the pulp-and-paper industry. These activities mainly depend on the stock of natural resources or produce industrial commodities with scale-intensive processes. In general, they are able to easily enter external markets in times of falling local demand. The sectors that declined in output included textiles and clothing, metallurgy and machinery, electro-technology, and transportation equipment. These are sectors either with high levels of unskilled (textiles) or skilled (machinery) labor, or with rapid technological advances (electronics). They were also severely affected by the trade liberalization of the 1990s.

Economic restructuring in the 1990s meant a new round of decline of "knowledge intensive" sectors. Recent research (for example: Hausmann, Hwang et al. 2005) has shown that production and trade patterns may have a significant influence on growth (much as structuralist theorists pointed out decades ago) and that specialization patterns in Argentina are not conducive to high growth (see, for instance, Guerson, Parks et al. 2006). As seen below, FDI has not contributed to solving this problem since, in fact, it has mostly reinforced existing trade and production structures.

Winners and losers also existed within the business sector. Affiliates of MNCs were the main "winners" in the restructuring process (Chudnovsky and López 2001). The number of MNC affiliates among the 500 Argentine leading firms increased from 219 in 1993, to 318 in 2000, to 340 in 2003, mainly through the takeover of public or private domestic firms. Their share in total output increased from 60 percent in 1993, to 79 percent in 2000, to 82 percent in 2003 (estimated from INDEC's data). Similar trends characterize the manufacturing sector in particular. In fact, the MNC share in manufacturing output during the 1990s was notably higher than during the ISI stage. In 1963, MNC affiliates accounted for 46 percent of total value added and 36 percent of employment for leading industrial firms. In 1997, the equivalent figures were 79 and 61 percent, respectively.

In contrast to MNCs' growing weight in the Argentine economy, local conglomerates, while pursuing heterogeneous strategies and exhibiting heterogenous performance, lost, as a whole, the central role they had played since the late 1970s. Although some of these conglomerates disappeared or shrank drastically, others (such as Techint and Arcor) strengthened their positions in the domestic market, often concentrating their activities on their "core business." At the same time, these successful conglomerates increased their presence in external markets, both through exports and FDI (Kosacoff 1999).

Before the reforms, most SMEs had obsolete machinery, inefficient production layouts, lack of skilled human resources, an excessively diversified product mix, little or no export experience, few cooperation linkages with other firms and organizations (including those offering technological or entrepreneurial services), weak quality control systems and marketing capabilities and a management style strongly dependent on the technological and other expertise of the owner. Naturally, these deficiencies seriously affected their competitive potential and, in any event, SMEs were generally more exposed to market failures in fields such as finance, technology, information and others (see Gatto and Yoguel 1993; Yoguel 1998).

The SMEs' adaptation to new market conditions was especially difficult. Many of them went bankrupt, while others lost market share, had to retreat to the lower end of their respective markets, sold their businesses or became importers in whole or in part. However, there was a group of dynamic SMEs, estimated at around 20 percent of the SME manufacturing sector, that had sufficient technological capabilities, management skills and human capital stocks to survive and expand in the domestic market and, in many cases, even to export (Yoguel and Rabetino 2002).

It is no wonder that, while large and foreign-owned enterprises (especially those participating in the privatization process and generally in the provision of services) largely supported the Menem government's policies, local manufacturing firms (and SMEs in particular) were less enthusiastic about them.

Exports grew significantly during this period, especially after 1994, favored by the regional integration process in MERCOSUR, improved international prices for commodities (at least until 1998), growth in agricultural output and the maturation of some large industrial and energy projects. As a result of these factors, exports doubled between 1993 and 2000. However, as imports grew far more than exports, Argentina ran significant trade deficits in most of the Convertibility years. Trade deficits were financed by growing inflows of foreign capital in the forms of both portfolio capital and FDI.

Trade deficits led to huge current-account deficits (an average of 3.5 percent of GDP between 1992 and 2001), one of the many warning signs on the macroeconomic horizon during the 1990s. Other gathering storm clouds were the deterioration of fiscal accounts, growing foreign indebtedness and relatively low levels of savings and investment (between 1991 and 2001, savings averaged 15.5 percent of GDP, while fixed investment averaged 18.5 percent). Meanwhile, unemployment became a serious problem after 1995, when it reached almost 20 percent of the labor force. In addition, poverty increased and income distribution became more unequal beginning in the mid 1990s.

All of these problems emerged in the context of a fixed and overvalued exchange rate, fostered by the nominal rigidity imposed by the Convertibility regime. In the early 1990s, the real appreciation of the peso—explained largely by the nominal fixity of the exchange parity in 1991 under still-inflationary conditions—was still considered an equilibrium phenomenon. They based this argument mainly on the fact that reforms implemented since the beginning of the Convertibility regime had led to significant productivity improvements that might justify the appreciation of the peso. In contrast, by the end of the decade and in view of the external shocks mentioned above, different estimates supported the idea that the real exchange rate was overvalued in relation to both its historical value and its "equilibrium value."[4]

By the late 1980s, under ominous macroeconomic conditions, with important business interests having serious difficulties adapting to the new rules of the game, and with growing social discontent as a result of the economic reforms, the Argentine economy suffered the external shocks of the Russian and Brazilian crises of 1998 and 1999. The two main consequences of these crises were, first, a "sudden stop" in capital inflows, and second, a new round of peso overvaluation due to the Brazilian devaluation of 1999, but also to the US dollar appreciation (in relation to the euro). Under these conditions, external debt indicators (in relation to GDP and to exports) reached dangerous levels, increasing the country's risk premium and resulting in growing capital flight. Argentina suffered three years of recession, along with deflation. By the end of 2001, the country was in the worst crisis in its history.

The nature and evolution of FDI inflows

In sharp contrast to the previous decade, when FDI decreased dramatically, Argentina was one of the main destinations for FDI inflows in the developing world during the 1990s. Between 1992 and 2001 direct investments of over US$ 76 billion flowed into the country, with a peak of more than US$ 23 billion in 1999 (see Figure 5.1).[5] For several years during this decade, annual inward FDI flows accounted for over two percent of GDP and 10 percent of gross fixed-capital formation.[6]

Profit remittances were very high throughout the decade, and in some years surpassed total profits (i.e., profit reinvestment was negative). In fact, remittances were higher than profits over the period 1995–2001 as a whole. Although it has been suggested that high profit remittances by privatized firms were largely responsible, these figures may also reflect a short-term bias on the part of foreign investors. While it may be understandable that remittances were high in the crisis year of 2001, the same does not apply for high growth

Figure 5.1. FDI Flows and Profits in Argentina (1992–2006)

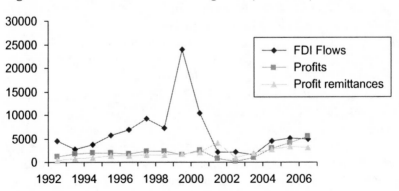

Source: Author's elaboration based on data from the National Direction of International Accounts (Argentina).

years such as 1997 or 1998. High profit remittances obviously lowered the positive impact of FDI on the balance of payments.

Most FDI inflows were related to takeovers, initially of public firms and then of private domestic enterprises, that accounted for around 60 percent of FDI inflows in the 1990s. Although the mergers and acquisitions (M&A) boom reflected worldwide trends, it was also fostered by changes in the domestic business environment. Data from Argentina's Secretariat of Industry, Commerce and Mining show that M&A exceeded US$ 70 billion between 1990 and 1999, with US$ 22 billion due to privatizations. Cross-border M&As totaled over US$ 58 billion during the same period (nearly 83 percent of all M&A activity).

FDI came mainly from the United States and Spain, whose firms purchased many privatized enterprises. Other important sources of investment were France, Italy, the Netherlands, Germany and the United Kingdom. There were also some major inflows from Chile (largely attracted by privatizations). Neither Japan nor other East Asian countries made significant investments in Argentina (Table 5.1).

The oil industry attracted one-third of FDI inflows between 1992 and 2001, while the manufacturing sector received around 21 percent.[7] Chemicals

***Table 5.1.* FDI Inflows to Argentina by Origin, 1992–2004 (% Change)**

Country	1992–2001	2002–2004
Europe	62	14
Germany	2	10
Spain	39	2
France	10	−9
Italy	4	4
Netherlands	4	12
United Kingdom	2	−11
Others	2	5
North America	25	13
United States	24	12
Others	1	1
Central America and Caribbean	1	5
South America	5	21
Chile	4	1
Others	1	20
Other Regions	6	47
TOTAL	100	100

Source: Author's elaboration based on data from the National Direction of International Accounts (Argentina).

(especially petrochemicals), auto, and food and beverages attracted most manufacturing FDI. The rest went into services, partly due to privatizations in communications, electricity and natural gas, as well as into banking, retail trade, etc. (Table 5.2).

As during the ISI period, market-seeking strategies were predominant among MNCs affiliates.[8] However, most foreign firms also took advantage of the opportunities created by MERCOSUR and in some cases (e.g., the auto industry), had efficiency-seeking objectives.[9] As seen below, they were also more prone to engage in foreign trade than domestic firms.

Structural reforms created an FDI-friendly environment. FDI had already been strongly deregulated in 1976 by the military dictatorship's Law 21382. The Menem administration completed this task, removing almost all the few remaining sectoral restrictions still allowed under the 1976 regime. After this round of reforms, no approvals, formalities or registration procedures of any kind were required for FDI operations. There were neither discriminatory withholding taxes on income nor taxes on profit remittances or dividends from FDI.

This investor-friendly approach was followed by the signing of 51 bilateral investment treaties, the endorsement of the failed Multilateral Agreement on Investment (MAI) proposed by OECD countries, and generous concessions in

Table 5.2. **FDI Inflows to Argentina by Sector, 1992–2004 (% Change)**

Sector	1992–2001	2002–2004
Petroleum	34	35
Mining	1	4
Manufacturing Industry	21	42
Food, Beverages and Tobacco	7	7
Textiles	0	0
Paper	1	3
Chemicals, Rubber and Plastics	7	8
Cement and Ceramic Products	1	1
Base Metals and Base Metal Products	1	15
Machinery and Equipment	1	−1
Automotive Industry and Transport Equipment	4	9
Electricity, Gas and Water	12	4
Commerce	5	1
Transport and Communications	9	−10
Banks	10	7
Others	7	17
TOTAL	100	100

Source: Author's elaboration based on data from the National Direction of International Accounts (Argentina).

the negotiations leading up to the General Agreement on Trade in Services (GATS). Following the mandate of the Agreement on Trade-Related Aspects of Intellectual Property Rights (TRIPS) negotiated in the Uruguay Round of GATT, the old Argentine patent law (Law 111 of 1864) was modified in 1995. Among other changes, patent protection was extended to pharmaceutical products, despite the opposition of the leading domestic manufacturers.[10]

Privatizations also attracted FDI. The Menem government considered privatization a powerful way to gain a quick reputation with the local and international establishment. This was crucial for a government—belonging to a party with a populist tradition—that had taken office in the midst of hyperinflation.

Encouraged by the requirement that consortia buying at public auctions had to include a partner with previous experience in the same sector, a high percentage of public utility firms ended up controlled by foreign investors. Most privatizations, however, involved joint ventures between foreign concerns and large domestic conglomerates. Typically, the foreign partner took responsibility for the technical and operational side of the business, while the domestic partner (usually holding a minority interest) remained in charge of its administrative and financial side. Foreign banks often participated as providers of finance, particularly through external debt-to-equity swaps. As the years passed, however, foreign banks and many domestic conglomerates sold their shares.

Trade liberalization also helped to attract FDI, given the change in MNCs' strategies worldwide. MNCs went from establishing stand-alone subsidiaries aimed at penetrating domestic markets with high levels of local content to creating integrated global networks pursuing efficiency and specialization gains through trade flows among subsidiaries, as well as subcontracting. While protectionism was favorable for attracting FDI during the ISI period, openness was more adapted to the new MNCs strategies.

Other policies with positive impacts on FDI attraction included: (1) the deregulation of sectors such as oil, fishing, mining, foreign trade operations, wholesale and retail trade, land, water and air transport and insurance, and (2) reforms to the technology transfer regime, eliminating the need for government approval of contracts between parent firms and their local subsidiaries.[11]

Some specific investment incentives were also put in place. In mining and forestry, tax stability was granted, along with some fiscal incentives, to investors. In the automobile sector, a special trade regime was adopted, consisting of import quotas, investment and balanced trade requirements for established manufacturers, minimum content rules for locally produced vehicles and preferential import tariffs for domestic producers. The program aimed at promoting specialization and fostering competitiveness among established car manufacturers in order to take advantage of the rapid increase in domestic demand that followed stabilization.[12] The automobile sector also had a common trade regime with Brazil. This did not, however, prevent "incentives wars," especially in the second half of the 1990s, when a number of major projects—largely, but not exclusively in the automobile sector— received huge incentives from Brazil's national and state governments (see Chudnovsky and López 2002). It is very difficult to disentangle the effects of the various factors attracting FDI, especially considering that different factors were important for different kinds of investors. However, on the whole, Argentina's main advantages were the abundance of natural resources, the size and growth of the domestic market, privatization, price stabilization, trade liberalization, and, to a lesser extent, integration in MERCOSUR (Chudnovsky and López 2001; Chudnovsky, López et al. 2002).[13] Neither cheap labor (wages in US dollars were relatively high in Argentina during the 1990s) nor loose enforcement of environmental regulations were key factors in attracting FDI. The "investor-friendly approach" may have been a necessary precondition for the FDI boom, but, in itself, would not have had a sizeable impact in the absence of these other attractive conditions.

FDI After the Convertibility Crisis

The end of Convertibility brought a major breakdown for the Argentine economy and society. From 1999 to 2002, real GDP declined by more than 18 percent. There was also a banking crash, resulting in default on the external debt and a huge peso devaluation during a period of sharply increasing unemployment and poverty rates. This unleashed a deep political crisis.[14]

After the devaluation, the new government of interim President Eduardo Duhalde, who took office in January 2002, implemented, among other measures, the denomination in pesos of internal contracts and obligations and of public services rates. In many cases, privatized utilities' rates had been fixed in US dollars during the 1990s. Along with "pesification," public services rates were also frozen. Bank deposits and credits denominated in US dollars were also "pesified," but asymmetrically, with the government compensating the banks for the difference. Banks became objects of popular anger and legal suits because of the pesification of the deposits.

An economic recovery started in the second quarter of 2002 and since then, GDP has grown steadily. While GDP growth was negative in 2002, over the following four years the economy grew at around nine percent per year. It took until 2006, however, for GDP per capita to surpass the 1998 level.

Furthermore, although unemployment and poverty rates fell, they have remained very high by Argentina's historical standards.

GDP growth was fueled by both consumption and investment. According to data from the Economic Commission for Latin America and the Caribbean (ECLAC), gross capital formation as a percent of GDP increased from a low of 11.3 percent in 2002, to 20 percent in 2005, but remained lower than the 1998 level of 21 percent.

The increasing total value of exports since 2003, aided by very high international prices for Argentina's main export commodities, made it possible for the country to maintain a relatively large trade surplus, even as imports started to grow again with the economic recovery and increasing investment. The trade surplus has led to positive current-account balances since 2002.

FDI flows were very low from 2001 through 2003, and while they recovered somewhat in 2004 and 2005, they fell slightly again in 2006 (see Figure 5.1).[15] In any case, Argentina clearly lost attractiveness for FDI; its share in world FDI inflows fell from nearly 1.5 percent in the 1990s to less than 0.5 percent between 2001 and 2005.

The end of Convertibility brought about conflicts between the government and foreign investors in two areas: in banking, due to the "asymmetric" pesification, and in privatized services, because of the rates freeze. In the former case, many firms brought suits against Argentina in the International Centre for Settlement of Investment Disputes (ICSID) (see Bouzas and Chudnovsky 2004).[16] Hence, it is no surprise that some investors in banks and privatized companies sold their equity mainly to domestic investors and other Latin American firms. This disinvestment was more than balanced, however, by new investments in different areas, including some large takeovers of private Argentine firms by Brazilian firms. Although no recent data are available on the subject, the presence of MNC affiliates in the Argentine economy today does not appear to be very different from in 2001.

A major shift in the origins of FDI, however, took place compared to the 1990s pattern. The share of Europe and the United States shrank drastically, from 62 percent to 14 percent and 24 percent to 12 percent of total FDI, respectively. For some particular countries (e.g., United Kingdom, France), FDI flows to Argentina were actually negative (disinvestment took place). FDI from South America and from Central America and the Caribbean soared between 1992 and 2001 and again between 2002 and 2004, from five percent to 21 percent and from one percent to five percent of total inflows, respectively (Table 5.1). Brazil and Mexico were the leading sources of investment from these regions.[17]

As for FDI destination sectors, petroleum continued to attract more than one-third of inflows. The main change in FDI patterns, however, was that, after devaluation and the consequent shift in relative prices in favor of tradable sectors, industry doubled its share (from 21 percent in 1992–2001 to 42 percent in 2002–2004) at the expense of services (Table 5.2). The metals and metal products sectors attracted the bulk of manufacturing FDI, mainly due to the acquisition of local plants by foreign firms.

The Impacts of FDI on Sustainable Development in Argentina The Economic Impacts

The macroeconomic impacts of FDI are related mainly to growth and investment. Bittencourt et al. (2006), using both Granger causality tests and panel data models, find no evidence of positive or negative impacts of FDI on growth and investment. The fact that most FDI came through M&As and that relatively few greenfield investments took place during the 1990s could explain the lack of a positive impact on total investment levels.

On the microeconomic side, the most recent and methodologically rigorous research on the subject is that of Chudnovsky et al. (2007), who focus on Argentine firms that were taken over by MNCs during the 1990s. The taken-over firms are the treatment group, and the firms that remain in domestic hands are the control group. The latter mimic a "counterfactual" scenario; that is, they allow us to know what would have happened to taken-over firms if they had not been acquired by foreign buyers.

Data from two innovation surveys were used for this research. The first survey covered the period 1992–96 and included 1,639 firms (INDEC-SECYT 1998). This sample represented 53 percent of sales, 50 percent of employment, and 61 percent of exports of the manufacturing sector in 1996. The second survey covered the period 1998–2001 and included 1688 firms (INDEC-SECYT-CEPAL 2003) representing 65 percent, 42 percent and 80 percent of sales, employment and exports, respectively, in 2001. The analysis was based on panel data and estimated difference-in-differences models.[18]

The variables of interest were labor productivity, trade (imports and exports) and innovation. Both innovation inputs (i.e., R&D activities) and innovation outputs (i.e., introducing a new or improved product or process) were studied. The main findings of this paper are:

1. Labor productivity increases after a domestic firm is acquired by foreign investors. The growth in productivity takes place gradually, starting the year the firm changes ownership.

2. Exports and export propensities (i.e., exports as a percentage of sales) increase after the firm changes ownership. The findings are similar in the case of imports and import propensities. As in the case of productivity, the increase in foreign trade levels takes place gradually, starting at the time of the takeover.

3. Takeovers by foreign investors have no effect on the expenditures and intensity of R&D in the acquired firms, but they increase the probability of introducing a new (or improved) product or process.

4. There is no evidence of horizontal or backward spillovers. The only exception is for positive backward spillovers on innovation output (meaning that firms that supply to sectors where a takeover has taken place may have been induced to launch new products and processes).

Summing up these results, we can state that the new owners of former domestic firms seem to have transferred inputs (such as organizational and production technologies) to the acquired firms. This allowed the acquired firms to launch new products and to increase labor productivity and trade more than domestically owned firms. However, research and development activities seem to have been unaffected by takeovers.

While the direct effects of FDI through takeover seem to be positive, the indirect effects on Argentine manufacturing industry are less encouraging. Spillovers only arise in the case of innovation outputs, meaning that domestic firms need to upgrade their technological assets to become MNCs suppliers.

Moreover, while MNC affiliates trade more than their local counterparts, a sort of "asymmetric integration" within global trade flows is clearly visible; foreign firms export mostly to other Latin American markets while importing inputs and final goods from developed countries. The "technological content" of their exports is clearly lower than that of their imports (Chudnovsky and López 2004).

Finally, in a study focused not only on taken-over firms but on all foreign-owned firms, based on the same data set mentioned above, domestic firms with high absorption capabilities appeared to reap positive spillovers from MNCs competing in the same sector (Chudnovsky, López et al. 2006.) (To measure absorption capabilities, the study employs an index including variables related to R&D expenditures, capital goods and intangible technologies, the use of modern organizational techniques, and the relevance of training activities.) This suggests that the probability of receiving positive spillovers from FDI presence is mostly related to factors internal to the domestic firms in host countries.

The failure to find any negative spillovers may be a result of the bankruptcy of some firms due to competition from MNC affiliates and, therefore, the inability to capture the performance of these firms in the surveys. At the same time, if the firms that exit are those with low capabilities, as seems likely, this strengthens our conclusions regarding the importance of developing domestic capabilities. In the absence of information on firms that exit, however, this cannot be rigorously demonstrated.

Social and Environmental Impacts

Chudnovsky et al. (2007) deal with the impacts of FDI on unemployment and wage inequality. In the first case, on the basis of the same innovation surveys and econometric techniques mentioned previously, they find that—contrary to what is often assumed in Argentina and elsewhere about FDI through takeovers—there is no evidence that total employment decreases (or, for that matter, that it increases) as a result of the acquisition of a domestic firm by a MNC. The available literature emphasizes other variables, such as macroeconomic evolution, as the chief causes of unemployment in Argentina (Frenkel and Damill 2006). While a foreign takeover has no impact on total employment, however, it has a significant effect on its composition, since the share of skilled labor in total employment increases after the acquisition.

In the case of wages, the study tests whether those sectors where FDI presence deepened during the nineties were also the sectors where, *ceteris paribus*, larger increases in wage inequality were observed. Data on wages came from the Permanent Household Survey, a typical labor force survey with information on wages, employment status and individual and family characteristics (age, gender, family size, etc.). The authors show that wage premiums for skilled workers increase with the FDI presence in the industry where they work. During the 1990s, in those industries where the FDI presence increased the most, wage inequality also widened the most (in favor of the most skilled workers). However, the impact of FDI on wage inequality is small, and it does not seem to be the main cause of the increase in income inequality during the last decade, which has been attributed to factors such as trade liberalization, unequal access to education and unemployment (Gasparini, Marchionni et al. 2001).

These results do not include some other FDI impacts, which cannot be properly measured with available data, namely: (1) Innovation surveys, as noted above, do not include firms that closed during the 1990s. If those firms closed due to MNC competition, an indirect negative effect on employment could have taken place; (2) The impact on unemployment of FDI in services (including privatized utilities) was not estimated; (3) If FDI is positively associated with outsourcing, it is possible that people whose activities were outsourced saw their jobs lowered in "quality" (for instance, because of the fact that instead of being employees of a big corporation with formal jobs, they became employees of smaller firms in which informal employment is more usual). While these potential impacts have not been tested, severe social problems in Argentina should be attributed mainly to other factors.

Regarding the environmental impacts of FDI, Chudnovsky and Pupato (2005) find, on the basis of data from the 1998–2001 innovation survey, that firm size and technology acquisition expenditures increase both the probability of undertaking environmental management activities and the "quality" of environmental management.[19]

They find that foreign firms are more prone to undertake environmental management activities and to generate positive environmental spillovers, inducing the adoption of simple, clean, production management methods in domestic firms with high absorption capabilities. However, somewhat surprisingly, foreign ownership is associated with a relative decrease in the quality of environmental management.

Going beyond econometric studies, no systematic evidence exists in favor of the hypothesis that MNCs came to Argentina attracted by low environmental or labor standards (as seen before, there were other and more relevant attraction factors for FDI). However, according to media reports, some "environmental refugees" may have invested in Argentina, mainly in the mining sector.

In general, no evidence exists for the claim that FDI per se has been a key factor contributing to pollution problems or environmental degradation in Argentina. Phenomena not discussed in this paper, such as concerns about the effect of the expansion of transgenic soy in Argentina's agriculture or the management of nonrenewable resources (petroleum and gas), if they are a problem, are due primarily to inadequate domestic regulations rather than FDI.

However, serious environmental problems are still present in the country and the contribution of FDI, although seemingly positive, has been modest. More research is needed to reach more reliable conclusions about the actual and potential impacts of FDI on Argentina's environment.

Conclusions and Policy Lessons

Summing up, FDI was not a panacea for Argentina's economy in the 1990s, but also has not been the chief cause of social problems such as unemployment, increasing income inequality or environmental degradation.

However, from the evidence discussed here, it appears that Argentina missed the opportunity to reap more benefits from the large FDI inflows that the country received in the last decade. While MNC affiliates showed better microeconomic performance than local firms, the latter reaped almost no spillovers from the foreign presence.

Furthermore, FDI did not appear to contribute to diversification of the country's productive structure, improvement of its trade specialization pattern, access to new markets in developed countries or growing capital formation. Its impacts on the balance of payments, in turn, were not as positive as expected due to high profit remittances.

From these findings, a policy agenda emerges. First, FDI impacts depend to a large extent on the capabilities of domestic firms in host countries. Hence, it is a priority to improve the competitiveness of local firms (especially SMEs) in Argentina. Such firms may benefit from governmental technical assistance, provision of information, linkages with universities and research institutions, supplier development programs, etc. Government programs may also mitigate market failures, especially lack of access to credit, that could be affecting SME performance. This could help local firms take advantage of the potential spillovers generated by FDI presence, compete better with foreign firms in their respective markets, and develop closer ties with MNC affiliates (as suppliers, clients, partners, etc.). The key message is that industrial, technology, and enterprise policies aimed at enhancing local capabilities are probably at least as important as direct FDI policies for improving the impacts of foreign investment on the host economy.

Second, policy efforts in the FDI area must focus not only on the quantity of FDI received, but also on its quality. Argentina is well known to international investors. If, as expected, the economy keeps growing in the coming years and if, as is desirable, domestic institutions are improved, the rules of the game become more stable, and policy swings become less frequent, the Argentine economy may attract significant FDI inflows in the future. However, quantity is not enough from the point of view of Argentina's broader development objectives.

In the 1990s, most FDI was market-seeking and took place through M&As. At present, efforts should be made to attract more greenfield investments, as well as FDI aimed not only at taking advantage of the domestic market, but also at integrating local affiliates into intra-corporate value chains through efficiency-seeking investments. However, efficiency-seeking FDI should not come at the expense of local linkages, as it often does in Mexico and Central America, since this makes productivity and technology spillovers almost impossible.

The goal of FDI policy should be to induce MNCs operating in Argentina to restructure their affiliates' operations to fit global corporate competitiveness objectives. This means, for instance, that MNCs affiliates in Argentina could get world or regional "product mandates;" that is, products that are assigned exclusively to Argentine affiliates for exporting to certain countries or regions (and eventually to the whole world).

This should not, however, come at the expense of local ties. Programs for the development of local suppliers should be established as a way to increase the local content of MNC affiliates' production without losing efficiency; local suppliers could even become world suppliers for the respective MNCs if they attain sufficient scale and competitiveness levels. It is also important to foster innovation activities by MNC affiliates, as is the case for many foreign affiliates operating in Brazil. This involves not only in-house R&D but also research linkages with universities and research labs in Argentina. Fiscal or financial incentives could be employed for both purposes (development of local suppliers and promotion of domestic innovation activities). The same policy instruments could be useful in encouraging MNCs to improve their environmental management systems and to diffuse their environmental knowledge and practices to local firms.

Regarding the objective of transforming the productive structure, MNCs will not invest in knowledge-intensive sectors unless specific government signals are in place. Recently, many MNCs have invested in Argentina in software and information services, a sector favored by many policy interventions in recent years. Creating desirable signals does not necessarily mean granting huge amounts of money to foreign investors, but creating a favorable climate for investment in new and technologically dynamic activities.

Policy measures in the abovementioned areas should not be taken only at the national level. MERCOSUR could coordinate government policies to enhance domestic capabilities and improve FDI quality. However, this kind of coordination has not happened so far. In fact, different MERCOSUR governments have competed for FDI through fiscal incentives, a phenomenon that peaked in late 1990s (Chudnovsky and López 2002). Some form of discipline against competitive investment incentives is needed in MERCOSUR, while governments consider common policies in FDI-related areas, such as innovation, environment or development of suppliers.

A recent study shows that MERCOSUR countries could expect increases in FDI inflows from entrance into the Free Trade Areas of the Americas (FTAA) or the signature of an EU-MERCOSUR agreement (López and Orlicki 2005). The same study suggests that Latin American South-South flows could be strongly stimulated by the FTAA, but that we should not expect MERCOSUR countries to become more attractive for North America-oriented "export platform" FDI, considering their distance from the United States and Canada. MERCOSUR countries, however, could attract more FDI from northern countries to take advantage of access to other Latin American countries in the FTAA. Moreover, the results of the study suggest that a Latin American and Caribbean regional integration agreement would have roughly the same effects as the FTAA on FDI received by MERCOSUR countries, while signing bilateral regional integration agreements with the US would not foster more FDI inflows.

While FDI to MERCOSUR countries may increase if the FTAA or an EU-MERCOSUR agreement is signed, caution is needed when forecasting the probable magnitude, origins and nature of additional FDI inflows. Furthermore, nothing guarantees than an increase in FDI "quality" could follow from the signing of the agreements, since coordinating investment policies with the US or the European Union would mostly involve granting guarantees to foreign investors, but would hardly include the kind of "pro-development" policies discussed above.

Finally, MNCs are not a substitute for local entrepreneurs. There are very few cases of successful MNC-led development strategies (e.g., Singapore, Ireland), and those examples took place under very unusual conditions. Argentina's large conglomerates shrank as a group in the last ten years, but a few of them survived and expanded and could be the basis to build a new domestic business elite, jointly with other new emerging big firms that have been growing recently. In this regard, granting these firms access to long-term credit, under conditions similar to those faced by MNCs in their home countries, could be a first step towards the creation of a new business leadership. This, in our view, is necessary to build a viable, long-term, sustainable development strategy in Argentina.

Chapter Six

FOREIGN INVESTMENT AND ECONOMIC DEVELOPMENT IN COSTA RICA: THE UNREALIZED POTENTIAL

José Cordero and Eva Paus

Introduction

After a long history of dependence on a few traditional exports, followed by import substitution in the 1960s and 1970s, and a debt crisis in the early 1980s, Costa Rica launched an aggressive attempt at diversifying production and exports in 1985. The new approach to development consisted of two main elements: pursuit of free trade agreements and the attraction of foreign direct investment (FDI). Costa Rica has been remarkably successful in attracting FDI. It is the only country in Latin America where most FDI has gone to manufacturing over the last decade, and it stands out even further for its ability to attract FDI in high-tech sectors.

In this article we analyze why Costa Rica was an attractive destination for transnational corporations (MNCs), and the impact FDI has had on economic development in the country. We show that FDI in the Free Zones has had a beneficial impact primarily at the macroeconomic level, through employment and trade balance effects. At the microeconomic level, however, the impact has been rather limited as backward linkages and technological spillovers are small in both absolute and relative terms.

The limited extent of backward linkages from FDI is due to the limited potential for spillovers for part of the foreign investment as well as to the limited domestic absorptive capacity for linkages. Ultimately, we argue, the lack of a coherent long-term development strategy has hindered the ability of the country to take more advantage of high-tech FDI. On the one hand, the government did not adopt proactive policies to address existing market failures, which make it difficult for national producers to become competitive input suppliers. And on the other hand, an approach that aims at attracting high-tech FDI is not compatible with trade liberalization and provision of tax exemptions to MNCs in the industrial and tourism sectors. By reducing tax revenues, this strategy hurts the government's ability to create and maintain an adequate stock of country-specific assets of the type that are required for the continuous attraction of FDI flows. The lack of government revenue is also hurting the country's ability to protect the national parks and wildlife areas that have been so important in the flow of tourism.

We argue that trade and FDI policies have to be articulated in the context of a larger development strategy that is aimed at expanding the country's knowledge-based assets so as to foster structural change and productivity growth, which generate employment and income in higher value-added processes and products. Government policies have to adjust the incentive structure that is currently heavily skewed toward foreign investment favoring national producers, so as to provide a more level playing field.

Where MNC Strategies Meet Costa Rica's Location-Specific Assets Background

Historically, all Latin American countries have depended on a small number of export commodities to generate economic growth. Costa Rica is no exception. In the early1600s it exported cocoa to South America (Greñas 1985), and during the late 1700s and into the early 1800s, tobacco to Nicaragua, Panama and Mexico (Fonseca 1998). But it was only with coffee, around 1830, that the country became integrated into the world markets (Acuña and Molina 1991). In the late nineteenth century, banana production started in the Atlantic region of the country, and for the next 60 years, the country remained dependent on the foreign exchange revenue mainly generated by these two commodities. Toward the end of the nineteenth century, Minor C. Keith won a concession to build a railroad connecting the Central Valley to the port of Limon, in the Atlantic region. The project was completed in 1890, and Keith initiated large scale banana plantations with his United Fruit Company. This was the first time the Costa Rican government pursued the arrival of large-scale foreign investment, both for the development of infrastructure and for the exploitation of natural resources.

The history of Costa Rica's development and the nature of its integration into the world economy in the twentieth century is marked by three major episodes: the abolition of the army and the development of a social democratic model in the late 1940s and early 1950s, the pursuit of import-substituting industrialization within the context of the Central American Common

Market in 1962, and the structural adjustment policies adopted after 1985 (Cordero 2004).

The abolition of the army and the introduction of social reforms during the late 1940s and the 1950s provided broad-based access to education and health care, and the creation of a strong institutional framework allowed social and political stability. This system, which made Costa Rica different from most other Latin American nations, was consolidated during the years of the ISI strategy, generating considerable economic growth and structural change during the 1960s and 1970s. With the debt crisis of the early 1980s, however, the limitations of the ISI approach became more evident and the strategy changed, as in many other developing countries.

During the Monge Administration (1982–1986), and especially after the structural adjustment program was signed with the World Bank in 1985, successive Costa Rican governments retrenched from direct involvement in economic production, abdicated proactive policies and pursued gradual market liberalization across most sectors. The decline of the average tariff rate from slightly over 60 percent in 1985 to 11.7 percent in 1995 and 5.8 percent in 2004 reflects Costa Rica's ever-greater integration into the world market (Paus 2005: 138).

Costa Rica's liberalization strategy has had two main goals: (1) increasing the country's participation in international trade, and (2) attracting higher quality foreign direct investment (FDI). With respect to the first goal, successive governments sought to improve the conditions under which the country participates in international trade. The distinguishing feature has been the pursuit of a multitude of free-trade agreements that, according to national authorities, would mitigate the vulnerability to unfair trade practices. Agreements have been signed with Mexico, Canada, Chile, and the Caribbean Community (CARICOM). Although the Pacheco Administration (2002–2006) signed the Central American Free Trade Agreement (CAFTA) with the United States, it is not yet clear, at the time of this writing, whether CAFTA will indeed be ratified.

With respect to the second goal, the focus has been on an increase in the number and quality of foreign investment projects within the industrial sector, and more recently in the service sector. In the expectation that higher-tech FDI in manufacturing would generate considerable development benefits, the Costa Rican government established Free Zones (FZs), or Zonas Francas, in the early 1980s. These offer producers the possibility to import inputs free of duty and to be exempted from taxes for twelve years; 100 percent for eight years and 50 percent for another four years. In addition, in 1982, the United States Agency for International Development (USAID) established and funded a foreign-investment-promotion agency, the Coalición Costarricense de Iniciativas para el Desarrollo (CINDE), the first of its kind in Latin America.

Since its inception in 1982, CINDE has been a private, not-for-profit organization, with no funding from the government. CINDE's independence from the government has the advantage that it can pursue its mission of FDI promotion regardless of the potential vicissitudes of changing governments. The very same independence, however, also reflects less of a commitment by the government. In the 1980s, CINDE had annual budgets between $4 million and $8 million, ran seven international offices in Europe, Asia and the United States and employed 400 people at the height of its operations. When Costa Rica no longer qualified for USAID funding, CINDE's budget was reduced to the interest income from the initial endowment. The Costa Rican government did not compensate for any of the shortfall in funding. In 2006 the organization had an annual budget of slightly more than $1.5 million, a staff of 29 people and one foreign office (in New York City).

In recent years, tourism has become an increasingly more important aspect of Costa Rica's integration into the world economy. There are special tax incentives for investment in tourism, just as there are tax incentives in the Free Zones. In the discussions that follow, we will consider tourism separately, not only because it straddles the areas of both trade and FDI, but also because its rapid growth is posing serious challenges to environmental sustainability.

FDI flows

Although FDI in Costa Rica increased during the 1980s, it was not until the 1990s that it really took off. The average annual inflow of FDI rose from $40 million during the 1980s to $416 million during the period 1990–2004 (see Table 6.1). During the nineties, increased FDI in Latin America was often the result of large-scale privatization efforts, particularly utilities. Not so in Costa Rica, which stands out as the big exception. Based on available data, it is the only country in Latin America where most FDI went to the manufacturing sector. Between 1996 and 2005, FDI in the manufacturing sector accounted for 68 percent of total FDI inflows. That compares with an FDI share in manufacturing of 21 percent in Argentina, 28 percent in Brazil, 11 percent in Chile, and 48 percent in Mexico (ECLAC 2005: 40). What sets Costa Rica apart even further from most Latin American countries are significant amounts of foreign investment in high-tech industries, namely in electronics and medical instruments.

Though there had been sizeable foreign investments in the electronics sector before, most notably Motorola in the 1970s and DSC Communications Corporation in 1995, the big jump in FDI in electronic equipment came with Intel Corporation's $300 million investment in 1997. Intel's decision to build a microchip assembly and testing facility outside of San José played a huge

Table 6.1. **Basic Economic Data for Costa Rica (1970–2004)**

	Net FDI Inflows			Investment Rate	Real GDP Growth
	Millions of Current U.S. $	% of GDP	% of GFCF	GFCF as a % of GDP	Based on Constant Colones
Average 1970–1979	44	2.3	10.1	22.7	6.4
Average 1980–1989	70	1.8	8.8	20.3	2.2
Average 1990–2004	416	3.1	16.1	19.9	4.7

Source: Calculated based on World Development Indicators, accessed April 25, 2007.

role in the magnitude and nature of foreign investment flows to Costa Rica, as it put the country on the map for transnational corporations in the high-tech sector. In 2006 there were 51 foreign companies operating in the electronics sector in Costa Rica (CINDE 2006: 8).

And even though Baxter had been operating in Costa Rica since 1987, it was only with Abbot's investment in the late 1990s and the publicity following Intel's investment decision that FDI in the medical-supply sector surged. By 2006, there were 22 foreign producers of medical devices in Costa Rica, including Boston Scientific and Inamed. More than half of them had arrived after 2003 (CINDE 2006: 8).

Between 1997 and 2006, FDI in the manufacturing sector accounted for 54 percent of all FDI inflows (see Table 6.2). Other important destinations of FDI were the tourism, real estate and services sectors. Costa Rica has become an increasingly attractive tourist destination, with beautiful beaches on the Pacific and Atlantic and ample opportunities for ecotourism. That has attracted a considerable amount of FDI in the tourism sector, especially in Guanacaste and Puntarenas. But in recent years, FDI in tourism has been overshadowed by the purchase of real estate by foreign private citizens who want another home in a beautiful spot of the world. Between 2004 and 2006, foreigners' purchases of real estate amounted to a staggering $763 million, 25 percent of total FDI inflows. As a result, real estate prices have skyrocketed, and the challenges to sustainable development are looming increasingly large.

FDI in Information Technology-enabled services (IT) has grown substantially over the last few years, primarily in terms of employment, though, rather than in size of investment. In 2006 foreign companies in the service sector employed 15,000 people compared to 11,000 in electronics and 6,000 in medical devices (CINDE 2006: 8). The main companies and areas in the service sector are Procter & Gamble (Global Business Services), Baxter (Baxter Americas), and Intel (Intel SSC) in shared business services; Hewlett Packard and IBM

Table 6.2. **Net Foreign Investment in Costa Rica by Sector (1997–2006)**

	1997	1998	1999	2000	2001	2002	2003	2004	2005	2006*	1997–2006
Millions of U.S. $											
Agriculture	38.1	41.9	49.9	−11.2	1	−8.6	−36.3	50.6	37.1	37.6	200.1
Agroindustry	6.5	14.7	10.4	11.5	5.2	2.8	8.4	−0.3	29.6	9.4	98.2
Commerce	17.6	39.3	9.2	17.4	8.3	15.2	6	23.9	47.6	45.4	229.9
Industry	270.6	423.5	355.9	296.2	231.4	482.7	386.8	456	344.9	428.7	3676.7
Services	−7.3	6.6	12.7	14.6	57.4	52.8	83.2	17.3	73.3	60.1	370.7
Financial system	−0.2	22.1	93.4	27.1	43.1	17.2	2.2	22.6	40.9	321.6	590
Tourism	79.3	61.4	84.7	52.1	111.5	76	88.3	41.4	53.5	144.1	792.3
Real estate	0	0	0	0	0	21	31	178.4	234.6	350	815
Other	2.3	2.1	3.3	0.9	2.4	0.3	5.6	3.9	−0.5	13.9	34.2
Total	406.9	611.6	619.5	408.6	460.4	659.4	575.1	793.8	861	1,410.80	6,807.1
Percentage breakdown											
Agriculture	9.4	6.9	8.1	−2.7	0.2	−1.3	−6.3	6.4	4.3	2.7	2.9
Agroindustry	1.6	2.4	1.7	2.8	1.1	0.4	1.5	0.0	3.4	0.7	1.4
Commerce	4.3	6.4	1.5	4.3	1.8	2.3	1.0	3.0	5.5	3.2	3.4
Industry	66.5	69.2	57.4	72.5	50.3	73.2	67.3	57.4	40.1	30.4	54.0
Services	−1.8	1.1	2.1	3.6	12.5	8.0	14.5	2.2	8.5	4.3	5.4
Financial system	0.0	3.6	15.1	6.6	9.4	2.6	0.4	2.8	4.8	22.8	8.7
Tourism	19.5	10.0	13.7	12.8	24.2	11.5	15.4	5.2	6.2	10.2	11.6
Real estate	0.0	0.0	0.0	0.0	0.0	3.2	5.4	22.5	27.2	24.8	12.0
Other	0.6	0.3	0.5	0.2	0.5	0.0	1.0	0.5	−0.1	1.0	0.5
Total	100.0	100.0	100.0	100.0	100.0	100.0	100.0	100.0	100.0	100.0	100.0

* preliminary.
Source: (Grupo Interinstitucional de Inversión Extranjera Directa 2006; Grupo Interinstitucional de Inversión Extranjera Directa 2007).

in back-office services; SYKES, Fujitsu, and People Support in call centers; Cypress Creek and Via Information Tools in software development; and Align Technology, Photocircuits, Holland Roofin, and Gensler in design and R&D.

Although the vast majority of FDI in Costa Rica has been greenfield investment, there are two notable exceptions. The first one is Heineken's purchase of a stake in the Costa Rican beverage company Florida Bebida in 2002, and the second one is Scotiabank's purchase of Grupo Interfin in 2006. US corporations have generally been the largest foreign investors, accounting for more than 60 percent of all FDI between 1997 and 2003 (Paus 2005: 144).

Costa Rica's location-specific assets

Given the small size of the Costa Rican market, FDI in manufacturing and IT-enabled services is mostly efficiency-seeking and not market-seeking. So why did Intel decide to build a microchip factory in San Jose rather than somewhere else in Latin America? And—more generally—why has Costa Rica been able to attract efficiency-seeking FDI in electronics, medical devices and IT-enabled services? The answer is threefold: (1) good fortune, because of the country's location; (2) the legacy of past investments in human capital and infrastructure, and a stable political system; and (3) attractive tax and tariff conditions in the FZs combined with proactive foreign investment promotion through CINDE.

Costa Rica has a strategic location, as a bridge between the United States and Latin America as well as the Atlantic and the Pacific. Proximity to the United States reduces the delivery time for goods exported to the US, and it is a strategic asset for nearshoring of IT-enabled services, especially given similar time zones.

Human capital is one of the most important factors in attracting high-tech FDI to a developing country.[1] Thanks to past investment policies in education, Costa Rica's adult literacy rate is close to 100 percent, and primary school enrollment is nearly universal. A considerable number of people have some knowledge of English, a result of the introduction of foreign language instruction in primary schools in 1994 and the prevalence of English-speaking tourists. Costa Rica also provides stability, economically, politically and with respect to capital-labor relations, again mostly due to the social democratic model and strong institutions developed in the past.

According to the CINDE website (<http://www.cinde.org>, accessed in May 2007), hourly wages in Costa Rica range from $1.80 to $4.11, including fringe benefits. Costa Rica ranks well in labor costs when compared to other Latin American nations, though not so well relative to Asian competitors (see Table 6.3). So far, the higher wages in lower-tech activities could still be

Table 6.3. **Comparison of Relative Gross Wages (2002)**

Country	Laborer		Professionals		Management	
	General	Skilled	Junior	Senior	Lower Middle	Upper Middle
India	32	36	27	30	30	41
Philippines	44	47	34	38	36	48
Malaysia	60	64	47	52	49	66
China	50	58	47	56	58	85
Costa Rica	100	100	100	100	100	100
Chile	118	113	87	97	93	114
Mexico	169	137	101	107	97	136
Panama	119	181	116	128	99	123
Singapore	174	173	120	123	109	136
Ireland	333	288	173	161	121	137
U.S.A.	306	292	194	192	164	197

Source: CINDE, http://www.cinde.org/eng-recursohumano.shtml

compensated with political stability, health services for workers, infrastructural support to firms (telecommunications, constant and reliable flow of electricity, infrastructure) and, often, higher labor productivity.

Last, but not least, Costa Rica has the longest-standing institution in Latin America charged with marketing the country to foreign investors. Initially, CINDE went after any investment it could attract. The main response came from clothing companies due to the tariff advantages under the Caribbean Basin Initiative and US tariff provision HTS 9802. By the early 1990s, however, Costa Rica was losing competitiveness in clothing to other countries in the Caribbean and, in addition, CINDE lost an important portion of its funding coming from USAID (Rodriguez-Clare 2001). As a result, CINDE decided to concentrate efforts only in the sectors in which Costa Rica was thought to have greater advantages: first, the electronics sector, then medical devices, and currently, also IT-enabled services.

It was CINDE's focus on the electronics sector and its pursuit of Intel which led to an Intel presentation at CINDE headquarters in November 1995 and subsequent visits by Intel teams to Costa Rica. According to Rodriguez-Clare (2001), the country, which was originally not in the long list of possible candidates, became a top contender after Intel's visit in 1996. The company's interest in diversifying locations eliminated the Asian nations from the list, and the final options were reduced to Chile, Brazil, Mexico and Costa Rica. The final choice was based on the availability of human capital, the lack of labor unions in the private sector, the interest in the promotion of the electronics sector and the fact that a well defined set of incentives for Intel and other MNCs already existed within the context of the FZ system.

But of critical importance for Intel's final decision was the personal involvement of then President Figueres. After the first encounter with representatives from Intel, Figueres appointed José Rossi, Minister of Foreign Trade, as the point person to coordinate all efforts needed to satisfy Intel's demands and tilt the MNC's decision in favor of Costa Rica. The small size of the country turned out to be an advantage, as it allowed for quick, integrated, collective action once the political will and the necessary power to enforce it were there. The Minister of Foreign Trade brought together the heads of the Ministry for Environment and Energy, ICE (the Costa Rican Electric Utility Company), the Ministry for Transport and Public Works, the Ministry of Finance, the Ministry of Science and Technology, the Ministry for Education and the Technical Institute of Costa Rica (Spar 1998: 17). And it was this cooperation and concerted effort which allowed the Costa Rican government to successfully address Intel's concerns about infrastructure (improved road access to the airport and uninterrupted access to electricity at reasonable prices), about education (availability of a sufficiently large labor force with the requisite technical skills) and about financial incentives (applicability of one percent tax on assets on corporations in the Free Zones).

The Intel case makes very clear the possibilities and limitations of CINDE. The agency was instrumental in getting Costa Rica on Intel's radar screen and in coordinating the first steps with other institutions once the MNC showed a clear interest in investing in the country. But it did not have the political muscle to do what in the end needed to be done, and was done, by an institution closer to the higher echelons of political power.

Bringing Intel to Costa Rica should not be seen in hindsight as the result of a long-planned strategy that finally bore fruit, as some analysts of the time portray it. Clearly there were planning elements involved, but what was important in the end was the coming together of somewhat autonomous elements, due to very strong individual efforts and cooperation among key agencies. From Costa Rica's perspective, Intel's arrival was the outcome of a fortuitous set of circumstances, in which the President's involvement and his directives to make things happen were critical. But unfortunately, the grand collective effort faded away once Figueres left office in 1998.

The process leading up to Intel's investment in Costa Rica provided an ideal opportunity to institutionalize modes of cooperation and an agreed-upon division of labor among different institutions and ministries to define, in a systematic way, FDI's role in Costa Rica's economic development and the role of different players, public and private, to ensure that the potential development benefits of FDI would materialize. Unfortunately, it was a lost opportunity. There were elements of a strategy and efforts by different actors, but never a coherent, well-coordinated strategy.

The FDI-development nexus

When analyzing the impact of FDI on development, economists typically distinguish between effects at the macroeconomic level and effects at the microeconomic level. At the macro level, FDI helps mitigate the foreign-exchange constraint and allows more flexibility in handling the current-account deficit, contributes to more stable prices and foreign exchange markets, increases investment and creates more employment opportunities. At the micro level, FDI's largest potential contribution to development lies in the advancement of domestic knowledge-based assets through spillovers.

In the case of Costa Rica, we find that the most important benefits from FDI have been on the macro side, with a positive contribution to investment, the balance of trade, employment and wages. With respect to the promotion of knowledge-based assets, however, the benefits have been small so far. Though there have been some important learning spillovers, backward linkages have been very limited, and we have seen little movement up the value chain by the MNCs in Costa Rica. Rather, among the large MNCs in high-tech production in Costa Rica, the trend has been to diversify into IT-enabled services rather than into more advanced production activities.

While the size of the country imposes inherent limitations on the degree and breadth of domestic sourcing, we argue that the main reason for the lack of greater advancement in backward linkages and in movements up the value chain is the absence of an integrated development strategy. Free trade and FDI inflows do not make a development strategy. When domestic linkage capability is insufficient due to widespread market failures, targeted government intervention is needed to raise that capacity so that domestic companies can reap knowledge spillovers from FDI.

Macroeconomic impacts of FDI

Investment

At the macro level, one would expect FDI flows to have a favorable impact on investment rates in the recipient country. With the increase in FDI, MNCs have become much more important for investment and economic growth in Costa Rica. While the average investment ratio during the period 1990–2004 was slightly below the average rate of the 1980s, the share of FDI in gross fixed-capital formation nearly doubled, from 8.8 percent to 16.1 percent (see Table 6.1). In spite of the data, it is unlikely that FDI has crowded out national investment. Correlation is not causality.[2] But it is clear that the accumulation of domestic capital has not kept pace with economic growth: in 1985 (the year the structural adjustment program was signed with the World Bank), private capital formation represented 22.8 percent of GDP, while public capital formation represented 4.7 percent of GDP. In 2005, these figures had gone down to 15.9 percent and 3.1 percent, respectively.[3]

Balance of trade

To assess the impact of FDI on Costa Rica's balance of trade, we look at the trade performance of the Free Zones, as Costa Rican authorities keep detailed separate data on companies in the Zona Franca regime, but not on MNCs overall. Even though only about 45 percent of MNC output comes from the Zona Franca (Monge et al. 2004, 15), ZF performance is an acceptable proxy for MNC performance in the higher-tech sectors, since most of the foreign investment in manufacturing and IT-enabled services is in the Zona Franca.

The Zona Franca regime was created in order to promote rapid export growth. And it has succeeded in doing so. According to data from the Central Bank, in 1991 traditional products (coffee, banana, sugar) accounted for 40 percent of Costa Rican exports, while the Zona Franca accounted for only 13 percent. In 2005, however, the Zona Franca exported $3.7 billion, more than half of the country's export revenue, while the share of traditional exports had dropped to a little over 11 percent of the total. Exports of electrical machinery have been the main force behind the huge increase in ZF exports (see Table 6.4). And Intel has been responsible for most of these exports. Between 2001 and 2006, Intel accounted for 39 percent of Zona Franca exports and 20 percent of Costa Rica's total exports.[4]

But it is in the nature of the FZ system that producers not only export a lot, but also import a lot. The reason is that most MNCs set up operations in free zones in order to take advantage of low labor costs; there are no duties on imports, so they import the vast majority of all their parts and components from more advanced nations, and put them together by means of relatively labor-intensive assembly processes. In addition, at this juncture, some of the key inputs that are outsourced cannot be produced in Costa Rica. As a result, the impact of the ZF on the balance of payments is substantially smaller than indicated by the large export figures and shares. Still, over the last 10 years, the FZ has always had a trade surplus, while the nation's trade deficit has been growing consistently (see Figure 6.1). The ratio of the trade balance in ZF to the trade balance in the rest of the economy has ranged from 121 percent in 1999 to 16 percent in 2006.[5]

Table 6.4. Value-Added and Exports in the Zona Franca

	2001	2002	2003	2004	2005	2006
Value Added in Millions of U.S. $						
Machinery, electrical materials & components	309	358	321	387	449	422
Precision instruments & medical equipment	207	198	292	330	266	100
Agroindustry	91	116	125	135	101	70
Textiles, clothing, leather, and shoes	102	145	143	120	115	103
Services	27	116	153	224	322	329
Plastic, rubber & their manufactures	33	52	53	70	85	43
Chemical and pharmaceutical products	18	13	3	5	40	3
Metal products	14	11	16	18	22	15
Agriculture and lifestock	16	19	23	1	1	2
TOTAL	936	1,157	1,269	1,404	1,472	1,100
Exports in Millions of U.S. $						
Machinery, electrical materials & components	1,218	1,256	1,789	1,560	1,878	2,305
Precision instruments & medical equipment	330	412	529	541	585	676
Agroindustry	97	204	246	307	336	337
Textiles, clothing, leather, and shoes	404	425	347	334	328	306
Services	106	128	143	147	172	222
Plastic, rubber & their manufactures	67	81	93	139	163	189
Chemical and pharmaceutical products	40	39	51	68	68	67
Metal products	33	30	34	48	57	76
Agriculture and lifestock	18	21	27	25	23	20
TOTAL	2,381	2,665	3,327	3,242	3,699	4,314
Value Added as a Percentage of Exports						
Machinery, electrical materials & components	25.4	28.5	17.9	24.8	23.9	18.3
Precision instruments & medical equipment	62.7	48.0	55.2	60.9	45.5	14.8
Agroindustry	93.5	57.0	50.7	43.9	30.2	20.7
Textiles, clothing, leather, and shoes	25.3	34.1	41.1	35.9	35.1	33.7
Services	25.5	90.5	106.9	152.3	187.3	148.1
Plastic, rubber & their manufactures	49.5	63.4	56.7	50.6	52.4	23.0
Chemical and pharmaceutical products	45.2	33.4	5.2	8.1	59.1	4.2
Metal products	44.0	35.6	48.2	38.1	37.6	19.3
Agriculture and lifestock	86.7	92.6	83.7	4.3	3.0	9.6
TOTAL	39.3	43.4	38.1	43.3	39.8	25.5

* Value added = exports − imports + change in inventories − remittances − taxes − consultancy fees abroad.

Source: Proconer.

Figure 6.1. Trade Balance (TB): Zona Franca and the Rest of the Economy

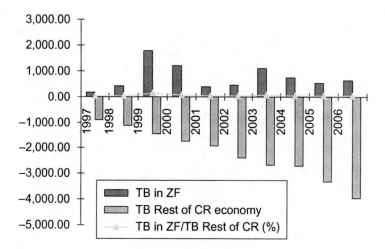

Source: PROCOMER and Central Bank.

Taxes

Since the early 1980s, the Costa Rican approach to development has been based on two pillars: the attraction of high tech FDI along with the promotion of tourism and the pursuit of trade agreements with other countries or regions. In the long run, it is difficult to attain both these goals at the same time. As highlighted earlier, human capital is one of the most important factors in the decisions of high-tech MNCs to relocate production to a developing country. Other important factors include a continuing and stable provision of electricity and an advanced telecommunications system. These location-specific assets are provided in Costa Rica by state universities and state enterprises. Investments in these institutions to improve the quality of the services provided depend heavily on the tax revenue collected by the central government. Since tourism is also an important part of the picture, the preservation of national parks, biodiversity and wildlife in the country also becomes a critical task. But again, these location-specific assets are maintained and protected through the tax revenue raised by the state.

However, trade liberalization, along with the participation in various trade agreements, has caused a significant decline in the tax revenue from foreign trade. Central Bank data show that the share of tax revenue from international trade went from 35 percent in 1987, to 24 percent in 1995, and to eight percent in 2004. In addition, the FZ system provides MNCs with tax exemptions on nearly all their activities. The Law of Incentives for Tourism

Development also provides firms in that sector with various tax exemptions and favorable treatment regarding income tax. This situation has made it increasingly difficult to raise tax revenues. In 2004, the tax ratio (the ratio of total tax revenue to GDP) was only slightly above 13 percent (see Table 6.5). Such a low tax ratio considerably reduces the government's ability to improve education and infrastructure, both for local development purposes and for the attraction and upgrading of FDI.

Some people have argued that this problem can be solved with higher economic growth. But that will not work in Costa Rica to the extent that higher growth is driven by activities that benefit from tax exemptions or reductions. Under these circumstances, higher GDP growth will not lead to a commensurate increase in taxes and the tax ratio. In 1997 and 1998, GDP increased by more than seven percent per year; but that success did not translate into a higher tax ratio (see Table 6.5). Not only did the tax ratio not increase when production rose, but the rates themselves are too low.

Agosín, Machado and Nazal (2004) show that in the mid-1990s, Costa Rica's tax ratio should have been 20.6 percent, given the level of its GDP

Table 6.5. Costa Rica's Tax Ratio, (1987–2004)

Year	Total Tax Income/GDP* (%)
1987	11.22
1988	10.97
1989	11.03
1190	10.81
1991	11.3
1992	11.88
1993	11.99
1994	11.59
1995	12.34
1996	12.55
1997	12.53
1998	12.56
1999	11.94
2000	12.29
2001	13.22
2002	13.22
2003	13.35
2004	13.36

* Total income as a percentage of GDP.
Source: Ministerio de Hacienda and Banco Central de Costa Rica.

per capita. The observed value, however, was only 12 percent. Turkey, one of the most underdeveloped countries of the OECD, had a tax ratio of 16 percent in 1975, higher than Costa Rica's tax burden. By 1990, Turkey reached 20 percent, and in 2004 the ratio passed 30 percent. In 2004, Finland, Sweden and Denmark registered tax ratios of 44 percent, 51 percent and 50 percent, respectively.[6]

It is clear that the tax structure does not mirror the changes the economy has experienced in recent years. As different activities have become dynamic, their contribution to tax revenue has not changed in any significant way. For example, in spite of huge real estate purchases by foreigners and infrastructure development in the Guanacaste region, the province's share in total tax collection is the same as it was in 2002 (Leiton 2007).[7]

The decision to offer tax exemptions to corporations in the FZ has been very important in persuading MNCs to invest in Costa Rica. These corporations demand, and use extensively, the resources provided by the public sector (human capital, electricity and telecommunications), but give little in return to contribute to the continuation and expansion of those resources. It is thus clear that the first and second goals of the Costa Rican approach to economic development are difficult to reconcile (Cordero 2006).

As we will argue later, it has been difficult to reap the benefits of technological externalities from FDI in Costa Rica; backward linkages and technological spillovers have been limited. Under such conditions, one needs to reevaluate whether the tax exemptions for foreign investors are justified. It is clear that the lack of tax revenue is hurting the capacity of the government to sustain the country-specific assets that the MNCs are looking for. Investments in electricity, for example, which had been programmed very carefully until the late 1990s, are lagging behind the growth of demand.[8] And although the country's literacy rates continue to be high by Latin American standards, literacy alone will not be enough to promote the development of a high-tech FDI sector. Public spending in social areas has also lagged behind the needs of the population. Poverty rates have not declined significantly for more than a decade (Trejos 2004). And the distribution of income has deteriorated considerably, with the Gini coefficient rising from 0.37 in 1990 to 0.42 in 2004.

Employment and value-added

Employment in the Zona Franca more than doubled between 1997 and 2005, from 16,677 to 39,009 (see Table 6.6). Out of the three sectors with the most FDI, employment in electrical equipment has been rather stagnant since the beginning of this century. In contrast, employment in the medical equipment industry has been rising at a steady pace. But the service sector, mainly

IT-enabled services, has provided the largest increases in employment. Employment in the clothing industry, which—like the service sector—is very labor-intensive, has continued to decline, as the industry is becoming increasingly less competitive compared to other Central American countries and key competitors in Asia.

Relative to Costa Rica's total labor force of 1,903,068 in 2005, 39,000 jobs amount to "only" 2.3 percent. But in addition to the creation of gainful employment, the employment component of the FZ is important for the local economy for a number of other reasons. First, it is through income taxes on these workers that the FZ, indirectly, has an impact on the government budget. Second, wages and working conditions in the Free Zones often tend to be better than in nationally owned companies. According to Monge Gonzalez, Tijerino et al. (2004: 24), between 1999 and 2004, the average salary in the Zona Franca was 20 percent higher than the average in the Costa Rican-owned manufacturing sector.

Higher wages and rising employment in the Zona Franca should be reflected in growing value-added. But the data show that that has not necessarily been the case. Based on Procomer's definition of value-added, value-added for the Zona Franca as a whole increased from 2001 till 2005, but dropped significantly in 2006, even though exports kept growing (see Table 6.4 again). Whatever the explanation for the drop in 2006 is, the important point is that value-added as percentage of exports has remained pretty much unchanged since the turn of the century.

FDI and the limited upgrading of national knowledge-based assets

The most important potential contribution that MNCs can make to the advancement of a developing country is at the microeconomic level. Through spillovers and linkages, FDI can expand the technological, production and marketing capabilities of national producers, thus increasing their competitiveness and ability to move up the value chain. However, such spillovers do not happen automatically. The empirical evidence on positive spillovers from FDI in different countries of the world is inconclusive. Some studies find positive spillovers (e.g., Kokko 1996; Sjoeholm 1999 and Haskel, Pereira et al. 2002); other studies find negative spillovers (e.g., Aitken and Harrison 1999 and Konings 2000), and yet other studies find no statistically significant spillovers in one direction or the other.

The competition effect is not an important channel for technological improvements in Costa Rica, since most FDI in manufacturing, especially in the high-tech sectors, is in the production of parts or finished goods which

Table 6.6. **Sectoral Distribution of Employment in the Zona Franca**

Sector	1997	1998	1999	2000	2001	2002	2003	2004	2005
Textil, design, leather & shoe	8,296	9,887	11,331	9,086	12,211	11,963	9,718	7,689	7,517
Services	3,654	4,186	1,320	1,372	2,631	3,922	5,463	6,985	8,577
Machinery, electronic materials & components	2,625	6,837	7,319	9,729	9,637	9,096	8,034	10,643	9,081
Others	1,324	1,745	2,203	2,515	2,211	2,085	1,956	1,772	2,152
Agroindustry	454	683	1,072	1,841	2,459	2,512	2,632	2,982	3,171
Precision instruments & medical equipment	135	212	1,576	2,101	2,678	3,512	4,063	2,371	5,113
Chemical & pharmaceutical products	102	113	137	129	148	94	87	114	136
Plastic, rubber & their manuf	65	223	967	1,009	887	977	1,003	1,568	1,593
Metal manufactures	22	397	416	363	755	384	650	740	893
Agriculture & cattle		3	20	45	467	509	698	749	776

Source: PROCOMER.

have not been produced in the country previously. In small developing countries, where FDI in manufacturing and IT-enabled services is mainly efficiency-seeking, the primary potential channels for spillovers are backward linkages, and training and education. We find that—to date—backward linkages have been very limited in Costa Rica, but that there have been positive effects through the training channel and the impact on curriculum development in the educational system.

Backward linkages

Backward linkages between MNCs and input suppliers in Costa Rica have been very limited to date. Although MNC purchases of domestic goods and services have grown in absolute terms, they have declined in relative terms. Between 1997 and 2005, MNCs' expenditures on national goods and services nearly quadrupled, from $99 million to $368 million (see Table 6.7). In relative terms, however, the picture shows very little progress: as a share of imports, national expenditures were 13 percent in 1997 and 12 percent in 2005; and as a share of exports they were 11 percent in 1997 and 10 percent in 2005 (see Figure 6.2).

The sectors with the largest amounts of FDI, the electronics and medical instruments industries, are also the sectors with the most limited development of backward linkages. In 2005, national expenditures accounted for two percent of imports in machinery and electrical equipment, and 7.8 percent in medical instruments.[9] And even those figures overestimate the use of purchases from national producers and service providers, since the data do not distinguish between national producers and foreign input suppliers located in Costa Rica. Available evidence suggests that MNCs' sourcing from national enterprises in Costa Rica is limited to printing, packing and services. Only a few Costa Rican companies have managed to become competitive material-input-suppliers to MNCs, mainly of plastic and metal parts. Foreign investment in natural-resource-intensive sectors (i.e., agriculture and agro-industry) has very high ratios of national expenditures to imports. But these are not the sectors with potentially dynamic high-tech activities.

The limited extent of backward linkages from FDI is due to limited potential for spillovers for part of the foreign investment and to insufficient domestic absorptive capacity for linkages. All foreign investments do not have the same potential to generate domestic linkages (Paus 2005). While FDI in high-tech productsholds out , theoretically, greater potential for spillovers than FDI in low-tech products, in the case of Costa Rica that potential is reduced considerably for two main reasons. First, most of the high-tech FDI is at the low end of the spectrum of technology intensity, involving assembly-type jobs, though in the case of Intel, testing and assembly of microchips is substantially

Table 6.7. **National Expenditure by Companies in the Zona Franca Regime**

	1997	1998	1999	2000	2001	2002	2003	2004	2005
Total (Mill. of U.S.$)	98.9	232.7	228	139.1	206.9	244.5	269.3	335	368.3
National expenditures as a % of imports									
Total	11.8	13.1	10.9	7.2	9.3	10	10.8	11.9	10.4
Machinery, electrical materials & comp.	6.6	5.8	4.4	2.7	3.1	2.4	2.6	2.6	2
Precision instruments & med. equipment	5.7	10.8	8.1	8.4	4	5	6.1	6	7.8
Agroindustry	63	64.1	44.7	74.3	82.7	77.7	86.2	84	78.1
Textiles, clothing, leather & shoes	5.4	12	15.3	4.7	6.2	5.7	5.5	7.6	6
Services	17.9	18.7	13.3	10.8	20.6	17.6	25.5	24	25.8
Plastic, rubber & their manufactures	15.7	33.7	27.3	33.4	25.2	27.4	15.5	24.4	24.7
Chemical & pharmaceutical prod.	54.8	34.2	32.2	30.4	36	28.3	41.4	47.2	23.3
Metal products	33.2	6	1.4	1.9	7	7.8	14.9	37.9	41
Agriculture, life stock	0	0	0	4.5	97.6	97.8	96.7	97.2	90.6

Figure 6.2. National Expenditures – Zona Franca

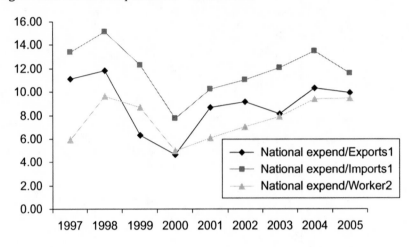

Source: PROCOMER.

more involved than "assembly" would suggest. Second, the large high-tech MNCs in Costa Rica (Intel, Abbot, Baxter) source the major inputs from the company-internal global network; that is., a lot of the production is internalized among the affiliates spanning the globe. In addition, many of the key inputs that are outsourced cannot be produced in Costa Rica at this juncture, either because the requisite scale is too large or the technology is too sophisticated.

In contrast to the large high-tech MNCs, however, many of the small- and medium-size MNCs in Costa Rica are eager to buy inputs domestically. For many of them, the investment in Costa Rica was their first investment abroad. Smaller MNCs do not have the global reach to internalize production across many borders. Thus, they have great interest in achieving cost reductions through local sourcing, as long as technological sophistication, quality and scale permit.

Unfortunately, even in areas where scale requirements did not constitute an obstacle to local supply provisions, Costa Rica's absorption capability for spillovers via input supply has generally not been sufficient. One of the reasons is that, under ISI, companies were protected by tariffs, but no reciprocal control mechanisms were in place to require producers to become internationally competitive. The experience of the successful Asian Tigers shows that control mechanisms involving export requirements were particularly effective. When the Costa Rican economy opened up in the 1980s, domestic producers turned out not to be competitive suppliers for MNCs.

But the pervasiveness of market failures made it unlikely that they would become competitive on their own. Many had imperfect information about needed technology and quality and faced high financial costs because of underdeveloped capital markets, and high risks because of the uncertain outcomes in the new competitive environment.

Most potential domestic input suppliers have been unable to meet quality expectations; they do not have the necessary technological know-how to meet minimum quality standards like ISO certification. Others have not attempted to become MNC input suppliers, as it is a high-risk undertaking, requiring investments in new machinery and technology with no guarantee of success. The demands on entrepreneurship are different in the highly competitive environment of a liberalized economy in the early twenty-first century, compared to the demands in the less competitive context of ISI.

The very existence of CINDE is based on the recognition of market failures; that is., information and coordination failures. Advertising the virtues of Costa Rica as a desirable investment location presumes that MNCs do not have sufficient information about the country's location-specific assets. And targeting foreign companies in prioritized areas reflects the belief that coordination failures are important; that is, that cluster formation in key areas will not happen on its own, but that it is desirable because of possible agglomeration effects.

But the recognition of market failures did not carry over to the development of national linkage capability, at least not in any significant and systematic way. Over the years, there have been several incipient proactive moves toward linkage creation in Costa Rica. At one point in the second half of the 1990s, there were at least three different programs. But they were partly competing with one another, they were not coordinated and they were mostly paper tigers. So they did not last long.

The establishment of Costa Rica Provee (CRP) in 2001 is the most promising attempt to date to promote indigenous linkage capability. CRP's formal integration into PROCOMER in 2004 is an important step towards the institutionalization of linkage promotion. CRP has been an effective matchmaker between national input suppliers and MNCs operating in Costa Rica., with the number of facilitated linkages increasing from 18 in 2003 to 140 in 2006. The value of first-time linkage contracts was $3.2 million in 2006.

Nonetheless, without greater resources—in terms of budget and human capital—CRP cannot bring about a qualitative jump in domestic linkage capability. In 2007, CRP had a staff of seven people and a budget of $275,000.[10] Furthermore, CRP provides training and consulting, but no access to financing. Access to credit at reasonable interest rates is still a hurdle for many small companies, who do not have the collateral needed for bank loans.

Here again, the need for more decisive and direct guidance from the government is crucial. Most of the business relationships that would entail the kind of technological externalities associated with FDI presuppose the existence of a minimum stock of assets and strengths in the areas that are more likely to attract the attention of foreign firms. Unfortunately, there has been no strategy in this area for a long time, and the promotion efforts of CINDE do not find the feedback and support that are required from the national authorities. The absence of a national strategy in these areas is partly the result of a severe lack of institutional coordination in areas related to science and technology. There is very little that Costa Rica Provee can do (on a significant scale) as long as the country does not have a strategy to create strengths in areas in which successful business initiatives might be developed.

Training and learning spillovers

Although high-tech FDI in Costa Rica has not induced many knowledge spillovers through backward linkages, it has generated some spillovers through training and education. High-tech producers in Costa Rica employ a larger percentage of skilled workers, which offers the potential for greater knowledge spillovers. At times, foreign companies provide training in skill areas that are not widely available in the host country, e.g., in computerized numerical control. Labor mobility will ensure that such knowledge then spreads more broadly. A 2004 survey of local input suppliers to MNCs showed that 6.2 percent of their managers, 27.6 percent of their engineers, and 31 percent of their technicians had previously worked for a transnational corporation (Monge et al., 2004).

In addition to the accumulation of skills and knowledge in the production process and the positive spillovers that come with labor mobility, foreign high-tech companies have had an important impact on upgrading the technical curriculum at Costa Rica's universities. That is particularly true for Intel. Both the engineering school at the University of Costa Rica and the Technological Institute of Costa Rica have contracts with Intel to collaborate on the development of curricula for technical careers. The goal is to provide the most up-to-date skills and knowledge needed at different levels, from technicians to engineers, which would support an expansion of the sector and—potentially—a move up the value chain within the sector as well.

Tourism

One of the areas which has been heavily promoted in recent years is the expansion of the tourism sector. It is seen as a very important part of the development process as it brings foreign exchange and purchasing capacity to the rural areas of the country.

The most important steps in this area were taken in the early 1990s, when a strong effort was made to promote Costa Rica as a nation with a strong commitment to protecting tropical forests, wildlife,, and biodiversity. The goal was to attract tourists to the country's natural beauty in a setting in which the most attractive places at the various beaches and mountains were still unexploited from the commercial point of view. The keyword was "ecotourism."

This approach rendered very favorable results: from 1995 to 2005 the number of tourists visiting Costa Rica more than doubled, from 785,000 to almost 1.7 million visitors. The number of foreigners visiting national parks also more than doubled in the same period, and the foreign exchange revenue generated by tourism increased from $660 million in 1995 to almost $1.6 billion in 2005. This number represents, in 2005, twice the value of traditional exports (which include coffee, bananas and sugar, among others) and more than half the value of exports from the FZ system.[11] As the industry flourished, hotel developments sprang up everywhere, especially in the coastal areas. As an example, just in the Papagayo peninsula area, 23 concessions were granted between 1991 and 1999.[12] These developments were stimulated by the incentives resulting from the Law of Incentives for Tourism Development.[13] This law declares tourism to be of public usefulness and lists the incentives provided to firms operating in the sector. The incentives are granted under a "tourist contract" and include various tax exemptions.

Just as human capital is critical for the attraction of high-tech FDI, natural capital is crucial for the attraction of tourism. The aim of most visitors to Costa Rica is to learn about and enjoy the beauty of the beaches, tropical forests and biodiversity. But the government is finding it increasingly difficult to adequately preserve these assets and to keep illegal hunters away from wildlife reserves and refuges. The reason? Insufficient government revenue, which leads to an inability to enforce the existing regulations.

But there is yet another aspect of the inconsistency of the country's approach to development; the arrival of tourists has put severe pressure on the airports, on the roads and highway system and on security. The capacity of the country's main airport had already collapsed in the early nineties; the number of passengers using this airport increased from 1.8 million in 1995 to 3.2 million in 2005. The pressure on roads has also been growing; the number of vehicles in circulation rose from nearly half a million in the mid-1990s to almost 1.5 million units in 2005. Investment in roads and highway expansion remains problematic, however, due to the budget constraints that the government faces.

The development of tourist activities, with new hotels in coastal and mountain areas, is increasing the pressure on the environment. The national plan for tourist development (2002–2012) foresees the creation of 1,800 new hotel rooms per year. But as indicated in the XXII Report on the State of the Nation, no assessment is available on the potential impact of this development, particularly in terms of the social and environmental impacts.[14]

Conclusions and Policy Suggestions

In this chapter we have analyzed the evolution of FDI in Costa Rica and its relation to economic development. FDI has had an important impact on Costa Rica's broad macroeconomic aggregates; it has contributed to the financing of the trade deficit (and thus indirectly to foreign exchange and price stability), it has countered the decline in national investment and it has generated export growth and employment.

However, to date, FDI has not contributed greatly to the advancement of the country's knowledge-based assets. Even though there have been positive effects through training and the impact on technical curricula at some of the main universities, backward linkages and the integration of national producers into global value chains have been very limited. The ratio of national expenditure to imports and exports has remained virtually stagnant since 1997.

The development of backward linkages is conditioned by the confluence of FDI spillover potential through domestic sourcing on the one hand, and domestic linkage capability, the country's absorptive capacity, on the other hand. While both sides play a role in explaining the scant development of linkages, we argue that the country's insufficient linkage capability has ultimately been the more limiting constraint.

In the presence of widespread market failures, most prominently imperfect information and coordination failures, together with high risk and high capital costs, it is not surprising that national absorption capabilities have generally been too low. Against the backdrop of the Washington Consensus, Costa Rican governments did not pursue proactive policies to work with private producers to overcome these market failures. One of the main reasons why the development potential of high-tech FDI has mostly gone unrealized so far is the glaring absence of a development strategy; a development strategy that would map out priorities and the role of different sectors and actors in achieving these priorities.

That has not happened in Costa Rica since the early 1980s, individual efforts and initiatives notwithstanding. Pursuit of free trade and attraction of FDI policies do not constitute such a strategy. There now exists a vast literature on the development failures of the Washington Consensus, including a critical assessment by key World Bank economists (2005). Rodrik (2001), among many others, has argued persuasively that we need a "trade policy as if development mattered." Trade and FDI policies have to be articulated in the context of a larger development strategy that is aimed at expanding the country's knowledge-based assets so as to enable structural change and productivity growth which generate employment and income in higher value-added processes and products (Abugattas and Paus 2006, Paus and Shapiro 2007). Government policies have to adjust the incentive structure, which is currently heavily skewed towards foreign investment, more toward domestic producers, so as to provide a somewhat more level playing field.

As global competition continues to intensify, especially with the rise of China and India, it is absolutely critical that the Costa Rican government articulate and follow a development strategy, which lays out priorities, formulates requisite policies and indicates a coherent, multi-agency approach towards implementation. The government, in close interaction with the private sector (Haussmann and Rodrik 2003, Rodrik 2004), needs to embark on a process of discovery of those activities that have the highest potential for successful interaction with FDI.

A new development strategy can only be achieved when the political factions in Costa Rica arrive at a new, sustainable coalition that can and will sustain such a project politically, as analyzed splendidly by Sánchez Ancochea (2004). Forging a new political coalition is not the only challenge, though. It is absolutely critical that the tax ratio be raised to allow for needed investment in education, infrastructure and social services. We have argued in this chapter that the liberalization policy with respect to FDI, tourism and trade has led to a reduction in the tax ratio which makes it hard to finance the very public investment needed to advance development and to set in motion a virtuous cycle of FDI-domestic linkages, higher value-added FDI, higher value-added national production, etc.

When Intel-Costa Rica celebrated ten years of operations in Costa Rica in March 2007, Intel president Craig Barrett criticized the lack of technological advancements in the country and the insufficient attention to progress in education (La República 2007). School completion and enrolment rates have become a growing concern; education of more engineers in a broader number of fields as well as greater availability of English-speaking employees are becoming increasingly important elements in eliminating the bottlenecks to further expansion of foreign investment in the IT-based services sector and to FDI in Costa Rica increasing in value. In the mid-1990s, only 18 percent of Costa Rican students in tertiary education were in the sciences, compared to 43 percent in Chile and 30 percent in Argentina (UNDP 2004: 176).

It is ironic, of course, that the very tax exemptions granted to Intel and other MNCs under the rules of the Zona Franca, means that these companies do not directly contribute to an increase in the tax revenue needed for significant improvements in infrastructure and education that they themselves benefit from. It is unfortunate that these companies do not appreciate the need to contribute to the generation of the country-specific assets they are looking for. But it is even more unfortunate that the government does not recognize the need for such a contribution either. The tax reform attempts that have been sent to the congress only timidly open up the possibility of taxes on MNCs, and with the fear that perhaps these firms will decide to leave the country in search of more favorable treatment in other developing countries. Of course, these fears are well grounded as firms (like the comments by Intel above) have made it very clear that they do not want to be taxed.

But it seems that policymakers have lost sight of the fact that the corporations operating in the FZ will only leave the nation if they can find another country in which lower wages and tax rates compensate for the higher productivity of the Costa Rican workers and the stability of the social and political system. The fact that special treatment for exports, e.g., tax exemptions for the Free Zones, will have to be eliminated by the end of 2008 provides a great opportunity for the Costa Rican authorities to establish a positive effective tax rate that will strike the right balance between generating revenue and not driving foreign investors away. And if the government wants to use tax reductions as a way to achieve targeted goals, then they should be linked explicitly to the advancement of the country's knowledge-based assets.

Stopping the tax-rate race to the bottom among developing countries ultimately requires the imposition of tax floors at a global level, a formidable challenge. The example of the Scandinavian countries shows that there is no necessary trade-off between taxes and competitiveness. In 2004, Finland, Sweden and Denmark reached tax ratios of 44 percent, 51 percent and 50 percent, respectively. These nations ranked first, third and fourth in the competitiveness report of the World Economic Forum for 2005 (EurActive.com 2005).

Insufficient tax revenue also makes it very difficult to sustain the natural and environmental capital that make the country so attractive to high-tech multinationals and tourists. In the tourist sector we find the same limitations as in the Zona Franca system; it is not clear which sectors are reaping the benefits of ecotourism, and there is no information on the environmental impact of hotel developments in protected areas. As in the case of the FZ, the institutions in charge lack a clear vision of where they want to go, and thus do not even generate the data that are required to assess the impact of their actions.

The Costa Rican government needs to define a coherent development strategy that takes into account the social and economic realities of the country in a global context of growing competitive pressures. The core of such a strategy has to be the advancement of the country's knowledge-based assets. And it is in that context that the role of FDI, and particularly high-tech FDI, has to be specified.

Important elements for the advancement of knowledge-based assets and a more lasting positive impact of FDI are an increase in tax revenues and a more fairly distributed tax burden. Since MNCs feed on the characteristics and specific assets of the local economy, the country needs to enhance all those features that have turned it into an attractive destination for high-tech FDI flows—political and social stability, a well defined institutional framework, an educated labor force and beautiful and well preserved natural areas.

This will only be possible through more and better investment in human capital, social programs for the disadvantaged and active government-private sector collaboration to identify and promote the most profitable and viable activities. Such a process will lead to the definition of the specific microeconomic policies required for a more dynamic local economy and for a closer interaction between national producers and MNCs.

The national system of science and technology has to be redefined, so as to attain a closer link between the needs of producers (local and foreign) and the development and improvement of location-specific assets. In this framework, the actions of an agency like CINDE have to cohere with the national development objectives, and the efforts of a better-equipped CRP program will be more likely to bring about a quantum leap in the country's linkage and absorption capabilities.

Finally, more resources are needed for the creation and maintenance of a reliable database of information on the evolution of the FZ (e.g., linkages, local purchases, types of workers hired or required), the evolution of the tourist sector and the condition of the national parks. This information will allow policymakers to assess the results of different microeconomic policies and investment projects and make the necessary adjustments in a flexible and speedy fashion, as internal and external conditions keep changing.

Part Two

POLITICAL ECONOMY OF NATURAL RESOURCES AND THE ENVIRONMENT

Chapter Seven

INVESTMENT RULES AND SUSTAINABLE DEVELOPMENT: PRELIMINARY LESSONS FROM THE URUGUAYAN PULP MILLS CASE

Martina Chidiak

Introduction

This chapter focuses on the recent dispute between Argentina and Uruguay over the installation of two pulp mills near the Uruguayan city of Fray Bentos, on the bank of the Uruguay River (a resource shared by the two countries). At present, only one of the pulp mills (involving investment by the Finnish firm Oy Metsä-Botnia Ab) is under construction at the originally planned location, since the other project (involving the Spanish company ENCE) has been relocated to another Uruguayan region. The Argentinean government claims that the Fray Bentos pulp mill will have severe environmental consequences, in particular for the nearby Argentinean city of Gualeguaychú, while the Uruguayan government argues that it will have no noticeable environmental effects.

This case has garnered increasing regional and international attention, as the dialogues, technical analyses, and legal disputes of the past two years have failed to arrive at a solution to the bilateral crisis.[1]

In fact, the conflict has been intensifying over time. Bilateral relations have been deteriorating even within the framework of MERCOSUR, the regional trade agreement into which Argentina, Brazil, Paraguay and Uruguay entered (with Bolivia and Chile as associate members) in 1991.

In an attempt to move the analysis beyond the details of the conflict and the opposing views of the two countries, this chapter adopts a regional perspective. It aims to highlight the main lesson from this dispute: the need to strengthen the institutional and regulatory capacities of the region in order to guarantee sustainable development benefits from FDI, and, in particular, to effectively regulate the potential environmental impacts of expanding forestry-based industry. The failure, so far, to achieve a resolution to this dispute or agreement on a mechanism for monitoring and regulating the environmental impact of the Fray Bentos mill suggests that the region is not yet able to ensure that the expanding pulp-and-paper industry (or FDI in this sector) will contribute to sustainable development.

This view can be supported from two perspectives:

First, the failure to reach a solution to the conflict is somewhat puzzling given the existence of at least two institutions created, among other things, for this purpose—the Uruguay River Statute signed by Argentina and Uruguay in 1975 and the regional agreements signed by Argentina and Uruguay in the framework of MERCOSUR (in particular, the Framework Agreement on Environmental Issues signed in 2001). The Framework Agreement on Environmental Issues agreement states that MERCOSUR member countries should cooperate for environmental protection and sustainable use of natural resources, as well as to meet international commitments on environmental matters (including through common policies). It also includes provisions to solve, through the MERCOSUR mechanism for dispute settlement, any controversy between member countries on environmental matters. This regional mechanism, however, has not been invoked for this case.

Second, the need for regional cooperation in order to effectively deal with potential environmental impacts of FDI has been neglected in this case. This bilateral dispute should be viewed in the broader context of international rules that have profound effects on local and regional regulatory issues: (1) investment protection rules, mostly developed at the bilateral or regional level (through bilateral investment treaties (BITs) and investment protection chapters of free trade agreements (FTAs)): and (2) international environmental rules stemming from multilateral environmental agreements (MEAs) as a response to concerns about transborder environmental impacts. Investment protection rules are important in this case since one of the foreign investors currently building the pulp mill in Fray Bentos, the Finnish company Oy Metsä-Botnia, is protected by the BIT signed by Uruguay and Finland in 2002. Multilateral environmental agreements, meanwhile, are important since Uruguay (like all other MERCOSUR countries) has ratified the Stockholm Convention on Persistent Organic Pollutants. MERCOSUR countries are bound to design new regulations to curb "unintended" emissions of dioxins and furans (pollutants of which pulp mills are a potential source) and to promote the use of best available technologies and environmental practices.

Bilateral dialogue virtually stalled between March 2006 and April 2007, and no efforts are currently underway to design a joint regulatory response to the potential environmental impacts of the pulp mill. At the time this article was concluded, Spain was trying to promote renewed dialogue, but no preliminary agreement—nor even any specific proposal—is yet in sight.

The window of opportunity for building the necessary regional institutional capacity and crafting a coordinated regulatory response is quite tight; the Botnia plant in Fray Bentos is expected to start operations in September 2007. Similarly, regulations to curb unintended emissions of dioxins and furans from new sources should be put in place by Uruguay (pursuant to Stockholm Convention on Persistent Organic Pollutants) by mid-2008. This suggests that the concerned parties may only realize that cooperation on regulation and monitoring was the best (and unexploited) option when it is too late.

The discussion is organized as follows:

The next three sections present some basic information on the case under consideration. The first section following describes the economic importance of the MERCOSUR region for pulp and paper production. The second section discusses the implications of the ongoing debate on FDI, BITs and sustainable development. The third section focuses on some stylized facts of the dispute and highlights the institutional weaknesses the dispute has revealed.

The fourth section discusses the commitments assumed by Uruguay and Argentina under the Stockholm Convention on Persistent Organic Pollutants and identifies two associated challenges. First, these commitments may lead to a potential conflict with foreign investors (due to the introduction of new environmental regulations after BITs were signed). Second, they pose an additional need for regional coordination of environmental policy in view of the limited national capacities to monitor releases of dioxins and furans. To conclude, the fifth section discusses the most important lessons from the case.

The Southern Cone's Role as Pulp-and-Paper Producer

Since the 1980s, South America has been one of the most dynamic and promising regions for forest-based industries such as pulp-and-paper. The Southern Cone (Argentina, Brazil, Chile and Uruguay), in particular, has increased its share of world pulp-and-paper production since the late 1980s due to a mix of favorable natural conditions (rapid growth and availability of low-cost land for forestry) and promotional forestry policies. So far, however, increasing "Southern Cone" output is mostly explained by rising production in Brazil and Chile, which jointly account for 70–90 percent of the sub-region's production.

Over the past decade, investment in Argentina has primarily taken the form of acquisition of existing pulp-and-paper plants, notably by foreign companies from MERCOSUR member or associate countries. For example, FANAPEL (Uruguay) took a majority stake in Celulosa Argentina; Celulosa Arauco (Chile) bought Alto Paraná (the main pulp producer) as well as Celulosa Puerto Piray. Another Chilean firm, CMPC, purchased the local company Papelera del Plata and in the 1990s began forestry operations in the provinces of Misiones and Corrientes. In addition, some investment went into new paper-product facilities, e.g., by Klabin (Brazil). Recent press sources also suggest that CMPC may have plans to build a pulp mill in Corrientes province.[2]

Argentina, Brazil, Chile and Uruguay increased their world share in roundwood production from seven percent in 1990 to nine percent in 2004, during a period of stagnant world output. In paper production, their three percent share increased to four percent over the same span, in spite of mounting world production (which grew 50 percent during the period). Nearly all of the Southern Cone's increase was accounted for by Brazil (the regional leader). Most impressive is the case of chemical pulp production. The Southern Cone countries increased their share from six percent to 11 percent (with their share of world exports reaching 24 percent in 2004). In chemical pulp, according to 2004 figures, Brazil and Argentina exported 50 percent of their production, while this proportion reached 90 percent for Chile.[3]

Unlike Chile and Brazil, where local firms are the main participants in the forestry sector, Uruguay expanded this sector through FDI.[4] In the 1990s, the country launched a broad strategy to attract foreign investment, comprising a new law for foreign investment (1998), adhesion to ICSID, the World Bank-affiliated international tribunal for investment-related disputes (1992) and the signing of 22 Bilateral Investment Treaties throughout the 1990s. In the forest industries, industrial and forestry-promotion policies also played an important role.[5] These policies have led to a surge of FDI inflows into the sector since the mid-1990s. The average annual inflow since then has hovered around US$300 million, i.e., more than double the previous peak of US$122 million (achieved between 1977 and 1982). The FDI stock more than tripled between 1990 and 2004—from US$670 million to US$2,110 million (Bittencourt and Domingo 2000; UNCTAD 2005).

Even if many other sectors grew under the new investment rules, the forestry case stands alone, since deliberate forestry-promotion policies have led to the rise of a previously nonexistent industry—eucalyptus-based forestry. This industry received most of the FDI going to the primary products sector in the first half of the 1990s. After nearly 15 years of planting, trees were ready for pulpwood production, spurring many pulp-processing projects. The two most prominent involve a Finnish company (Botnia) and a Spanish pulp producer (ENCE). Originally, the two projects were to be located near Fray Bentos (in the Department of Río Negro). These projects were expected to produce 1.5 million tons of eucalyptus bleached kraft pulp for the world market, and to lead to FDI inflows of US$1.5 billion (the largest investment ever hosted by Uruguay). The ENCE project is currently being redefined both in terms of scale and location, after the decision not to build the plant near Fray Bentos. For this reason, this article mostly focuses on the Botnia project (aimed at producing one million tons of eucalyptus bleached kraft pulp). According to recent estimates, the Botnia pulp mill will be ready to begin operations in September 2007. The two projects (or even the Botnia project alone) will rank Uruguay third among Latin American kraft pulp producers.

The Debate Over Investment Protection and Constraints on Environmental Policy

Since the 1990s, a growing international debate has explored the links between FDI and sustainable development and the effects of FDI-protection mechanisms on these links.

Many developing countries have signed bilateral treaties protecting foreign investment in the past 15 years. The "investment chapters" of free trade agreements (FTAs), such as NAFTA's Chapter Eleven, have been another important kind of bilateral or regional (as opposed to multilateral) mechanism for investment protection.

In MERCOSUR, two separate protocols were drafted for investment protection (one for intra-MERCOSUR investment, the 1994 Colonia Protocol, and one for foreign investment, the 1994 Buenos Aires Protocol). Neither, however, has entered into force, since the required full ratification by members was not reached. Argentina, Paraguay and Uruguay ratified the Buenos Aires Protocol, but it did not enter into force due to Brazilian nonratification; by contrast, none of the member countries formally ratified the Colonia Protocol.

Critics of both BITs and investment chapters of FTAs usually point out their bias towards the protection of investors' rights (e.g., through overly broad definitions of investment and expropriation that widen the scope for litigation), for generalizing benefits to all investors (via "most favored nation" clauses) and for "importing" institutions (in particular, introducing investor-state arbitration, by which investors may sue governments at international tribunals such as the International Centre for Settlement of Investment Disputes (ICSID) or the United Nations Commission on International Trade Law (UNCITRAL)). More generally, critics argue that such agreements seriously constrain governments' policy latitude, and may lead to a virtual freeze on regulation in order to guarantee a stable business environment (and avoid conflicts with investors). For a more detailed discussion, the interested reader is referred to Mann (2001) and Peterson (2003); Stanley (2004) offers an analysis of BITs focusing on Latin American countries.

In general, BITs and investment protection chapters of FTAs make no special provisions for areas in which governments may want to retain strong regulatory powers (e.g., environment, public health). Foreign investors have sued host countries because they considered new environmental regulations or policy decisions 1) indirect "expropriations" of their investments, 2) unjustified performance standards or 3) unjust treatment of investors according to minimum standards (Mann 2001; Peterson 2003).

In a number of cases, governments had to back down from their environmental policy decisions (e.g., Ethyl v. Canada, leading to Canada retreating from its ban on MMT imports) or compensate investors for economic losses due to environmental regulations, While this remains a concern in the environmental community, in the case Methanex v. United States, the Tribunal ruled that an environmental regulation cannot be considered an expropriation, reversing the precedent set in the earlier cases (Mann 2001; Mann 2005). In addition, some environment and investment chapters of FTAs are evolving to recognize host countries' rights to protect the environment and natural resources. For example, in the FTA signed between the US and Colombia, the environment chapter makes explicit reference to biodiversity protection and its importance for sustainable development, as well as to the parties' sovereignty regarding the use of natural resources. Furthermore, the investment chapter of this FTA states that investors may not sue the host country for regulatory changes affecting their activities if those changes pursue public-health or environmental-protection objectives.

Nevertheless, these exceptions are quite rare in the universe of outstanding FTAs and BITs. In some cases, environmental concerns have been included in FTA provisions or in specific protocols (e,g., those signed by Chile with the US and the Central America Free Trade Agreement (CAFTA) with the US), but without specific provisions to safeguard environmental regulations. Even more worrying, there is no international tribunal to adjudicate cases of noncompliance with the environmental provisions of BITs or FTAs (as mentioned by (Mann 2001), for the case of NAFTA).

The BIT signed by Finland and Uruguay made no specific provision for environmental regulations. Therefore, the Finnish firm Botnia could, in principle, sue Uruguay if the government established new environmental regulations for the pulp and paper industry (e.g., changing the standards set in the initial operation permits, denying a new permit due to a facility's inability to comply with more stringent environmental regulations, etc.).

Some analysts argue that such investment-protection mechanisms put too much emphasis on investors' rights and not enough on investors' obligations. In particular, foreign investors are granted "unlimited" protection through BITs or investment chapters in FTAs, but make only voluntary commitments on the environmental impacts of their operations abroad (i.e., they face no compulsory rules to meet the same environmental standards in their home base and foreign operations) (Von Moltke and Mann 2004). One example of this voluntary-commitment framework is the Revised OECD Guidelines for Multinational Enterprises (OECD, 2000), which allows complaints at national focal points (in investors' home countries or in host countries) in cases where companies fail to comply with environmental, human rights, or labor standards, or disclosure and transparency guidelines.

Foreign investors (and MNCs) face, in addition to local environmental requirements, those stemming from international financial institutions' project evaluations (e.g., those faced by Botnia and ENCE when they applied for International Finance Corporation (World Bank Group) funding for their pulp-mill projects) (see section IV below). However, both the OECD Guidelines' and international financial institutions' requisites rely on local legislation to determine the appropriate environmental standards. The World Bank Group's operational rules only required that the companies' environmental impact assessments indicated that they would apply best available technologies and meet national emissions standards (according to technology specifications, the evaluation of the local regulatory authority (DINAMA), etc.). This may not be sufficient in the pulp mills case if national regulations do not fully acknowledge regional environmental impacts (discussed in Section 4 following). This may well call for the participation of regional institutions in order to address environmental concerns created by investment and trade within the region, something that did not happen in this dispute (MERCOSUR was hardly involved).

The Pulp Mills Dispute

After more than a year of bilateral controversy, Argentina brought Uruguay to trial before the International Court of Justice (ICJ) under charges that Uruguay breached the terms of the Uruguay River Statute by unilaterally authorizing ENCE and Botnia (the local company name for the subsidiary of Oy Metsä-Botnia) to build the pulp mills. For its part, Uruguay presented claims both at MERCOSUR and before the ICJ due to roadblocking by Argentinean protestors, who interrupted traffic on the bridge connecting the cities of Fray Bentos (in Uruguay) and Gualeguaychú (Argentina) during most of the summer months over the past two years, severely affecting Uruguayan income from tourism.

It is puzzling that two partners in a regional trade agreement, with a long historic record of good relations, have failed to solve the conflict posed by the potential environmental impact of two pulp mills.

In principle, this is a controversy that could be solved at the technical and regulatory levels, provided appropriate technical institutions are available and involved. MERCOSUR features many working groups for technical and institutional cooperation that are relevant for this case: (1) two technical subgroups (among ten that report to the Common Market Group), one on Environmental issues (SGT N° 6) and one on Industry issues (SGT N° 7); (2) one Specialized Meeting on Science and Technology; and (3) a Technical Cooperation Committee. It is puzzling that none of these bodies was involved in efforts to create a dialogue in this case, regardless of growing importance of this sector in the MERCOSUR region.

From a pure cost-benefit perspective, this case poses a regional policy dilemma.[6] A preliminary analysis, mainly from the environmental impact assessments (EIAs) available, suggests that most economic and social benefits from the proposed pulp mills would accrue to Uruguay at the cost of some environmental impact (while some environmental risks may be not fully considered by Uruguayan authorities, as argued below), and that Argentina faces some environmental risk with no certain socioeconomic benefits from the projects. Some potential economic gains were spurned by the Entre Ríos province (in which Gualeguaychú is located) when it recently banned wood exports to the Uruguayan pulp mills; however, other provinces with eucalyptus plantations, like Corrientes and Misiones, may still benefit from such exports.

The initial conflict, temporarily reduced has subsequently mounted over time (see Table 7.1 for a chronology). For almost a year, analysts have stressed that the bilateral xsconflict may seriously weaken MERCOSUR ties. Even if the characteristics of this particular case, which has been a political "hot potato," could explain the reluctance of MERCOSUR (in particular at the Common Market Council, the main political body) to get involved, it is still puzzling that the case was not eventually brought to consideration under MERCOSUR technical or advisory bodies, such as the Common Market Group and its subgroups (save for the Uruguayan claim on roadblocking presented at the dispute settlement mechanism).

The main argument of each party before international tribunals has been to show that its share of damages is too high and unjustified:for Argentina, in terms of environmental risk if the Fray Bentos plant is built and starts

Table 7.1. **Chronology of the Pulp Mills Dispute**

2003	**October**
	Uruguayan government grants ENCE reliminary environmental authorization for the building phase (DINAMA, Res.342/2003).
	Civil Society representatives from Gualeguaychú express their concern over the environmental impact of the pulp mill to the Argentinean government
	Argentinean note of complaint to the Uruguayan government. Ad-hoc CARU meeting. Argentina questioned unilateral authorization by Uruguay for a project affecting a joint resource, regulated by the Uruguay River Statute.
2004	**March**
	Talks between the two governments lead to an agreement to this initial dispute.
	April
	The Foreign Relations Minister of Argentina declares in the Congress that, in the CARU Framework, Argentina will receive all the relevant information to determine whether to agree or not to the project authorization. Argentina agrees, in the CARU framewor
	May
	CARU meeting 01/04. Uruguay argues that the transcript from the meeting reflects that Argentina agreed to the authorization and considered the dispute closed (no transcript is available for consultation).
2005	**February**
	Uruguayan government grants Botnia preliminary authorization for the building phase (DINAMA, Res.63/2005)
	April
	Botnia starts building works near Fray Bentos.
	May
	The two governments agree on creating a joint high-level technical taskforce (GTAN) to evaluate the environmental impact of the pulp mills on the Uruguay River.
	June
	The Argentinean government sends a note to the World Bank Group asking the institution to refrain from funding the Botnia project (knowing that an application for funding had been presented by the company in 2004). As a result, Uruguay postpones the first
	August
	GTAN meetings start.
	December
	World Bank Group releases draft cumulative-impact study.
	Protestors from Gualeguaychú start road-blocking at the San Martín Bridge joining Fray Bentos and Gualeguaychú. Sporadic road blocking also occurs on the bridges joining Colón (Arg.)-Paysandú (Uru.) and Concordia (Arg.)-Salto (Uru.) during the summer.

(Continued)

Table 7.1. **Continued**

2006	**February**
	The Argentinean Parliament approves the Executive Power decision to bring the dispute with Uruguay before the International Court of Justice (ICJ).
	Uruguay demands a special meeting of the Common Market Group of MERCOSUR to discuss the economic impacts of road-blocking in Argentina. Argentina (holding the rotating presidency of MERCOSUR) ignores the request. Uruguay files a case under MERCOSUR disput
	March
	After a series of meetings and the exchange of information and notes, the GTAN could not agree upon a joint set of conclusions. Each government issues a separate report.
	Road blocking lifted on the bridges near Gualeguaychú (after 46 days) and Colon (after 34 days).
	The Uruguayan president invites Argentina for joint monitoring of the pulp mills.
	The Argentinean president asks his Uruguayan Counterpart to consider asking for a halt in construction on both plants for 90 days in order to give more time to assess their cumulative environmental impact. ENCE agrees to stop building, and shortly after a Bilateral talks came to a halt.
2006	**April**
	Independent expert review of the draft cumulative impact study released by World Bank Group (Hartfield report).
	Argentinean NGO (CEDHA) presents a claim before the Finnish focal point arguing that Botnia's operations in Uruguay did not comply with the OECD Guidelines for Multinational Enterprises.
	May
	Argentina presents two cases before the ICJ in relation with the bilateral dispute. One case demands the building at the Botnia facility stop, the other one accuses Uruguay of breaching the Uruguay River Statute by unilaterally granting authorization for
	July
	ICJ refuses to grant (at the demand of Argentina) an interruption of building at Botnia. The jury states that building operations did not imply "irreversible damage" to Argentina. ICJ decision on the other case presented by Argentina (over whether Uruguay
	September
	MERCOSUR Tribunal releases verdict over the Uruguayan complaint on road blocking is released. It recognizes that Argentina failed to fulfil its obligations under MERCOSUR by tolerating the road blockings but did not impose sanctions on Argentina (nor comp
	October
	World Bank Group releases final cumulative-environmental-impact study.
	November
	MIGA and IFC (World Bank Group) grant funding to Botnia project (US$170 million from IFC, and US$350 million guarantee by MIGA).

(Continued)

Table 7.1. **Continued**

	Finland's Ministry of Trade and Industry (national focal point for the OECD guidelines for Multinational Enterprises) dismisses the case presented by CEDHA. It finds that Botnia was not in noncompliance with the above-mentioned guidelines.
	December
	Road-blocking on the San Martín Bridge by protestors from Gualeguaychú resumes and lasts all summer (still in force in July 2007). Occasional blocking also occurrs on the other two bridges joining the two countries.
2007	**January**
	The ICJ does not accept Uruguayan claims for compensation for road blocking. The jury finds that road -locking did not impose "irreversible damage" to Uruguay.
	March
	Entre Rios Province enacts a law banning wood exports from the province to feed the Uruguayan pulp mills.
	April
	Botnia announcs that the plant is expected to start operations in September 2007.
	Under the mediation of the Spanish Government, Uruguayan and Argentinean representatives meet in Spain for preliminary talks over the dispute.

operations as planned; for Uruguay, if the Argentinean roadblocking protests, which inflict economic losses on Uruguay due to a fall in trade and tourism flows from Argentina, go on unchecked.

Even if each government wanted to put an end to the dispute, it might have faced high costs. In March 2006 Uruguay was in a difficult position to ask Botnia to halt construction and relocate its plant after having granted the preliminary authorization for building (and after construction had started). This would have either required very expensive compensation or considerable risk of a formal complaint under the BIT signed with Finland. On the Argentinean side, given the general approval that protestors from Gualeguaychú have enjoyed in the country, ordering (or eventually forcing) an end to the roadblocking would have been politically difficult.

Nevertheless, even when the conflict peaked in March–April 2006, no alternative to carrying on the dispute endlessly was apparently considered. The Argentinean report to the High Level Technical Taskforce in February 2006 identified many weaknesses of the EIAs presented by the two companies and of the standards set by the preliminary permit issued by the Uruguayan government. Most of the criticisms regarding the lack of information or precision in the EIAs were confirmed by the independent review carried out at the request of the World Bank Group (Hatfield Consultants 2006). For its part, the Uruguayan government repeated the invitation to Argentina to jointly monitor the projects, Neither party, however, proposed joint work on revising information requirements and standards in the final building and operation permits.

This is even more worrying considering the results of the independent review commissioned by the World Bank Group (Hatfield Consultants 2006). This report states that catastrophic environmental impacts are not to be expected with the technologies to be installed in the plants, but that assessing the actual environmental impact requires more detailed consideration of the plant design, contingency plans, environmental management and monitoring, as well as detailed regulatory requirements. The Hatfield report passes no judgment on local regulators' actions or their consideration of regional impacts (e.g., no comments on the unilateral building authorization by Uruguay are found, nor on whether environmental impacts on the Argentinean side were fully considered).

For almost a year (March 2006–April 2007), no political dialogue or joint technical efforts took place, since each party set very demanding conditions for restarting talks. The Argentinean government demanded relocation of the Botnia plant, while tacitly accepting roadblocking in spite of the Uruguayan complaints before MERCOSUR and the ICJ. The Uruguayan government, meanwhile, demanded the end of roadblocking, while allowing building of the Botnia plant to continue in spite of Argentinean complaints that the environmental impacts (in particular on the Argentinean side and on the Uruguay River) had not been thoroughly considered by the Uruguayan authorities.

Pending environmental concerns

Even setting aside the catastrophic-environmental-impact claim, as suggested by the Hatfield report, some environmental concerns posed by Argentina regarding the Botnia project seem relevant. These are summarized as folllows:

1. Water pollution risks near Fray Bentos (the Argentinean report from the GTAN also stresses that no details or quantified analyses of the expected impacts on the Argentinean side, in particular near Gualeguaychú, the closest city to Fray Bentos, are offered in the EIAs):

   • The main concern is related to dioxins and furans release. The Uruguayan government agreed in principle to the company's decision not to monitor these releases after the EIA indicated that no noticeable emissions of these pollutants would result from the selected technology (i.e., the emissions standards allowed by the chosen production technology). On these grounds, the preliminary authorization has not set a standard on AOX (Halogenated Organic Compounds), a measure of the presence of dioxins and furans and other persistent organic pollutants (POPs) in water effluents.

• Another concern is that even if the Uruguay River is a relatively "clean" watercourse, the occurrence of eutrophization episodes has been regularly verified, in particular during the spring and summer months. The analysis of emissions standards for phosphorous and nitrogen compounds does not seem to take this into account and does not limit the risks of increasing eutrophization episodes (with the associated risks of fish mortality and of negative impacts on tourism due to the presence of algae and foam).

These two concerns could be managed and solved in the framework of the Uruguay River Statute (and CARU) if parties were ready to negotiate. Eventually, the arguments and evidence presented by the two countries on these issues will be considered by the ICJ before it makes a decision.

2. Air quality concerns: The release of dioxins and furans could also occur through the air. The Argentinean government has made complaints about the monitoring requirements set by its Uruguayan counterpart. Even though a maximum limit for annual air releases of these pollutants was set, no specific requirements for monitoring such releases were indicated. This is cause for concern since Botnia has indicated in its preliminary monitoring plan that it does not intend to measure dioxin and furan releases continuously (on grounds that such emissions are expected to be negligible).

3. Possible threats to tourism:A third major concern of the Argentinian government is the potential impact of the pulp mill on tourism (in particular on Ñandubaysal, the Uruguay River beach that is closest to Gualeguaychú). This relates not only to air and water pollution risks but also to other impacts, such as odor and visual disamenities caused by the plant. Uruguayan authorities have required Botnia to prepare a mitigation plan for all major visual effects. The ICJ ruling will not address this since it will only focus on environmental impacts on the Uruguay River (covered by the Uruguay River Statute). From this perspective, consideration of environmental concerns about the pulp mills in the framework of MERCOSUR could have been more thorough (involving all transborder or regional environmental and visual effects).

Institutional aspects

It is remarkable that the institutional framework that could have prevented the conflict, but failed to do so, seems quite solid.

First, the uses of the Uruguay River in the area shared by Uruguay and Argentina are regulated by the Uruguay River Statute ratified by both countries in 1975. The Statute created the Uruguay River Administration Commission (CARU) to regulate bilateral cooperation in several areas (such as navigation, building works, ports building and operation, rescue operations, natural-resource management, pollution control, and research and dispute settlement). The water quality and pollution discharge standards are gathered in the Uruguay River Digest.

The Uruguay River Statute also incorporated other international principles and commitments, such as those adopted under MERCOSUR's Framework Agreement on Environmental Issues (2003). The Agreement aimed (among other things) at promoting sustainable development and preventing negative environmental impacts in member countries, particularly in border areas (FARN 2006).

Figure 7.1. Stockholm Convention on Persistent Organic Pollutants

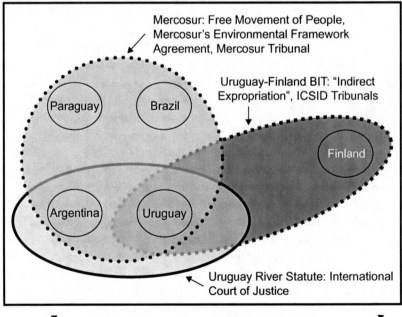

Under the Uruguay River Statute, each party must notify CARU of any building plan or project that may have an impact on the environmental quality of the river and must subsequently turn over all the information needed to evaluate this impact. Any party wishing to implement such a project must wait for the other party's comments before granting authorization, unless the other party fails to present such comments within 180 days. If the notified party finds that some relevant impact can be expected from the project, the parties have up to 180 days to solve the dispute bilaterally. After that period, they may resort to the International Court of Justice (as both parties to the dispute did in 2006).

Second, the MERCOSUR Agreement on Environmental Issues adopted the MERCOSUR mechanism for dispute settlement (best suited for trade disputes). Uruguay resorted to this mechanism to file a complaint on roadblocking in Argentina. In addition, there is a specific permanent technical workgroup (SG N° 6) on environmental issues made up by representatives from all member countries. This group provides a forum for dialogue and cooperation on environmental matters from a technical and legal perspective and meets at least twice a year. This technical forum was not involved in the controversy.

The ICJ will have to decide whether Uruguay breached the Uruguay River Statute when it gave preliminary authorization for building the pulp mills without previous consultation with Argentina. But there is more to this decision than is immediately apparent. If a project may pose environmental risks, the Uruguay Statute allows the party concerned about environmental impacts to demand information from the party promoting the project. The concerned party gets 180 days to present and sustain evidence of such impact. The lack of information on the dialogue between the two countries in the framework of CARU between late 2003 and the end of 2005 (no transcripts from the meetings are available) precludes us from saying whether Uruguay produced all the information necessary for Argentina to evaluate the pulp mills' environmental impact (after granting preliminary authorization for building) and if Argentina presented evidence of environmental impact in due time. This is probably what the ICJ will have to determine in the coming months in order to rule whether Uruguay breached the Uruguay River Statute when it authorized the construction of the pulp mills. This tribunal has already dismissed both the Argentinean demand for a halt in construction at the Botnia project and the Uruguayan claim on roadblocking in Argentina.

Both parties have failed to honor their regional commitments. If it is true that Uruguay failed to comply with the Uruguay River Statute by unilaterally granting authorization to build the pulp mills, it is also true that Argentina, by tolerating roadblocking, failed to comply with the rules of fluid movement of people, goods and currency agreed to in MERCOSUR.

In view of the previous decisions by the ICJ on this case, and given that building will soon be completed at Botnia's facility, it seems highly unlikely that this court will satisfy Argentinean demands to halt building and to ask Botnia to relocate the pulp mill, regardless of whether the Tribunal finds Uruguay guilty of breaching the Uruguay River Statute.

In such a context, what step should the Argentine authorities take next? First, the government should realize that the probability of a favorable ruling of the ICJ is quite low and face the need to switch to a new strategy. The best alternative would be to work in cooperation with Uruguay to guarantee protection of the Uruguay River environment (as well as environmental conditions around the pulp mill more generally) by reinforcing regulatory requirements for the operation phase—before the Botnia plant starts operations. The project has only received authorization for the building phase. To get an operation permit, the firm must successfully complete an Environmental Management Plan and a Monitoring Plan and the Uruguayan authorities must make a new decision (separate from the decision to authorize construction). As discussed below, setting operation permit standards and monitoring requirements poses important challenges in one particular regard: the release of dioxins and furans.

Environmental Protection v. Investment Protection?

Developing countries are responsible for the local implementation of their commitments under multilateral environmental agreements (MEAs). This implies the translation of international commitments into local regulations, as well as the enforcement of the latter. If any (foreign) investor fails to comply with such regulations, action has to be pursued through regular administrative channels at the national level. That is, institutions to safeguard environmental concerns covered by MEAs are not "imported" but domestic.

In regard to the pulp mills controversy, the most relevant MEA is the Stockholm Convention on Persistent Organic Pollutants (POPs). This convention set a list of 12 chemical substances that pose major environmental and health risks due to their toxicity, persistence (nondegradation), bioaccumulation, and transborder impacts. These impacts stem from the transport of these substances through air, water and migratory species, which allows effects far from the release site. The list of POPs targeted for phase-out includes dioxins and furans, which are not produced for sale, but rather are generated as "unintentional" releases from production processes. Among the sectors and activities that may lead to such releases are waste incineration, secondary metal production, uncontrolled combustion of biomass and waste, and the pulp industry.

Uruguay and Argentina (as well as all other MERCOSUR countries) ratified the Stockholm Convention in 2004. As a result, they are required to incorporate the Convention's provisions into national legislation (both countries have) and specific environmental regulations (still pending). With regard to unintended emissions of dioxins and furans, the Stockholm Convention states that the initial focus should be to minimize releases from industrial and waste incineration sources, and that best-environmental-techniques should be required for new sources (plants) no later than four years after the Convention's coming into force. Uruguay and Argentina each also have to present a National Implementation Plan (NIP) no later than two years after the Convention comes into force for each country stating they will meet their regulatory commitments.

Uruguay issued its National Implementation Plan in May 2006 (i.e., two years after the Convention entered into force), and is expected to institute best available technique (BAT) requirements for new sources of unintended emissions of dioxins and furans by May 2008. As stated in the NIP document, Uruguay faces many challenges to implementing the Stockholm Convention provisions, like most countries in the region (Government of Uruguay 2006). The first challenge arises from the lack of precise information regarding the actual releases of dioxins and furans in the country (the preliminary inventories of such releases, for the NIPs, resort to estimates following a standard toolkit developed in the framework of the Stockholm Convention). A second challenge stems from the fact that this environmental concern is new to the country (and not included in local environmental regulations). A third challenge relates to the lack of analytical capacities and equipment (in both the public and private sectors) to control and measure releases and concentrations of dioxins and furans. The lack of equipment is a more general concern in all MERCOSUR countries, as reflected in the Chilean NIP and as recognized by technical experts of the region (Government of Chile 2005; UNSAM 2006). Therefore, institutional and technical capacity-building will be necessary before the Stockholm Convention provision can be met at the local (and regional) level. The Uruguayan NIP stresses that, in addition to employing the necessary equipment, an interministerial taskforce should initiate a process of evaluating and drafting new regulatory provisions, organize monitoring routines and requirements and identify priority sectors and sources (Government of Uruguay 2006).

As discussed previously, a government's ability to fulfill its commitments under the Stockholm Convention may be hampered if the country has signed BITs that either limit the country's freedom to set national environmental policy or increase the risks of litigation if new environmental regulations are introduced. This suggests that a conflict may arise between compliance with an MEA and compliance with a BIT. In other words, the "importation" by developing countries of foreign institutions aimed at investment protection and at tackling global environmental concerns may clash.

Within the region, Uruguay's vulnerability to constraints by foreign investors is matched only by Argentina's (in view of the low levels of foreign investment and BITs in other pulp producing countries in MERCOSUR). Argentina has a long record of low enforcement of environmental regulations and faces complaints from both locals and foreign countries for not effectively controlling pollution from pulp mills. (Paraguayan citizens on the other bank of the Paraná River are affected by emissions originated in Argentinean pulp mills (UNSAM 2006)). A Chilean company accounts for most of Argentina's pulp production for sale, and Argentina signed a BIT with Chile in the 1990s.

Under the Stockholm Convention, some guidelines were developed regarding best available techniques (BATs) and best environmental practices (BEPs) that minimize the release of dioxins and furans from pulp production (UNEP 2006). As the EIAs, the independent review commissioned by the World Bank Group, and the Uruguayan government documents state, the BAT list includes both the elemental chlorine free (ECF) bleaching process (to be used by both Uruguayan pulp mills) and the allegedly "cleaner" totally chlorine free (TCF) processes. Some BEPs are also indicated for phases of production other than bleaching (e.g., knot removal, avoiding pulping of wood contaminated with polychlorinated phenols, using precursor-free additives in applications such as defoaming solutions, etc). The approach to technology in the Stockholm Convention is to update the list of BATs/BEPs regularly as more information becomes available (UNEP 2006). National regulations in other (especially industrialized) countries that already control POP use and release, consider either ECF or TCF technologies acceptable. ECF pulp mills in developed countries usually have the capacity to convert to TCF processes (which is a source of flexibility in case future Stockholm Convention provisions insist on TCF technology). This will probably not be the case, however, in the case of the ENCE and Botnia plants to be installed in Uruguay. Eucalyptus bleached kraft pulp produced with a TCF method does not meet the required brightness standards of world pulp markets.

Lessons

The discussion above suggests that there is some potential for conflict, when it comes to host-country implementation, between FDI protection rules and multilateral environmental agreements. In particular, new environmental regulations (for the pulpand papersector, among others) required in MERCOSUR countries to comply with the Stockholm Convention on Persistent Organic Pollutants could clash with some countries' commitments to maintain stable rules for foreign investors.

This poses a major regulatory challenge for most MERCOSUR countries, but in particular for Argentina and Uruguay (where foreign investors have a key role in the forest sector). In addition, the previous sections indicate that the design and implementation of new environmental regulations to control for "unintended emissions" of dioxins and furans (POPs being phased out under the Stockholm Convention) pose many technical and regulatory challenges to these countries.

Uruguay and Argentina should have faced this challenge through concerted regional action (e.g., in the framework of MERCOSUR or CARU). One potential advantage of this course of action would have been to balance investors' rights with investors' obligations under the international treaties and environmental agreements signed by the host countries. A second advantage would have been the ability to pool (scarce) technical resources and equipment for emissions controls and to develop a joint strategy to guarantee financing and secure the necessary equipment and training. Furthermore, such a strategy could improve individual countries' bargaining power in case of a controversy with a foreign investor over the introduction of a new environmental regulation.

Even though MERCOSUR features both a number of technical bodies (e.g., the Working Subgroup on Environment (SGT N° 6)) and institutional arrangements (e.g., the Framework Agreement on Environmental Issues) well-suited for joint efforts (such as dialogue and cooperation on environmental issues, or even joint regulation) it suffers from severe institutional weaknesses, particularly on non-trade issues. This could partly explain why MERCOSUR had little role in this bilateral dispute. All in all, the creation of regional rules (e.g., for the implementation of MEAs) and the strengthening of environment-related bodies in MERCOSUR should be a policy objective in itself.

The importance of finding a reasonable and quick solution to the bilateral dispute, in view of the growing importance of the pulp-and-paper industry in the region and the way this dispute could set a precedent for future environmental disputes among MERCOSUR members, was apparently overlooked by both parties to the dispute. The institutional failure evidenced in this conflict has been sadly neglected and constitutes the most worrying aspect for the future.

So far, the two governments seem to have paid little attention to environmental concerns and impacts. They apparently see the dispute as a matter of "national pride" with little consideration of its future implications. From their perspective, it is as if the final ICJ verdict could end both the conflict and the associated risks and problems.

By refusing to become involved in regulatory design prior to the granting of an operating permit to the Botnia plant, the Argentinean government may be running the risk of losing control over some environmental impacts. Bilateral or regional cooperation to guarantee minimal environmental impact of the Fray Bentos pulp mill through joint control seems the only practical solution to effectively tackle environmental concerns and risks.

Chapter Eight

FOREIGNERS IN THE FORESTS: SAVIORS OR INVADERS?

Nicola Borregaard, Annie Dufey and Lucy Winchester

Introduction

This chapter examines the environmental impacts of FDI in the forestry sector in two of the region's major producing countries, Chile and Brazil. One of the characteristics of the world economy over the last two decades has been the strong growth in FDI flows. More and more companies, in an increasing number of economic sectors and countries, now invest beyond the borders of their home countries; meanwhile, the governments of receiving countries are competing more and more to attract foreign investment.

By 2005, about a third of the stock of global FDI has gone to developing countries. Latin America accounts for 10 percent of the global FDI stock. Three countries, Brazil, Argentina and Chile, attracted 82 percent of FDI flows into the region between 1990 and 2002.

The economic benefits of FDI include technological innovation, increases in competitiveness, improvements in efficiency and transfers of intangible resources such as new forms of organization, administration and marketing.

Expectations regarding the environmental impacts of FDI are rather mixed. On the one hand, some argue that FDI brings negative environmental impacts, especially in developing countries that have lower environmental standards and could constitute "pollution havens." On the other hand, some claim that foreign firms help to improve environmental performance in developing countries by transferring both cleaner technology and management expertise in controlling environmental impacts.

The environmental impact of FDI in Latin America is a sensitive issue, as Latin American countries are characterized by natural-resource-based production and exports, primarily in the mining, forestry and fishery sectors. These are environmentally sensitive sectors, with significant potential effects of both resource extraction and processing.

Environmental effects from forestry are, by now, relatively well studied. There are various certification initiatives aiming at improving the social and environmental performance of forestry companies, including the Forestry Stewardship Council (FSC), the Programme for the Endorsement of Forest Certification schemes (PEFC) and national labelling initiatives including the CERTFOR in Chile and Certflor in Brazil.

Rather than discussing the different environmental impacts from forestry in general, the focus of this chapter is on the question of the environmental impact specifically attributable to foreign direct investment. Rather than examining individual projects in detail, which is beyond the scope of this chapter, we have taken a macro approach, based on a literature review and interviews, combined with a more detailed examination of selected large investment projects.

The chapter approaches the effects of FDI on the environment through a familiar three-part framework for identifying and evaluating environmental impacts from trade and investment. According to this framework effects can be differentiated into:

1. Scale effects: Positive scale effects occur when economic growth (in this case deriving from FDI) causes an increase in the demand for environmental goods and economic gains are used to tackle environmental problems. Negative scale effects occur in the absence of environmental regulations and management; economic growth increases the use of natural resources and the generation of pollution. On a micro level, scale effects can be any impacts on the environment of increases in the scale of individual operation

2. Technological effects: Positive effects from the use of environmental technologies in foreign operations as well as to positive spillovers to domestic firms.

3. Regulatory/policy effects: Potential effects on domestic environmental regulation. Positive impacts are pressures to tighten environmental regulation and enforcement, and negative impacts are downward pressures due to competition for foreign investment (the "race to the bottom").[1]

National and Foreign Investment in the Chilean and Brazilian Forestry Sectors

While Chile accounts for only 0.5 percent of forested land worldwide and 1.9 percent in Latin America, it is the second most important pulp producer in the region after Brazil (equivalent figures of 20.8 percent and 66.3 percent, respectively). Chile is the world's fourth-largest exporter of wood chips (8.9 percent of world exports) and fifth-largest exporter of boardword (FAO 2006). Brazil is the world's top tropical timber producer and sixth largest producer of pulp (BRACELPA 2007).[2] The Brazilian forestry industry accounts for 4.5 percent of the country's GDP and seven percent of its total exports. Its key activities include timber exploration, production of wood products, and production of pulp and paper.

Production in the Chilean and Brazilian forestry sectors

Chile

The Chilean forestry sector includes timber extraction as well as production of wood products and pulp and paper. According to the National Forestry Institute (INFOR), in 2005 there were over 30 million hectares of forested land in Chile, equivalent to 20.5 percent of the country's territory. Of this territory, 48 percent was virgin, 45 percent native forest and seven percent plantation. Despite the fact that forestry plantations make up the smallest portion of forested areas, they produce most of the raw material used by the forestry industry. Close to 98 percent of the timber used, as a component of the forestry industry, comes from plantations and only two percent from native forests.[3] Plantation acreage increased by 154.4 percent between 1979 and 1997 (from 739.6 thousand to 1,881.9 thousand hectares). The main planted species are radiata pine (accounting for 75.5 percent of forest plantation acreage) and eucalyptus (16.9 percent). Between 1997 and 2005 total plantation acreage increased by just under 10 percent to 2,078.6 thousand hectares (67.8 percent and 23.6 percent dedicated to radiata pine and eucalyptus, respectively). Since the year 2000, total expansion of land planted and dedicated to industrial plantations has been very limited, and industry experts believe that the total land dedicated to plantations is reaching its upper limit.

In Chile, the native-forest contribution to the added value of the forestry sector is far less than that of plantations. Of all the timber produced in the country in 2005, 20.3 percent came from native forests, of which 86 percent was used for firewood production and the remaining 14 percent for industrial materials. In industry, native forest wood is mainly used for sawnwood (71.1 percent) and boardwood (28.1 percent). The pulp production industry does not use native timber as a raw material. While native forest use in woodchip fabrication reached a peak in the mid 1990s (accounting for 74.2 percent of total industrial usage), since 2003 it has been entirely replaced by eucalyptus. The use of native forest is also decreasing for sawnwood. Currently, only 2.9 percent of the raw material comes from native forests (in contrast to the 1960s, when they were the principal source of raw materials for the sector) (INFOR 2005).

In Chile, plantation landholding is highly concentrated. In the case of radiata pine, 71.1 percent of the plantations is in the hands of the two percent of all forestry owners with holdings over 1,000 hectares. Two companies alone own more than 75 percent of these plantations. Similar conditions exist in the eucalyptus plantations sector. This ownership concentration reflects the concentration of production and vertical integration that characterize the forestry sector. The largest sawmills, panel companies, and pulp-and-paper companies are owners of the plantations that provide their raw materials. In the pulp production subsector, 100 percent of the production is concentrated in the hands of only two companies: Celulosa Arauco y Constitución SA (CELCO) and Compañía Manufacturera de Papeles y Cartones (CMPC) (Table 8.1). Similarly, in the boardwood subsector, 100 percent of the production is concentrated in three companies: Celulosa Arauco y Constitución SA (CELCO), Compañía Manufacturera de Papeles y Cartones (CMPC), and Masisa S.A.

In 1970, Chile's forestry sector represented only about 1.2 percent of GDP; by 2005, this percentage had increased to 3.3 percent. Effectively, in the mid-1970s the forestry sector began to increase in importance relative to national output, reaching values of over three percent of GDP by the mid-1990s, though dipping slightly in the latter years of the decade. Since the year 2000, the forestry sector's contribution to GDP has reached 3.2 percent to 3.4 percent. The comparative advantages that Chile has in timber production, the government's introduction of tree-planting incentives, the adoption of reforms to attract private capital to the sector, and the capacity of the industry to adapt to international market forces are factors that explain the success and development of the country's forestry sector.[4]

In Chile, sawed timber and furniture production stand out as the most important industries within the forestry sector, accounting for 50.6 percent of the sector's total output by value in 2005. The pulp-and-paper industry follows in importance (40.6 percent) and then forestry planting and timber

Table 8.1. **Chilean Pulp Exports by Company – 2005**

Company	Export (millions of US$)	Participation (%)
Arauco y Constitución SA	743.7	61.7
CMPC SA	460.8	38.3
Total	1,204.5	100.0

Source: Foreign Trade Statistics, PROCHILE.

extraction (8.8 percent). During the last ten years, the importance of the timber and furniture subsector relative to the pulp-and-paper industry has steadily increased.

Brazil

A major participant in the global short-fiber pulp market, Brazil has five million hectares in plantations. Most of the forest plantations are concentrated in thes south near the Atlantic coast, in the states of Bahia, Espírito Santo, Minas Gerais, São Paulo and Paraná (see Figure 8.1). About 40 percent of plantation output is used as raw material by the pulp-production industry, 35 percent is used as fuel for the iron and steel industries and 25 percent is for the log and sawnwood industries (Mendoca, 2000). By 2006, companies in the pulp-and-paper sector owned 1.7 million hectares of plantations (BRACELPA 2007), making the sector not only self-sufficient for raw materials, but also a supplier of wood to other industries.

Plantation acreage in Brazil has grown fast over the last few decades, especially in the 1970s and 1980s, after the government introduced reforestation plans and fiscal incentives for tree planting. In response to deforestation, the government encouraged the private sector to invest in plantations and did away with incentives to exploit native forests. The second Forestry Code, established in 1965, required large companies using forestry raw materials to replace the forests with new plantations, and required the iron and steel industries, transport companies and other parties using coal as

Figure 8.1. Production Evolution, Main Forestry Activities in Chile

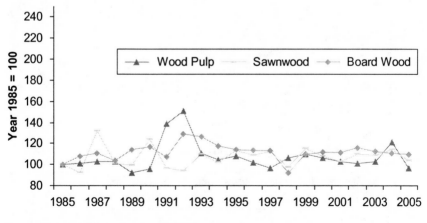

Source: Elaborated from data from INFOR.

a raw material to have their own forests to cover their consumption needs. The government also established a Fiscal Incentives Program for Forestation or Reforestation, which, for example, allowed individuals and companies to use 50 percent of their income tax payment for reforestation. Although the program was directed at small- = and medium-scale producers, the pulp-and-paper industry increasingly took advantage of its provisions (Mendoca 2000). In addition, in 1990 the government established different uses for different types of forest, depending upon whether they were National Forests, Extraction Reserves, "Indian" Reserves or Protected Areas. National Forests, Extraction Reserves, Indian Reserves and other protected areas are managed as a permanent estate, i.e., conversion to other land uses is not permitted. While multiple-use forestry is permitted in the first two, logging is normally prohibited in Indian Reserves and protected areas (Landell-Mills 1999).

In tropical timber, Brazil is both the world's largest producer and consumer, with 86 percent of the timber production from the Amazon being consumed internally and the State of São Paulo alone consuming more tropical timber than France, the UK and Spain combined.

The tropical Brazilian forests are mainly concentrated in the North, in the Amazon region, although there is also a less important forest zone in the tropical Atlantic region. Close to 40 percent of the land in the Amazon region is privately owned, and is principally dedicated to farms and rubber plantations. Only a small portion contains native forest. These forests primarily supply the log and sawnwood industries, accounting for 75 percent of the raw materials used by these industries (Landell-Mills 1999).

Figure 8.2. Production of Key Forest Products, BRAZIL

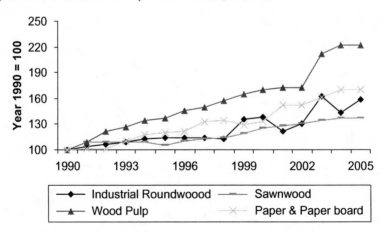

Source: Elaborated from FAOSTAT.

Table 8.2. **Production Evolution of the Main Forestry Activities in Brazil and Chile**

	Unit	Brazil				Chile				
		1990	2005	Increase 1990–2005	Annual Average Increase	1985	1990	2005	Increase 1985–2005	Annual Average Increase
		(Million)	(Million)	(%)	(%)	(Thous)	(Thous)	(Thous)	(%)	(%)
Industrial Roundwoood	Cum	74.3	118.1	59	3.1	211	349	2,111	900.5	12.5
Sawnwood	Cum	17.2	23.6	37	2.1	2,191	3,327	8,298	278.7	7.3
Wood Pulp	Tons	4.3	9.6	122.8	5.5	849	804	3,237	281.3	7.7
Paper & Paper board	Tons	4.8	8.2	71.3	3.7	w.d.	w.d.	w.d.	w.d.	w.d.

Source: Elaborated from FAOSTAT and data from INFOR.

The deforestation rate for year 2000 was 0.33 percent lower than the 0.5 percent rate for the 1990–1995 period (Landell-Mills 1999). About 2.3 million hectares of forests are cut annually for agricultural expansion and other purposes (May 2003). Although clearance for agriculture is the main driver of Amazonian deforestation, much of Brazil's tropical timber originates from deforestation. Concerns about deforestation and illegal logging have resulted in the introduction of trade restrictions by the government, as well as suspensions on forest management plans (Richards, Palmer et al. 2003).

Domestic and foreign investment in Chilean and Brazilian forestry sectors

Chile

Chile has a dynamic market-oriented economy characterized by a high level of foreign trade. During the early 1990s, Chile's reputation as a role model for economic reform was strengthened when the democratic government, which took over from the military in 1990, deepened the economic reform initiated by the military government. From an economic point of view, the era of military dictatorship (1973–1990) can be divided into two periods. The first, from 1975 to 1981, corresponds to the period when most of the reforms were implemented. Chile was transformed gradually from an economy isolated from the rest of the world, with strong government intervention, into a liberalized, world integrated economy, where market forces were left free to guide most of the economy's decisions. The period ended with the international debt crisis and the collapse of the Chilean economy. The second period, from 1982 to 1990, was characterized by economic recovery and a further movement toward a free-market economy, although at a slower pace than that of the early 1980s. By contrast to the "automatic adjustment" strategy used in the initial period of reforms, this period of reform relied on careful policy management. Three policy areas became critical in the implementation of the program: active macroeconomic policies, consolidation of the market-oriented structural reforms initiated in the 1970s, and debt-management policies geared toward rescheduling debt payments and making an aggressive use of the secondary market. There were several structural goals of the 1985 adjustment program: rebuild the financial sector, which had been nearly destroyed during the 1982 crisis; reduce import tariffs from the 35 percent level that they had reached during 1984 to a 15 percent uniform level; and promote exports through a set of fiscal incentives and a competitive real exchange rate.

In this overall context, in Chile, factors sustaining the growth of the forestry sector include the state's adoption of incentives for private investment, the international "opening" of the economy, the privatization process and the encouragement of foreign investment.

Decree 701 of 1974, later modified in 1998 (Law 19.561), falls into the first category and has been the most important instrument for the development of the country's forest wealth. The decree establishes total protection from expropriation of forestry land, establishes a subsidy of between 75 percent and 90 percent for reforesting costs and plantation management and introduces reductions of and exemptions from land taxes and utilities fees for companies exploiting native and planted forests.

The planting of nearly one million hectares of trees—principally radiata pine and eucalyptus—has been subsidized through this policy, generating both economic and environmental benefits for Chile. The forestry industry's easy access to capital and technology permitted extensive use of these subsidies. Between 1974 and 1995, small property owners and indigenous groups, however, received only 5 percent of the total funds allocated by the state. The modifications introduced in 1998, and again in 2000, were aimed at the extension of benefits to these small landowners, the creation of incentives for the prevention of desertification and soil degradation and the recuperation of eroded soil.[5]

In 1974, export tariffs were lowered and the ban on exports of raw or semi-processed forestry products was lifted. Between 1974 and 1978 the state privatized the forestry sector, with two national economic groups acquiring a large percentage of forestry property. In 1982 the state had to repurchase the properties in the face of economic crisis, and in 1984 carried out another privatization process. The Grupo Angelini took control of COPEC and its important forestry resources—Celulosa Arauco, Forestal Arauco, Celulosa Constitución and Forestal Constitución—and the Grupo Matte, already owners of CMPC, took control of Inforsa. In addition to the participation of domestic private interests, foreign companies also invested in the forestry sector.

The government also promulgated, in 1974, policies to increase the role of foreign investment in the Chilean economy. Decree 600 (DL 600) established equal treatment for domestic and foreign investors, free access for foreign companies to all markets and sectors, the elimination of payments for the consignment of utilities and an optional special tax regime for foreign investors. Between 1974 and 1999, FDI inflows under DL 600 totaled US$1,067 million; by 2005, an additional US$435 million in FDI entered the country. Since 1974, forestry FDI under DL 600 has accounted for 2.7 percent of all FDI under the decree (Table 8.3). As seen in Table 8.3, with the exception of the early 1990s, the forestry sector accounted for a very small fraction of total FDI under DL 600. Forestry FDI under the decree, as a share of the total, reached a peak in 1991 with 12.7 percent, but declined gradually to a 1999 share of only

Table 8.3. **FDI in the Forestry Sector and Total FDI, Chile (through DL 600)**

Year	Millions of Dollars		
	Forestry FDI (A)	Total FDI (B)	(A)/(B) (%)
1974–1989	114	5,111	2.2
1990	62	1.28	4.8
1991	125	982	12.7
1992	110	993	11.1
1993	120	1,736	6.9
1994	135	2,522	5.4
1995	86	3,031	2.8
1996	78	4,838	1.6
1997	64	5,225	1.2
1998	123	6,039	2.0
1999	63	9,226	0.7
2000	34	3,039	1.1
2001	60	5.02	1.2
2002	51	3,381	1.5
2003	176	1,286	13.7
2004	82	4,635	1.8
2005	11	4,635	0.6
Total	1,067	40.66	2.7

Source: Comité de Inversiones Extranjeras (Foreign Investments Committee) 2007.

Figure 8.3. Contribution of FDI in Forestry to Total FDI, Chile (through DL 600)

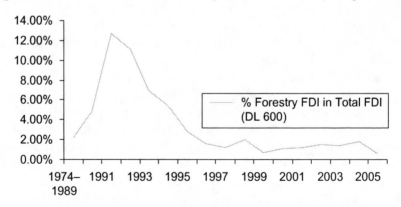

Source: Comité de Inversiones Extranjeras (Foreign Investments Committee) 2007.

0.7 percent. In the last decade, the forestry sector's share of total FDI under DL 600 has been fairly stable, except for 2003, when the paper-and-printing subsector attracted substantial inflows from the United States and Switzerland. While FDI investments in forestry reached US$176.5 million in 2003, these investments are not significant relative to the costs of production facilities in the sector: for example, a single new boardwood plant costs about US$50 million, and a new pulp plant costs nearly US$ 1,000 million.

Chapter XIX of the Compendium of Regulations for International Exchanges of the Chilean Central Bank has been far more important than DL 600 for FDI inflows into the forestry sector. This measure was introduced in 1985 in order to stimulate FDI and diminish foreign debt. Between 1985 and 1989, total FDI into the forestry sector under Chapter XIX was US$1,026 million, equivalent to 22.7 percent of the total FDI under this provision. This is five times the amount of capital coming into the country under DL 600, which only brought in US$190 million dollars between 1982 and 1989.

FDI inflows to Chile via Chapter XIX peaked at US$1,321 billion in 1989, dropping considerably in 1990 and in 1991, when this mechanism ceased to exist. The majority of foreign companies carried out investments in Chile through alliances with domestic companies already established within the sector. The New Zealand group Carter Holt Halvey partnered with group Angelini to buy 50 percent of COPEC. The UK-based Shell acquired Bosques de Chile SA, Aserraderos Copihue and Forestal Colcura Ltda., and established the company Forestal e Industrial Santa Fé in conjunction with US-based Scott Paper and Citibank (CEPAL 1999). An alliance between North American Simpson Paper Co. and CMPC created Celulosa del Pacífico SA, one of the most modern and important Chilean long-fiber cellulose companies. Finally, Japanese and North American companies undertook some minor land acquisitions for forestation. Both Shell and Simpson Paper, however, withdrew from the pulp business by selling all their assets to the Matte Group in 1998.

During the last 10 years, the Chilean forestry sector has seen considerable vertical integration and concentration of market shares by the Matte and Angelini Groups (CMPC and Arauco, respectively). This process brought the exodus of many of the foreign companies which had entered in the early- to mid-nineties. Foreign investment in the sector continues to exist, but on a small scale, compared to the large domestic companies. During the last five years, FDI from the United States has been concentrated within the boardwood subsector, in certain remanufacturing activities. Masisa S.A., which resulted from a merger between Nasisa and Terranova, related to the Swiss-based Schmidtheiny Group, and which is now owned by a 53 percent by GrupoNueva, also related to the Schmidtheiny Group, maintains a modest position in the boardwoods subsector.

Brazil

Although latest official data on FDI in the forestry sector in Brazil date from 2000, foreign investment is certainly low. GrFigure 8.4 shows FDI in the forestry sector relative to total FDI in Brazil between 1996–2000: it varies between 0.1 percent and 1.3 percent.

Between 1996 and 2000, timber products accounted for 39 percent of the FDI in the forestry sector, pulp and paper for 33 percent, and timber exploration for the remaining 28 percent.

Figure 8.4. Contribution of FDI in Forestry to Total FDI, Brazil

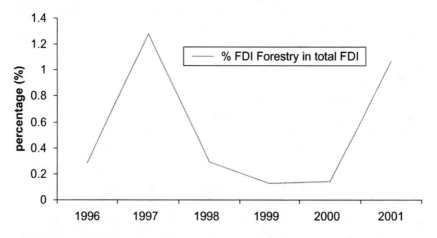

Source: Authors' elaboration based on data from Censo do Capital Estrangeiro, 1995 a 2000, the Departamento de Capitais Estrangeiros (FIRCE), Banco Central Do Brasil.

Figure 8.5. Distribution of FDI in Forestry by Subsector, Brazil (1996–2001)

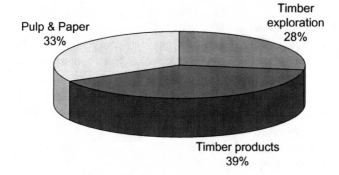

Source: Authors' elaboration based on data from Censo do Capital Estrangeiro, 1995 a 2000, the Departamento de Capitais Estrangeiros (FIRCE), Banco Central Do Brasil.

Andario and D'Avila (1999) suggest that there have been two important foreign investment flows to the forestry sector in the Amazon region, specifically in the states of Amazonas and Pará. The former, attracted by fiscal incentives in the 1970s and 1980s, came from countries consuming tropical timber, such as Germany, the US and China. The latter, during the second half of the 1990s, was dominated by Asian timber groups, who basically acquired existing companies and timber rights, generally exceeding one million hectares (Landell-Mills 1999). The investors in this case included the WTK Group (Malaysia), Samling Corporation (Malaysia), Rimbunan Hijau Group (Malaysia), KTS Group (Malaysia) and Fortune Timber (China). The main factor behind the arrival of the Asian companies was a shortage of inputs due to bans on logging or log-and-export activities in various Asian countries in the early 1990s.

Amazonas state has a strong export orientation and substantial presence of foreign-owned companies, while Pará state has mainly domestic companies supplying the national market.[6] The most important foreign-owned companies in the Brazilian tropical timber sector are Gethal (US), Carolina (Asia), Mil (Switzerland) and Braspor (Portugal). These companies are totally export oriented and in 1997 were responsible for 67 percent of all the timber exported from Amazonas state, accounting for 13 percent of all timber exported by Brazil (McQueen, Grieg-Gran et al. 2004). Cotton and Romine (1999) estimate that foreign companies in Brazil have been responsible for about three percent of timber extraction, 8–12 percent of semi-processed timber output and 25 percent of the sector's exports.

The pulp-and-paper industry, in the South of Brazil, achieved a high degree of competitiveness during the 1980s, making it very attractive to foreign investment. FDI into the sector reached more than US$18 billion in total between 1989 and 2006 (Mendoca 2000; BRACELPA 2007) and is projected at US$14.4 billion for the period 2003–2012 (BRACELPA 2007).

By 2006 FDI represented about 20.7 percent of the pulp production output (Valor Economico, 2007). Key foreign companies are Cenibra (Japan), International Paper (US), Norske Skog (Denmark), Rigesa (US) and the recently established Veracel, which is a 50-50 joint venture between the Brazilian Aracruz and the Swedish-Finnish Stora-Enso. The main producers, however, are domestic companies, such as Aracruz, Votarantim and Klabin. Figure 8.6 presents the share of total output for each of the main companies in the pulp sector in 2004.

FDI in the paper subsector, on the other hand, represented 16 percent of total output in 2004 (Valor Econômico 2007).

As noted in Figure 8.6, the Brazilian pulp-and-paper industry is a highly concentrated sector. Although there are 220 companies producing pulp and paper in the country, only nine companies account for more than 87 percent

Figure 8.6. Share of Main Companies in Pulp and Paper (2004)

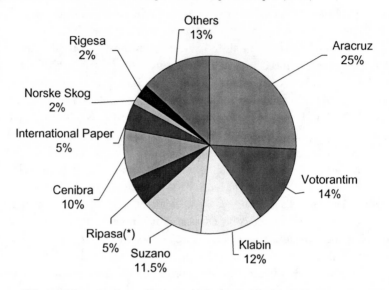

Source: Elaborated from dos Santos Rocha and Togeiro de Almeida 2007.

of the total output (Valor Econômico 2007). Six out of the nine key companies were vertically integrated (i.e., produced both pulp and paper).

FDI and Environment in Chilean and Brazilian Forestry Sectors

In Chile, FDI in forestry has not had the same economic significance as FDI in other industries, such as mining. Foreign involvement in the sector has, however, permitted investment flows in periods when domestic finance has been scarce (such as the late 1980s), or in which the industry faced specific capital flow constraints (such as the 1990s)[7].

At first view, the environmental impact of FDI in the forestry sector would not appear to differ from that of domestic investment. Whether foreign or domestic, large investment projects have been the main focus of environmental concerns. In the late 1990s, these were potential foreign investment projects that raised concerns about the sustainability of native-forest exploitation.[8] In this decade, these have been domestic projects (CELCO-Validivia and CELCO-Itata) that have raised concerns related to industrial pollution.

Domestic and foreign companies are implicated in the same types of environmental problems—especially native forest substitution—as well as the same social issues, such as property rights and the rights of indigenous people. Environmental certification has advanced rapidly, with most large companies, both domestic and foreign, having gained both International Organization for Standardization (ISO) 14001 approval and some kind of sustainable management certification by one of the major forest certification schemes. Several experts interviewed argue that there is no significant difference between FDI and domestic investment in terms of environmental management and impact.[9] Authors such as Donoso (1999) explicitly argue that foreign and domestic investment did not differ in exploitation and substitution of native forests.

Today, many domestic as well as foreign companies are certified under ISO 14001. In the area of sustainable forest management, however, foreign companies obtained Forestry Stewardship Council (FSC) certification while domestic companies in Chile concentrated on the national CERTFOR certification. This latter certification is recognized by Programme for the Endorsement of Forest Certification schemes (PEFC), though it is widely viewed as less rigorous than FSC certification.[10] With the buyout of many of the foreign investments, some plantations certified through FSC are now owned by domestic companies.

In Brazil, as the previous section suggests, FDI in the forestry sector has little economic significance compared to domestic investment. In environmental performance, the differences in performance between foreign and domestic companies depend on whether these are located in the tropical wood or pulp-and-paper sectors.

In the tropical wood sector, it seems that today the worst environmental offenders are domestic companies. Foreign companies are less likely to be involved in illegal logging—the key environmental concern in the sector—are more law-abiding and are more likely to embrace environmental standards such as ISO 14000 and FSC. Even though there were important worries about negative environmental impacts associated with massive Asian FDI, these never materialized.

In the pulp-and-paper sector, on the other hand, domestic companies tend to perform better than their foreign counterparts in terms of emissions and effluents. Moreover, although today there are no significant differences among FDI and national companies regarding the adoption of environmental management or compliance with the law, it seems that the latter lead the introduction of more advanced environmental approaches.

Analysts emphasizing the similarity, in environmental behaviour and impacts, between domestic investment and FDI in the forestry sector have failed to account for some differences, both positive and negative. One difference is in the use of different environmental certification schemes by foreign versus domestic companies.[11] Another relates to the use of transgenic species. Finally, some differences relate to the lag in domestic companies' introduction of environmental management systems.

Scale Effects

Chile

Most new investment projects in the pulp-and-paper sector in Chile make use of the latest technologies, including filters, closed loops, evaporation and recycling, thereby reducing emissions or effluents.[12] The environmental impact assessments (EIAs) for investment projects, however, indicate that there will always be emissions, effluents and solid waste, and in this sense, any new project brings new environmental damage. Given that each investment project is different, producing different products and being located in different geographical settings, a quantitative environmental comparison between domestic and foreign investment is impossible.

One important kind of environmental impact in the forestry sector is deforestation and native-forest substitution. In Chile, the role of foreign-owned companies in native-forest substitution has never been explicitly treated or isolated from the overall picture of deforestation/substitution.[13]

Another issue regarding scale effects is the alternative uses of land. Haltia and Keipi (2000), for example, compare the net environmental benefits from forestry versus cattle-farming investment in Chile and Brazil, concluding that forestry investments, especially pine and eucalyptus plantations, involve significantly larger environmental benefits than cattle farming. This suggests that scale effects are not only negative but also positive, especially when compared to other land use alternatives. The positive effects include prevention of soil erosion and CO_2 sequestration. These effects can be strengthened if forest operations are based on plantations, and these do not replace native forest, but are planted on land previously destined to agriculture.[14]

Individual foreign investment projects, implying not only a previously unknown scale for native forest exploitation, but also dealing, in some cases, with forest species that have been little researched, usually fall into the large-scale category, as in the cases of US-based Trillium and Boyse-Cascade. These projects imposed new challenges for environmental enforcement, required new regional policies or land use policies, and involved considerable uncertainties. These are explained in the section of regulatory effects, given that both projects finally abandoned their logging plans.

Enforcement issues continue to be of great concern for large-scale investment projects, now primarily of a domestic nature. In 1996, the Comisión Nacional del Medio Ambiente for Chilean Region X (COREMA) accepted the environmental impact study drafted by Celulosa Arauco y Constitución (CELCO-ARAUCO) and approved construction of a US$1 billion kraft-bleached-type paper pulp mill on the Rio Cruces near San José de la Mariquina and what was to later become the Carlos Anwandter Nature Sanctuary. COREMA's approval was subject to two conditions: (1) a company guarantee that hazardous waste would be treated in an environmentally safe way (tertiary treatment) and (2) a company promise to develop a monitoring and follow-up plan for its waste products. Since the mill began full operations in February 2004, however, it has faced repeated complaints from the public concerning noise and odors.[15] It has also been accused of being responsible for water pollution and the loss of black-necked swans and other wildlife in the Nature Sanctuary. Even though, after extensive research by the National Commission on Environment, it was not possible to establish a cause-effect relationship for the death of the black-necked swans, there have been fines to the operation on the grounds of unauthorized effluents.[16]

Brazil

In Brazil, as shown previously in Table 8.4, forestry sector output has increased in the last two decades, both in timber and, especially, in pulp and paper. Forestry is an environmentally sensitive sector and, thus, any expansion may increase the pressure on the ecosystems. Although there is no information on what proportion of such expansion is attributable to foreign companies, the former section makes it clear that FDI—either in tropical timber extraction in the North or in the pulp industry in the South—has not been a dominant factor.

Tropical timber extraction in Brazil is associated with deforestation and illegal logging. According to Macqueen et al, (2004) about 20 percent of timber extraction in the Amazon is clearly illegal. The Asian capital inflows of the mid-1990s were linked to illegal extraction of tropical woods (Viana 1998; Andario and D'Avila 1999). The fears prevailing in the mid-1990s about the Amazon being invaded by Asian companies with poor environmental practices, however, never materialized. Most illegal logging involves the small domestic companies that account for the bulk of tropical timber production. Richards, Palmer et al. (2003) argue that foreign-owned companies are less likely to be involved in illegal logging (are more law-abiding) than domestic companies due to fear of eviction.

While the vast majority of timber companies in the Amazon are small- and medium-size enterprises, foreign-owned companies are usually large. This may exacerbate some of their negative environmental effects (McQueen, Grieg-Gran et al. 2004).

The pulp-and-paper sector is very concentrated, with nine companies accounting for about 87 percent of domestic pulp production. This means the size of each company's operations tends to be very large. But the largest ones are domestic companies. Although important environmental improvements have been introduced in the sector in recent years, resulting in reduced emissions and effluents per unit of output, there is always some pollution. This means that any increase in production puts additional pressure on the ecosystems.

The key environmental issues in processing operations involve water effluents, airborne emissions, and odors. Sueila dos Santos Rocha and Togeiro de Almeida (2007) compare the environmental performance of foreign-owned and domestic companies in pulp and paper. They analyze efficiency in water consumption, effluent pollution levels, and emissions of malodorous gases for a set of nine companies, representing 86 percent of Brazil's total pulp production in 2004. They find that domestic vertically integrated pulp-and-paper companies (i.e., Votorantin, Suzano and Ripasa), on average, perform better in terms of emissions and effluent levels than foreign companies.[17] About the level of individual companies, the Danish company Norske Skog shows the best performance for all the analysed indicators while the US-based International Paper produces the worst environmental indicators.[18]

Impacts on timber extraction also matter, since the sector uses wood as an input. By 2006 pulp-and-paper companies owned 1.7 million hectares of eucalyptus and radiata-pine plantations (BRACELPA 2007). The environmental community raised concerns in the past about impacts of the expansion of industrial plantations linked to the pulp-and-paper industry on watersheds and biodiversity (IIED 1996). Again, however, this is attributable to both domestic and foreign companies that have responded to government incentives policies. On the other hand, there have been important increases in productivity in the wood for pulp (63 percent for eucalyptus and 58 percent for pine between 1980 and 2005) (BRACELPA 2007), which means that not all the expansion in pulp production has been accompanied by equivalent growth in the plantations feeding the industry. Moreover, most companies today hold some type of environmental certification for their plantations (see next section).

Technology effects

Chile

It goes beyond the scope of this chapter to establish quantitatively and in detail the differences between foreign and domestic-owned companies in terms of emissions or effluents and the adoption of related technologies.

However, a literature review and expert interviews allow us to draw some broad conclusions.

There is no clear difference between foreign and domestic owners in the development of new process and production technologies. New technologies have been developed and introduced by each of these groups.[19] A study on the pulp-and-paper industry in Chile suggests that there is no substantial difference between foreign and domestic facilities (Herbert-Copley 1998). The study shows that the dominance of outside supplier and equipment firms and engineering companies has left limited scope for dramatic differences in mill design. Export market pressure has a common influence on both foreign and domestic firms, which leads to similar types of environmental changes (e.g., decreases in the use of bleaching). The role of lenders has also influenced companies' behavior, since international agencies have tied funding to environmental performance.

FDI has had an impact on the introduction of the Clean Development Mechanism in the framework of international programs on climate change in the forestry sector in Chile.[20] The two projects first incorporated in the Register of Activities Implemented Jointly (AIJ)[21] of the Intergovernmental Panel on Climate Change (IPCC), were presented by Chilean–foreign company consortiums.[22] Regarding the first forestry-related projects implemented under the Kyoto Protocol, however, in 2005 all are Chilean-based: three biomass projects, two by Arauco and a third by a small forestry company from Magallanes (Russfin Forestal).

On the other hand, in Chile, one of the most important policy instruments for spurring technological progress in the environmental area is the Clean Production Agreement. Today there are 95 companies (three cellulose plants and 92 sawmills) in the forestry sector that have signed clean production agreements with the National Council for Clean Production. There is no difference in the participation rate of foreign-owned or domestic companies.

On the other hand, according to the environmental organization RENACE, Forestal Monte Aguila (owned by Shell) was the first company to use transgenic species on its plantations. (The plantations were later burned and the use of transgenic species discontinued due to FSCcertification and other issues.)

The ISO 14000 standards set target indicators to guarantee the sustainable management of forests and environmental management of production processes. In Chile, more than 1.2 million hectares of forest plantations are currently managed in agreement with this system, this being equivalent to 60 percent of the country's total plantation acreage (CORMA). Differences between domestic and foreign companies regarding ISO standards are not discernible.

However, there are subtle differences between the use of the international certification FSC and the domestic certification scheme CERTFOR. The initial interest in forest certification has been attributed to guidelines from European parent companies.[23]

There are currently 422 thousand hectares of forests (principally plantations) certified under the Forest Stewardship Council (FSC), representing 15 companies, with another 26 having certification for Chains of Custody.[24]

Since its creation in 2002, the CERTFOR standard has certified a steadily growing area of forests. Today, the system has a certified forest area of nearly 1.6 million hectares, including all plantations owned by large domestic companies. The trend towards certification of chains of custody (CoCs) started in 2004. Numerous companies joined in 2005 as a result of stricter international labelling demands. To date, the system includes fourteen certified CoCs. The main goal of CoCs is to guarantee a connection between the input of certified wood to a process and the products exiting that process. To achieve a chain of custody and to be able to label the final products as certified, each unit responsible for the wood, from the forest up to the minor distribution channels, must have a CoC certificate that endorses that the wood came from forests handled under recognized criteria of sustainability.[25]

Different authors as well as experts interviewed note that both domestic and foreign companies have pursued certification.[26] The first attempts at achieving certification were, in fact, taken by foreign-owned companies. In Chile, the first company ISO 14001 certified was Santa Fé, at that time owned by Shell. Some years later, three foreign-owned operations were among the first certified under FSC.[27] Today, ownership of these operations has passed to domestic hands, making it very difficult to trace differences in certification to differences in preferences between foreign-owned and domestic operations.

Finally, there are very slight differences between domestic and foreign companies with regard to sustainability reporting. The half foreign originated Masisa SA (related to the swiss-based Schmidtheiny Group) has, since 2005, been alone in making sustainability reports registered under the Global Reporting Initiative (GRI). The large domestic companies Arauco and CMPC, however, have, since 2005 and 2006, respectively, also made sustainability reports according to GRI guidelines, but have not registered them officially under the GRI.

Brazil

Technology effects for Brazil, including the embrace of higher environmental standards, the use of environmental technology, and the implementation of environmental management techniques, can be evaluated by looking at the level of environmental certification in the sector.

According to May (2003), the certified forest segment in Brazil began to emerge in the late 1990s in response to consumer concerns, such as the impacts of plantations on watersheds and biodiversity, poor working conditions on plantations and fears of the export-led deforestation of the Amazon. The certification process linked to the Forest Stewardship Council (FSC) is perceived principally as a reinforcement of existing regulatory requirements, such as observance of environmental and labor law, but also introduces new practices (May 2003).

The pulp-and-paper and industrial charcoal segments were the first to adopt ISO 14000 environmental management and FSC certification. Today all major operations, whether they are foreign-owned or domestically owned have ISO 14000 and some sort of environmental forest certification (see Table 8.4). Although no big differences are now apparent between foreign and domestic companies, the latter played a key role in the initial adoption of voluntary environmental standards in the sector. In 1998 the domestic company Klabin became the first enterprise to receive FSC plantation forest certification in Latin America, for its operations in Paraná. At the time, a number of major pulp-and-paper enterprises in Brazil were seeking certification according to ISO 14000 environmental management norms (May 2003). With the considerably more rigorous FSC certification of Klabin's operation, the rest of the sector was soon incentivized to follow suit

Table 8.4. **Adoption of Environmental Standards in the Brazilian Pulp-and-Paper Industry**

Name	ISO 14000	FSC	CERFLOR
DOMESTIC			
Aracruz (including Veracel which 50% owned by Stora-Enso)	Yes	No	373,938 ha
Votorantim	Yes	70,529 ha	No
Klabin	Yes	361,972 ha	No
Suzano Bahia Sul	Yes	243,242 ha	No
Ripasa(*)	Yes	77,066 ha	No
FOREIGN			
Cenibra	Yes	233,779 ha	223,778 ha
International Paper	Yes	Yes	29,941 ha
Norske Skog	Yes	No (not sure whether it has own plantations)	??
Rigesa	Yes	No	35,000 ha

Source: Elaborated from (dos Santos Rocha and Togeiro de Almeida 2007); http://www.fsc.org.br/; http://www.inmetro.gov.br/qualidade/cerflor.asp

One of the unique factors in Klabin's certification was the extension of its management area to third-party suppliers, and its provision for resolution of land-tenure disputes. Outsourcing has presented a problem for certified wood-products manufacturers. If a certified company obtains supplies from firms whose forests are not certified or have disputed titles, it is required to split its industrial processing operations to assure the chain of custody of certified products. By extending the certified area to include external suppliers, Klabin guaranteed that its flow of certified raw material would be sufficient to fill orders, and at the same time helped to resolve land-tenure disputes in its surrounding area.

Most certified companies in the pulp-and-paper sector have FSC certification, which is considered the most stringent standard. The Brazilian company Aracruz and the foreign Norske and Rigesa companies are certified under the national certification scheme CERFLOR. CERFLOR was promoted by some industry leaders, especially Aracruz, that did not want to comply with the more stringent FSC norms. CERFLOR's standards are similar in name to those established by FSC in Brazil, but are considerably more flexible in regards to observance of international environmental norms, socio-cultural impacts and labour relations with third party suppliers (May 2003).

Regarding the introduction of environmental practices and technologies in processing, dos Santos Rocha and Togeiro de Almeida (2007) find that while all the companies in the pulp-and-paper sector in their sample have at least one plant certified under ISO 14001, more Brazilian-owned plants are certified than foreign-owned plants. Moreover, the authors also argue that while all pulp-and-paper companies have environmental management systems and technologies at the intermediate level (i.e., efforts are made to prevent pollution), Brazilian companies were leading the transition towards a more advanced level.

Forest management certification only covers a small percentage of total tropical-timber extraction in the Amazon region. According to McQueen, Grieg-Gran et al. (2004), only 20 to 30 operations producing a total of about 500,000 m^3/year, approximately 1.7 percent of the timber produced in the Amazon, are certified under FSC. However, despite the scant adoption of forest-management certification, foreign-owned companies, particularly those of European origin, have embraced environmental technologies to a greater extent than their national counterparts. Authors such as Richards, Palmer et al. (2003), note that foreign companies in tropical timber in Brazil have greater financial and technical capacities than their Brazilian counterparts. They also note that, among those companies in Amazonas state that have a greater export orientation and are more exposed to foreign ownership, environmental certification is becoming significant for reasons of international

Table 8.5. **Adoption of Environmental Certification Schemes by Foreign Companies in Tropical-Timber Industry**

Company	State	Country of Origin	Certification Scheme
Amacol	Para	US	None
Amaplac and WTK Forestal	Amazonas	Malaysia	None
Braspor	Amazonas	Portugal	FSC
Cifec	Amazonas	China	None
Compensa	Amazonas	China	None
Eidai	Amazonas e Pará	Japan	None
Eldorado	Pará	France	FSC
Gethal	Amazonas	Germany	FSC
Janus Brasil	Pará	US	None
Jaya Tiasa Carolina Maginco Selvaplac	Amazonas e Pará	Malaysia	None
Lawton	Pará	US	None
Mil Madereira	Amazonas	Switzerland	FSC
Nordwisk	Pará	Danish	FSC
Robco	PArá	US	None
Terra/Equatorial Resources	Pará	US	None

Source: Based on (McQueen, Grieg-Gran et al. 2004); http://www.fsc.org.br/

market access. The first company to be certified under the FSC scheme was the Swiss company Mil Madeireira (or Precious Woods Amazon) in 1997.

In Pará state, likewise, foreign companies such as Gethal Amazonas were the first ones to be awarded FSC certification, in the year 2000. However, the Brazilian firm Cikel Brazil Verde also adopted FSC certification early on, in 2001. May (2003) highlights both firms as among the first major timber companies in the Brazilian Amazon whose forest management systems were FSC certified. Both companies have also gained chain of custody certification, and are now expanding the management areas under their control to better respond to growing demand for certified wood products.

In all these cases, access to overseas markets (US and EU) represents the main factor behind the decision to certify their forests. Another factor influencing this decision is capital investment. When the US fund manager GMO Renewable Resources purchased Gethal, the buyers insisted that the company first complete FSC certification, perceiving this as a precondition for successful market penetration for its tropical plywood (May 2003).

Domestically owned companies, on the other hand, are mostly small-scale and family-based companies with low levels of technical and managerial capacity and communication skills (Richards, Palmer et al. 2003). A report commissioned by the government of Brazil in 1996 surveyed 34 logging companies in Paragominas, Pará state, which is dominated by domestic firms. It found that none met the requirements of the International Tropical Timber Organization. The report concluded that the timber industry in Paragominas was purely extractive, with no forest management of any sort.[28]

Regulatory Effects

Chile

While a lack of environmental enforcement capacity can result in significant environmental damage from large-scale investment projects—both foreign and domestic—these large-scale projects can, at the same time, raise awareness of environmental problems and spur pressure for change.

Two previously mentioned large foreign investment projects—Trillium and Boyse-Cascade—have spurred debate on the need for refinement of the EIA system, the lack of a clear legislative framework and of enforcement on native forests, a lack of regional planning and an absence of policy debate around overall sustainable-development objectives.[29]

Donoso (1999) regarded the large foreign-forest investment project Cascada as an opportunity for native-forest management, emphasizing existing problems but pointing out the company's voluntary commitments regarding requirements on their suppliers, as well as materials and training provided to forest owners and workers. Experts such as Armesto (1999) have proposed concrete legal changes in the context of the new foreign-investment projects. Armesto proposed a legal requirement to protect one hectare of forest for each three hectares of forest where activities are undertaken. However, since neither of the two large foreign investment projects that induced this policy debate has ultimately materialized, the impact of these proposals is unclear.

Both projects, Trillium and Boyse-Cascade, were submitted to the EIA system and were discussed in a public participation process as well as subjected to the technical assessment of the regulatory agencies. Especially due to the high degree of uncertainties regarding the growth rates and other biological data of the species and the ecosystems involved, these processes each took several years. Finally, the precautionary requirements imposed by the regulatory authorities on the projects in order to confront the uncertainties, combined with the pressure of environmental groups as well as financial constraints, led the companies to abandon their projects.

No policy or legislative changes have occurred directly related to, or immediately after, the increased policy debate around the projects, but an indirect effect has certainly existed.

Brazil

The current weak enforcement of legislation in Brazil can imply significant environmental impacts from forest projects—both foreign and domestic. The evidence is mixed regarding FDI in tropical timber. On the one hand, the accusations against Asian companies of illegal timber extraction suggest negative regulatory effects. On the other hand, the early adoption of FSC certification by foreign-owned (mainly European–owned) companies suggests positive regulatory effects, as the FSC process is principally a reinforcement of existing regulatory requirements. May (2003) suggests the adoption of certification by these companies could also have positive effects on companies oriented to the domestic market.

More widely, Richards et al. (2003), find that foreign-owned companies in Amazonas state are generally more law-abiding than domestic companies due to fear of eviction.[30] They find a much higher level of private-sector corruption in the Pará sawmilling industry, which is dominated by relatively small-scale and family-based domestic companies. These companies face an oligopsony of timber traders who retain most of the rent. Such conditions tend to make domestic companies more rent-seeking (and likely to try to cut compliance costs) in their behaviour than foreign companies.

Moreover, in the case of the Asian companies, the rather larger size of the foreign-owned operations, their poor past environmental records, and their greater exposure to international scrutiny have helped to raise awareness of environmentally damaging practices and spurred pressure for change. Illegal logging activities by Asian companies attracted the attention of legislators. The Chamber of Representatives analysed the situation and possible courses of action, approving several legal responses including: [31]

1. The 1998 Environmental Crimes Law increasing the power of environmental protection agencies like the Brazilian Environmental Institute (IBAMA).
2. Stricter regulatory enforcement and higher penalties, reducing the level of illegal logging.
3. Returning considerable private forest to the state.
4. Adopting better enforcement techniques (e.g., Matto Grosso state using remote sensing and GIS technology in environmental enforcement).
5. The federal initiative to introduce long-term National Forest logging concessions (FLONAs).

For the pulp-and-paper sector, the available evidence does not indicate a negative regulatory effect. The research of dos Santos Rocha and Togeiro de Almeida (2007), suggests that although foreign companies do not perform better than national ones, they do not use Brazil as a "pollution haven."

Table 8.6. **Scale, Technology and Regulatory Effects of FDI in Forestry Sector, Chile and Brazil**

Scale, Technology and Regulatory Effects	Chile	Brazil
Scale Effects	*Native forest substitution*: No studies isolating foreign owned companies, but overall no significant impact over the last two decades. *Deforestation*: no clear evidence, requires further research to analyze smaller scale foreign operations. *Alternative land uses*: potentially positive effects for plantations versus agriculture in prevention of soil erosion and capturing of CO_2. For large scale projects (both foreign and domestic), *enforcement and environmental compliance* issues exist (see also regulatory effects).	Tropical Timber: *Ecosystem stress*: in overall, FDI has a lower participation than domestic companies but the intensity in the use per unit likely to be higher due to the larger size of operations. FDI less likely to involve illegal logging. Pulp & Paper: In average, FDI has a smaller size of operations than domestic companies. *In average*, domestic companies perform better in terms of their emission and effluent levels Both FDI and domestic companies supply from plantations.
Technology Effects	*Overall:* Foreign companies slightly more connected to latest technological development, this report proves this for several soft technologies.	Tropical Timber:

	Environmental certification: Today no discernable differences between domestic and foreign companies. First steps towards implementing certification often initiated by foreign owned companies.	*Environmental certification*: FDI was first awarded FSC certificates and is more likely to embrace better environmental technologies.
	Development of new technologies: No distinction between foreign and domestic owners.	Pulp & Paper:
	Clean Development Mechanism: foreign company that was the first to incorporate a project in the Register of AIJ of the IPC.	*Environmental certification*: although today no perceived differences among FDI and domestic companies, the latter were the first in introducing FSC certificate.
	Sustainability reporting: slight differences discerned between domestic and foreign companies.	*Environmental management*: domestic companies leading transition towards more advanced environmental approaches.
		Tropical Timber:
		FDI more likely to be law abiding.
		FDI greater exposure to sensitive markets led to introduction of new legislation and greater law enforcement by the government.
		Pulp & Paper:
		Both FDI and domestic companies are law abiding and in some cases FDI ahead of legislation.
Regulatory Effects	FDI in forestry has had no apparent effects on *environmental policy*, or *regional planning*.	
	However, large scale FDI projects have stirred environmental policy and regulatory debate.	

Source: Authors' elaboration.

These researchers observe that the two foreign companies operating in Sao Paulo, at least, had a level of environmental performance higher than that required by the Brazilian law.

Policy Recommendations

Since the late 1990s, there has been an intense debate about the effects of natural-resource FDI on the environment. FDI supporters argue that foreign companies tend to introduce better environmental technologies and environmental management practices than domestic companies, while those skeptical about FDI suggest that the former have more rent-seeking goals and therefore they are not interested in controlling the environmental impacts of their activities. However, as the above analysis suggests, neither of these views is completely true for FDI in the forestry sector in Latin America.

Given the mingling between domestic and foreign ownership in the forestry sector, it is a challenge to identify and draw clear lines between domestic and foreign operations. Moreover, compared to domestic companies, foreign-owned companies in the forestry sector account for a small proportion of national forestry production. However, there are some subtle differences worth mentioning:

Regarding scale effects, although the increasing scale puts greater pressure on natural resources, the domestic companies in Chile and Brazil are those that account, by far, for most national production. Moreover, at the level of the scale of individual operations, there is no evidence that foreign investment is always of larger scale, or especially related to products with severe environmental impacts. Indeed, with the exception of FDI in timber extraction in the Amazonas region of Brazil, where foreign operations tend to be larger than their domestic counterparts, the largest companies operating in the pulp-and-paper sector in Brazil are domestic. Moreover, in terms of pollution per unit of output, although a foreign-owned company boasts the best performance, on average, the domestic companies perform better in terms of both emission and effluent levels. In Chile, the two largest native-forest operations proposed in the last decade involved foreign companies, but they did not come to fruition due to environmental requirements by the government and environmental pressures by NGOs.

Regarding technology effects, the use of environmental technologies and management seems very similar for foreign and domestic companies in both countries. However, there are differences in the two countries in terms of the type of investors that initially pushed for the introduction of better environmental practices.

In Brazil, it seems that FDI—especially of European origin—played a big role in pushing the introduction of certified environmental management in the tropical-timber sector. In the pulp-and-paper sector, however, a Brazilian company played the key role in the initial adoption of voluntary environmental standards. In Chile, the first steps towards implementing internationally based certification were taken by foreign-owned companies. Domestic companies prefer the domestic certification scheme CERTFOR.

The results of this analysis suggest, as some previous studies have, that foreign companies are more heavily focused on international requirements and on reputation.[32] If elevated international requirements were not matched by local pressure, however, foreign companies might put their environmental reputations ahead of real environmental commitments ("greenwashing"). The early interest of foreign companies in international certification schemes should be emphasized, as well as the success of domestic certification schemes in Chile and Brazil, the CERTFOR and the CERTFLOR, respectively, with regard to the elevated percentage of certified plantations in the total of plantations.

Sustainability reporting seems to follow a similar pattern, with foreign companies, especially European companies, enjoying a slight head start over the domestic companies.

On regulatory effects, the existence or lack of an environmental regulatory framework is important in several ways: in attracting foreign investment, in closing the gap between foreign and domestic companies in environmental management and finally, in preventing environmental damage. In general, there is no evidence linking FDI in the forestry sector with negative regulatory impacts. In Brazil, foreign companies in tropical timber extraction tend to be more law-abiding than domestic companies and, where foreign companies have been targeted by NGOs due to bad practices, this has induced tougher environmental laws and enforcement, not a drop in regulation. In the pulp-and-paper sector, domestic and foreign companies are generally law-abiding and foreign companies do not use the country as a "pollution haven." In Chile, large foreign-investment projects have spurred discussion on the necessity of a native-forest law, even as existing regulation proved effective in confronting the environmental risks imposed by the large investment projects.

However, the research also suggests that it is too simplistic to make a distinction only on the basis of the domestic or foreign ownership of the companies. There are other factors for policymakers to consider in attempting to maximize the positive contributions of companies operating in the forestry sector and minimize the negative ones. Robust environmental laws and enforcement are the most important factors affecting companies' environmental performance. The existence of economically oriented policy incentives, such as the DFL 701 in the case of Chile is affecting the environmental impact of both domestic and foreign companies alike. Global insertion and exposure to international markets also seem more important than country of ownership. Other factors influencing the environmental results of companies in the forestry sector include the environmental policies of headquarters, parent companies or key shareholders; reputation; pressure from environmental groups; the costs of environmental management systems and technologies; access to credit; value chain governance and land ownership concentration.

Companies that orientate their production to environmentally sensitive markets (e.g., the EU and US) tend to introduce better environmental practices and technologies, providing proof of their environmental credentials through recognized certification schemes.

Among the foreign companies in the sector, there are differences in environmental performance depending on country of origin (e.g., whether the FDI comes from OECD or non-OECD countries). Indeed, whereas European and North American investors tend to be at the forefront of environmental management, Asian companies show significantly less interest in the environment.

All this suggests several points for policy intervention for those governments aiming to increase the contribution of investment, whether foreign or domestic, in the forestry sector. The most important include:

1. The need for ex ante environmental assessments of economically oriented forestry policies.
2. The need for robust environmental regulation and adequate resources for their enforcement.
3. The need for government policies facilitating private companies' adoption of better environmental practices and technologies, including by establishing national environmental standards, improving access to credit especially for smallest companies and providing environmental training.
4. The need for awareness-raising on environmental issues in general and environmental certification in particular to increase public pressure for better environmental practices and enforcement:

   • More domestic attention to environmental certification programs is necessary in both countries, especially given the increased share of domestically sold products in Chile, for example. The result of this would be twofold: on the one hand, increased public recognition that certification would exert more pressure on non-certified companies to initiate certification and more pressure on the certified companies to maintain themselves in the system; on the other hand, with more

NGOs, and with the general public and the media knowledgeable about certification, monitoring of forestry activities in general would increase.
- Further research on the current perception of the certification schemes by clients and consumers would be necessary in this case.

5. The need for better practice on information disclosure and handling:

- On the part of the public sector, greater availability of statistics on FDI by sector and company.
- On the part of private or public institutions, continuous updates of statistics on certification and sustainability reports.

Chapter Nine

BUCKING THE TREND: THE POLITICAL ECONOMY OF NATURAL RESOURCES IN THREE ANDEAN COUNTRIES

Leonardo Stanley

Introduction

Over the past 25 years, Latin American governments have undertaken a structural-adjustment process including, among other actions, the elimination of trade barriers, privatization of large public domestic firms and deregulation of markets. This move towards deregulation and market reform has included a new embrace of foreign direct investment, even in the strategic oil and gas industries. Considering the former regulations and polices in this sector introduced during the nationalization wave of the 1970s, the transformation has been amazing: foreign investors have not only been welcomed but have even granted proprietary rights over extracted oil. Most Latin American oil-and-gas-producing countries agreed to fix royalties at very low levels. Furthermore, the 1990s witnessed the rise of bilateralism (bilateral investment treaties (BITs) plus International Centre for Settlement of Investment Disputes (ICSID) jurisdiction), which transformed the institutional framework governing the relationship between foreign investors and host states.

Paradoxically, after a decade of market-friendly reforms and neoliberal policies, the beginning of the new millennium was marked by economic crisis, social conflict, and political turmoil.

The Andean countries (Bolivia, Colombia, Ecuador, Peru and Venezuela) are usually grouped together for analytic purposes. However, the countries on which this chapter focuses (Bolivia, Ecuador and Venezuela) share some particularities, calling for an analysis separate from the rest (Colombia and Peru).

First, although political instability was a common feature of all countries in the region (Solimano 2003), this subgroup of countries moved towards a new kind of populist politics. Venezuela moved in this direction first, after Hugo Chavez came to power in 1999, signaling the collapse of the political duopoly of Acción Democrática and COPEI. In Bolivia, the transformation came with the election of Movimiento Al Socialismo (MAS) leader Evo Morales in December 2005, after two years of political turmoil that saw three presidents fall from power (G. Sánchez de Lozada, C. Mesa and E. Rodriguez). In Ecuador, another political outsider, Rafael Correa, recently won the presidential election of November 2006, backed by a new political party (Alianza País - Patria Altiva y Soberana). Hopefully this administration will close seven years of recurrent political crises, starting with the 1999 crash, which have taken down four administrations (J. Muhaud, G. Noboa Gejareno, L. Gutierrez and A. Palacio).

Second, these three Andean countries are also different in their approach to integration with world markets (Fairlie Reinoso 2005). Whereas Colombia and Peru are both engaged in talks with the US on free trade arrangements (FTAs). Bolivia, Ecuador and Venezuela are moving in another direction (pro-Mercosur).[1] This strategy is quite striking when considering the FDI partners of the two groups of countries. Cumulative FDI data for the period 1992–2001 show that US investors accounted for the largest individual-country shares of FDI in Bolivia (42.4 percent), Ecuador (58.7 percent) and Venezuela (34.8 percent), whereas in Colombia and Peru this was not the case. For Ecuador and Venezuela, a similar pattern exists for international trade: the US market accounted for 62.9 percent of Ecuador's total oil exports in 2005 (PetroEcuador, 2006). The figure for Venezuela is even more stunning: the country ranks as the fourth-leading supplier of imported crude and refined petroleum products to the US. By contrast, Bolivia's is less dependent on the US market. The main companies involved in this country's hydrocarbon sector are EU-based or regional (e.g., PETROBRAS from Brazil), and its biggest external market is currently Brazil.

Third, from an economic perspective, energy-related income is crucial for all three countries, with oil and natural gas exports serving as the main source of foreign exchange. For Venezuela, oil accounts for more than three-fourths of total exports. The importance of energy exports is less dramatic for the other two countries. Still, Bolivia ranks as an important regional player in the natural gas market and trade figures show a high share of hydrocarbon-related exports for both Bolivia and Ecuador. In terms of public revenues, oil- and gas-related income is highly significant for all three countries. For Bolivia, natural gas provided an average of 34 percent of current government revenue during the 1990s, though most of this came from local gas taxes rather than natural gas

Table 9.1. **Selected Countries, Main Statistics (2005)**

Concept	Unit	Bolivia	Ecuador	Venezuela
Population	Million	9.42	13.21	26.55
GDP	Current U$S – Billion	9.3	36.5	140.2
Change in GDP	2005 vs. 2004	4.05	3.93	9.33
GNI per capita	Atlas Methodology – Current U$S	1,010.0	2,620.0	4,820.0
GNI per capita	PPP – International U$S	2,710.0	4,110.0	6,540.0
Hydrocarbon Exports/ Total exports	Percentage	46.3	56.9	87.2
Hydrocarbon Revenues	Share over Total Fiscal Revenues (%)	25.3	30.0	55.2
Oil Production	Barrels	15,416.9	194,169.0	1,098,218.3
NG Production	Thousands m^3	12,716.5	1,608.0	34,755.5
Per capita oil production	Barrels of oil produced/ population	16,354.0	146,975.0	413,548.0
Per capita NG production	Cubic feet produced/ population	13,489.0	01,217.0	13,088.0
FDI	US$ Million	−241.6	1,646.1	2,583.0
FDI - Natural Resources	Percentage	71%	90%	34%

Source: Data from World Bank Database, ECLAC Database, (Jimenez and Tromben 2006).

exports (Andersen and Messa 2001).[2] The equivalent figure was slightly higher in preceding years (1982–92), when hydrocarbon-related income accounted for 42 to 50 percent of government revenues (Sánchez Albavera 1997). In Ecuador, oil accounts for 40 percent of public sector proceeds, whereas for Venezuela, the share reaches 50 percent (Jimenez and Tromben 2006).

All three countries considered in this chapter share another characteristic: their relationship with foreign investors is presently under stress. In all three, the governments have introduced legislation to regain control over natural resources, bypassing previous legislation and moving away from previous contracts. Paradoxically, instead of prompting a legal battle at international tribunals (as allowed by the bilateral agreements signed in the 1990s), foreign firms have accepted the new rules and agreed to renegotiate contracts.

What explains this behavior? Do developing countries now have more bargaining power vis-à-vis foreign corporations than before? Or are conditions in the oil-and-gas sector important to this outcome (i.e., is this an exceptional case)?

These are some of the questions motivating this chapter. In the search for answers, attention is paid first to the oil-and-gas industry, its main markets and players, and a brief historical account of the evolution of the contractual frameworks in the industry. In the next section, the evolution of FDI in the selected countries is summarized. The third section provides an analysis of the relationship between host states and foreign investors and how this relationship has evolved over the past decade (including a brief description of BITs). In the fourth section, the recent institutional breakdown and current situation are described, and some clues offered as to why foreign investors have not opted (at least not yet) to sue host countries. The final section draws a few conclusions.

The oil and gas markets exhibit some features that impact heavily on the relationship between host governments, multinational companies, and state-owned companies. With more than 80 percent of world reserves in hands of state-owned firms, multinational corporations' (MNC) ability to dictate the rules of the game cannot always be taken for granted. At present, the bargaining power MNCs enjoyed in the 1990s has all but disappeared. Soaring prices have tempted governments to increase the tax burden on energy firms, almost worldwide. "The average tax rate paid by oil and gas companies operating in the UK today," notes the United Kingdom Offshore Operators Association (UKOOA), "is 57 percent, with all those companies paying corporation tax at a special rate of 50 percent, and around 140 of the UK's older offshore fields subject to a further tax, the Petroleum Revenue Tax (PRT) at 75 percent."[3] Even UK Prime Minister Gordon Brown is tempted to tax windfall gains.

From an "institutional" perspective, one might be tempted to conclude after recent events that Venezuela ranks as one of the worst places to invest in the oil sector. However, some informed commentators disagree. According to Rahim, a consultant at Washington-based PFC Energy, the wrong place to invest "is not Russia or Venezuela, but Britain, which is constantly tinkering with its tax rates." He argues that "recent tax changes in Britain cost oil firms more money than similar measures in Venezuela" (*The Economist* 2007).

Oil and Gas: Markets and Players

For most countries around the world, oil and natural gas are considered strategic assets. The geopolitical importance of oil has long been recognized by academics and policymakers. The three countries considered in this chapter are all important players in one (Bolivia and Ecuador) or both (Venezuela) markets.

Bolivian oil was first discovered in the 1920s by Standard Oil of New Jersey. In 1939 President David Toro nationalized the company's Bolivian holdings and created the state-owned oil company Yacimientos Petroleros Fiscales Bolivianos (YPFB). During the 1950s the Bolivian government offered new concessions (under very generous terms) to foreign firms in order to promote hydrocarbon-related exports (Bulmer-Thomas 1994). As a consequence, Gulf Oil Company began to invest in the country. It, too, ended up being nationalized, by President Alfredo Ovando in 1969.[4]

Table 9.2. **Oil and Gas Reserves**

Resource	Source	Date	Measure	Bolivia	Ecuador	Venezuela
Oil	BP Statistical Review[a]	Year-End 2005	BB	No data	5,060	79,729
	Oil & Gas Journal[b]	January 1, 2007	BB	0.440	4,517	80,012
	World Oil[c]	Year-End 2005	BB	0.456	5,145	52,650
Gas	BP Statistical Review[a]	Year-End 2005	TCF	26,122	No data	152,320
	CEDIGAZ[d]	January 1, 2006	TCF	26,133	3,178	152,384
	Oil & Gas Journal[b]	January 1, 2007	TCF	24,000	0.000	152,380
	World Oil[c]	Year-End 2005	TCF	26,700	0.350	150,890

Source: Energy Information Administration – US Government.
[a] BP p.l.c., *BP Statistical Review of World Energy June 2006*, except United States. Oil includes crude oil, gas condensate, and natural gas liquids.
[b] PennWell Corporation, *Oil & Gas Journal*, Vol. 104.47 (December 18, 2006). Oil includes crude oil and condensate.
[c] Gulf Publishing Company, *World Oil*, Vol. 227, No.9 (September 2006), except United States. Oil includes crude oil and condensate but excludes natural gas liquids.
[d] Centre International d'Information sur le Gaz Naturel et tous Hydrocarbures Gazeux (CEDIGAZ), *Natural Gas in the World, End of July 2006*.

Bolivia ranks second in natural gas reserves among Latin American countries (after Venezuela). Although the first gas field was discovered in the Department of Santa Cruz during the 1960s, hydrocarbons did not become the country's principal export until the 1980s, when tin prices plummeted (Loza 2002; Vargas and Sánchez-Albavera 2005).[5] Argentina was the main external market for Bolivian natural gas from 1972 until the 1990s. After the collapse of the Argentinean market, Brazil emerged as the principal regional buyer of Bolivian natural gas.[6] The original contract between Bolivia and Brazil, signed in 1991 with a term of twenty years, called for Bolivia to supply eight MCM/day during the first year, with an annual increase projected to double exports by year eight.[7] The base price was set at US$ 0.90 per MBTU with the price to be adjusted each trimester following the price path of a basket of three international fuels, and a "take or pay" clause obliging Brazil to pay for at least 65 percent of the contractual daily quantity even if it chose not to accept such a quantity. Negotiations over the pipeline were concluded in February 1993, fixing capacity at 30 MCM/day. In addition to the quantities initially fixed, both governments later agreed on an additional supply of six MCM/day for electricity generation with a price fixed at US$ 1.20 per MBTU, a slight increase on the original price.

Encouraged by the new hydrocarbon legislation introduced in 1996, several oil firms decided to invest in Bolivia (Spanish Repsol-YPF, French TOTAL,

Figure 9.1. Bolivia: Natural Gas Reserves (1996–2003)

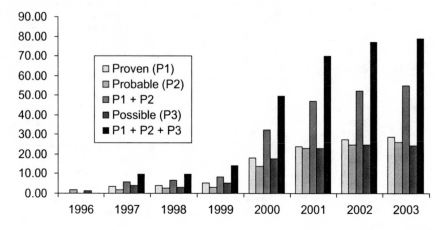

Brazilian PETROBRAS, US Exxon Mobil and British BP, among others). Hydrocarbon-related foreign investment accounted for 40 percent of total FDI incoming to Bolivia during the period 1993–2002.

Most of the investments were concentrated in the two departments with the most promising geological conditions (UNDP 2005). Since 1999, known Bolivian reserves increased substantially (see next figure),[8] with proven plus probable reserves (P1 + P2) rising from 5.69 TCF (Trillion cubic feet) in 1997 to 54.8 TCF in 2003 (and 79.06 TCF, if probable reserves are considered).

At this point, the Bolivian government faced strategic dilemmas about how to diversify markets and whether to move downstream into the industrialization process. Some policymakers favored transforming Bolivia into the dominant energy supplier for the Southern Cone of South America. Others touted the advantages of transforming the country into a world player, selling excess natural gas to new markets (e.g., California).[9]

Oil exploration and exploitation erupted in Ecuador at the time of the first oil shock, basically after important discoveries in the Oriente region. In 1971 the Ecuadorian government launched the Corporación Estatal Petrolera Ecuatoriana (CEPE), later becoming PETROECUADOR. At the same time, the government bought a stake of the Texaco-Gulf consortium, and renegotiated the concession contract with the Anglo-Ecuadorian Oil Fields Company. However, oil-related FDI inflows remained prominent in the early 1970s, and oil exports have soared since then (Gelb 1988).

During the nineties, the Ecuadorian government introduced a new foreign-investment policy generating a sharp increase in FDI in the hydrocarbon sector. The main policy objectives were to modify the oil contract system (in order to increase firms' incentives), open downstream activities to private

Figure 9.2. Oil Production by Type of Firm (1993–2005)

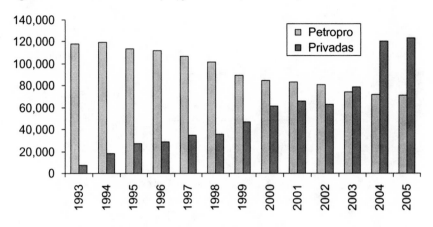

investment and expand the Trans-Ecuadorian Oil Pipe System. As a consequence, production from private oil companies increased substantially, surpassing PETROECUADOR in 2003, as shown in the Figure 9.2.

In contrast to new investors, who focused on new fields, most PETROECUADOR production continued to rely on mature oil fields. Falling production might also reflect insufficient investment and also highlight bad performance records at the state-owned company, Banco Central del Ecuador (BCE 2006). Alongside PETROECUADOR, many foreign firms—Spanish Repsol-YPF, Canadian Alberta Energy and City Investing, Italian AGIP and US Occidental Petroleum (Oxy)[10]—have become important players in the Ecuadorian market over the past decade.

Foreign investment in exploration and exploitation increased spectacularly (from US\$ 90 million in 1991 to US\$ 1,120 million in 2001), allowing foreign companies´ production to rise from 7,500 barrels per day in 1993 to 62,000 barrels per day in 2002 (UNDP 2005). Known reserves, meanwhile, increased from 2,115 billion barrels in the mid-1990s to 4,630 billion in 2004, as the following Figure 9.3 shows.

By 2007 Ecuador ranked fourth in the region in known reserves, and accounted for 4.5 billion barrels of proven reserves, and production reached 528,473 barrels per day by 2005. In recent years, thanks to high oil prices and soaring production, Ecuador's crude exports increased significantly. Foreign companies accounted for almost 60 percent of total exports (PetroEcuador).

Venezuela became a major oil exporter in the early 1920s, following important oilfield discoveries by Standard Oil of New Jersey and Royal Dutch Shell in the 1910s (Haussman 1995). The leading industrial nations and foreign investors, attracted by Venezuelan oil, gained a high degree of

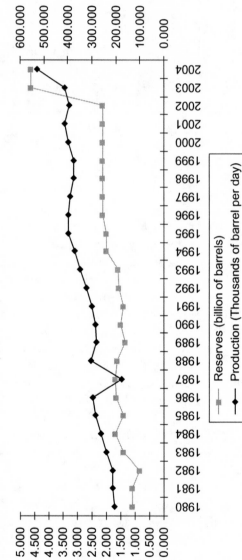

Figure 9.3. Ecuador: Oil Reserves and Production (1980–2004)

influence on the country's political elite. Under President Juan Vicente Gomez's government (1908–1914, 1922–1929), foreign oil companies even shaped the oil law (Bethel 2002).

In the 1940s, Juan Pablo Pérez Alfonso (by that time the country's Minister of Development), signed the first "50/50" formula.[11] He also introduced a more activist role for the government, beginning to market in-kind royalties on the open market, rather than selling them back to MNCs at below-market prices. Later on, in 1972, the Venezuelan government passed a number of laws and decrees that gave the country effective administrative control over every phase of the oil industry (from exploration to marketing), and raised the effective tax rate to 96 percent. The following year, a new law was passed canceling former concession contracts, although with adequate (but restricted) compensation. On January 1, 1976 Venezuelan President Carlos Andrés Pérez enacted the Hydrocarbon Nationalization Law, taking possession of the country's oil wealth and enlarging the role of Petroleos de Venezuela, S.A. (PDVSA). [12]

During the 1990s the Venezuelan government introduced massive changes to the hydrocarbon legislation, the so-called "opening process," in order to attract foreign investors. The objective was twofold: firstl, to keep the industry close to the state of the art by incorporating new technology and skills from abroad; second, to increase the state-owned oil company's access to new markets. To this end, the government passed two new laws: an organic law opening the domestic gasoline market and other hydrocarbon-related products, and a law to promote the development of the petrochemical, coal-chemical and other related sectors. The opening process took place in three different rounds: in the first round (1992–93) three contracts were awarded; in the second round (1993–95) eleven more were granted; and, in a final round in 1997, three other agreements were added. During the first two rounds, the government secured foreign investment of over US$ 2 billion; and during the third, which was a big success, added inflows of US$ 2.17 billion. These operational agreements allowed private firms to participate in 32 oil fields. By the mid 1990s, under Rafael Caldera's government, the opening process, previously confined, was also extended towards the Orinoco belt.[13]

Venezuela is a top world player in both the oil and gas markets. A leading member of OPEC, the country ranks as an important oil producer and one of the top exporters (Agnani and Iza 2005). Venezuela also has important reserves of natural gas, ranking first in Latin America, and is one of the leading natural-gas producers in the Western Hemisphere.

Venezuelan's proven oil reserves increased from 17,870 BB (billion barrels) in 1980 to 56,300 BB by 1988. Since then, reserves have increased annually at very low rates, but after exceptional increases in 1998 (a 10 percent increase) and 2001 (5.87 percent) they now stand at about 80,000 BB.

Table 9.3. **Hydrocarbons Reserves in Latin America (as of January 1, 2007)**

Country	Oil		Natural Gas	
	Billions of Barrels	Participation	TCF	Participation
Argentina	2,468	2.1	16,090	6.3
Bolivia	0,440	0.4	24,000	9.4
Brazil	11,773	10.2	10,820	4.2
Colombia	1,453	1.3	3,996	1.6
Ecuador	4,517	3.9	0,000	0.0
Mexico	12,352	10.7	14,557	5.7
Peru	0,930	0.8	8,723	3.4
Trinidad and Tobago	0,728	0.6	18,770	7.4
Venezuela	80,012	69.5	152,380	59.7
Total	**115,150**	**100.0**	**255,302**	**100.0**

Source: Oil & Gas Journal.

Figure 9.4. Venezuela: Proven Reserves (1980–3007)

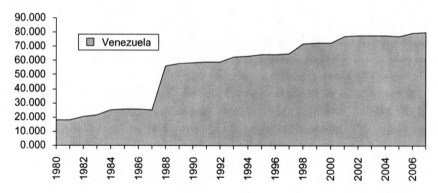

To the above figures, one may add heavy-grade oil reserves at the Orinoco belt of about 235,000 billion barrels. Consequently, total reserves add up to about 315,000 billion barrels. Venezuela's claim to be the world's number one country in terms of reserves may prove correct.

A final comment in relation to hydrocarbon reserves has to do with host country strategies. In the case of Bolivia, the country's strength relates to its neighbors' weakness: energy anxiety has made Brazil willing to accept renegotiated contracts, and scarce resources have led Argentina to rush for new sources of natural gas. However, looking into the future, the main strategic asset of Bolivia might be related to its geographical position, something that sounds paradoxical, but true. Venezuela's bargaining power will continue (or even increase, if reserves in the Orinoco Belt are developed) as long as prices remain at present levels and the world's reliance on hydrocarbon continues. Finally, the future may look less optimistic for Ecuador, as the country doesn't enjoy the geographical or market advantages of the other countries.

Rules and Institutions

At the beginning of the past century, most Latin American governments cultivated foreign investment by granting vast reserves of hydrocarbons (oil and gas) and minerals to private companies. Most FDI flows were directed at public utilities' operations and, in the three countries analyzed, especially focused on the exploitation of natural resources. Under the liberal model in place at that time, the region's governments made little effort to control or restrict international private capital transactions.

However, since the 1950s, most states in the region adopted a more protectionist approach. And in the late sixties and seventies, after the decolonization process, a massive nationalization wave took place in Latin America. Since then, FDI has been a hot topic. On the one hand, investors have asked for "more protection" at multilateral fora. On the other, for those sympathetic to developing countries' positions, the main point was how to set "MNCs codes of conduct" in order to countervail their former power. Host countries' attitudes towards foreign investors can be summarized in their support of a "New Economic Order" in a series of UN resolutions emphasizing the sovereignty of nations with respect to foreign investors and in the Andean Pact (AP) Decision 24/71.[14] The debt crisis of the 1980s and the generalization of the bilateral scheme, based on bilateral investment treaties (BITs), put an end to this debate.

As mentioned above, the three countries under study have always relied on primary exports for foreign-exchange revenue. However, this "primary-export development" strategy has been particularly disappointing for them (Bulmer-Thomas 1994). The fall of export commodity prices and the eruption of the Latin American debt crisis generated a more inviting attitude towards foreign investors among the region's governments, who began to view FDI as the new hope for the development process. The movement towards FDI liberalization was exemplified by AP Decision 220 (later expanded by AP Decision 291).

The 1980s saw a collapse in oil prices (along with other commodity prices), and a significant increase in world oil supply. Under these conditions, some flexibility was introduced to promote FDI, but contracts did not change substantially.[15] It was not until the 1990s that countries in the region (with the exception of Mexico) began to loosen their previously rigid entry conditions for the oil-and-gas sector. However, restructuring was far from homogeneous (Sánchez Albavera 1997). Differences were mainly related to each country's attributes, such as reserves, production/consumption ratio for hydrocarbons and by-products, technological level and experience in the national oil-and-gas industry, among others. Another important transformation in the contractual relationships between oil companies and host states allowed foreign investors to enter the industry under new contractual forms: associative contracts and service contracts in Venezuela and private investment promotion, among other legal forms, in Ecuador (Sánchez Albavera 1997; UNDP 2005).[16] An even more acute change took place in Bolivia, where the capitalization process ended the former public monopoly of YPFB and the state-owned company was opened to private investors.[17]

The bilateral scheme

Although the bilateral treaty system began in the late 1950s, this legal framework only proliferated in the late 1980s and 1990s. The change was not only legal. The international political environment changed substantially during those years, with developing countries' bargaining positions diminishing (UNCTAD 1999). Following the worldwide trend, all three countries considered in the present chapter were very active in signing BITs.

From a theoretical viewpoint, BITs were introduced in order to overcome dynamic inconsistency problems (i.e., as a commitment device). In contrast to trade, direct investment involves the acquisition or creation of productive capacity, thus implying a long-term perspective. Hence, once investment becomes "sunk" in a particular location, the host country may have a strong incentive to change the "rules of the game" (engage in "holdup"). In order to attract FDI, developing countries may wish to signal that they are "investor friendly" by adopting tax incentives and subsidies favoring MNCs, embracing market liberalization and signing BITs. From this perspective, economic factors play a minor role in providing incentives to foreign investors. Instead, political goodwill—demonstrated by importing institutions from abroad—is key.[18]

In practice, the bilateral system emerged due to the pressure exerted by capital-exporting countries. After the defeat of multilateral accords on foreign investment, BITs became the second-best solution for foreign investors seeking more guarantees and security. Bilateral agreements introduced a new institutional scheme biased in favor of foreign investors, backed by the neoliberal views dominant during the 1990s (Sornarajah 2006).

Although BITs vary across countries, most of them share similar features when it comes to foreign investment (e.g., the same basic standards in regard

Table 9.4. **BITs Signed and In Force**

Country	N° of BITs – Signed	N° of BITs – in Force	Before 1990s	During the 90s	After 2000	TBIs Partners
Bolivia	22	18	0	18	0	Argentina; Austria; Belgium and Luxembourg; Chile; China; Costa Rica; Cuba; Denmark; Ecuador; France; Germany; Italy; Republic of Korea; Netherlands; Paraguay; Peru; Romania; Spain; Sweden; Switzerland; United Kingdom; and USA.
Ecuador	28	21	2	17	2	Argentina, Bolivia, Canada; Chile, Costa Rica; Cuba; Dominican Republic; Egypt; El Salvador; Finland; France; Germany; Honduras; Italy; Netherlands; Nicaragua; Paraguay; Peru; Romania; Russian Federation; Spain; Sweden; Switzerland; United Kingdom; USA; Uruguay; and, Venezuela.
Venezuela	25	21	0	20	1	Argentina; Barbados; Belgium and Luxembourg; Brazil; Canada; Chile; Costa Rica; Cuba; Czech Republic; Denmark; Ecuador; France; Germany; Indonesia; Italy; Lithuania; Netherlands; Paraguay; Peru; Portugal; Spain; Sweden; Switzerland; United Kingdom; and Uruguay.
Total	**75**	**60**	**2**	**55**	**3**	

Source: Author's elaboration based on UNCTAD Database.

to treatment, transfer of funds, expropriations and mechanisms for dispute settlement). Expropriation clauses included in these agreements generally include some standard "prompt, adequate and effective compensation" or "just compensation" formula. By contrast, BITs differ on the definition of "indirect expropriation," government actions not expropriating private property outright, but substantially impairing the value of an investment.

Other important clauses are those dealing with the investor-state investment dispute mechanism, which allows foreign investors to make claims against the host country before multilateral institutions, such as the International Centre for the Settlement of Investment Disputes (ICSID) or the United Nations Commission on International Trade Law (UNCITRAL). The impact of this arrangement can be seen from the recent experience of Argentina: once a country changes the "rules of the game," foreign investors may launch a legal offensive against it.

From this perspective, one would expect Bolivia and Venezuela to be frequent targets of complaints before ICSID tribunals (as Argentina was after the collapse of the Convertibility Plan in 2002). However, this has not been the case.

During the 1990s, increasing availability of capital (both portfolio investment and FDI) and foreign exchange constraints in host countries (particularly in Latin America) enabled foreign investors to extract legal concessions from host states in developing countries. At present, oil firms have lost bargaining power relative to countries with (important) hydrocarbon reserves, such as Bolivia and Venezuela. Host-country leverage is evident in Venezuela's new contracts with foreign oil companies. The new arrangement stipulates that all disputes arising in the future must be settled in domestic courts, not in international tribunals such as ICSID (Vis-Dunbar 2006). Although foreign investors' first instinct, when faced with changed policies in Bolivia and Venezuela, was to intimidate host countries with the threat of claims before ICSID or other international tribunals, most of them finally accepted the new "rules of the game."

Foreign investors' treatment and FDI inflows: The recent facts

Regardless of the policies followed and institutional changes introduced, FDI to the Andean region has *increased* sharply since the beginning of the 1990s (see Table 9.5 following). Since then, and especially after 1997, Venezuela has become the region's main recipient of foreign investment. Using the latest data available, FDI inflows almost doubled in 2005 over the previous year's figure (ECLAC 2006).

This performance has remained unchanged in recent years (i.e., since Chavez has taken office). In 1999, the natural-gas sector was opened to

Table 9.5. **FDI Inflows, in $ US Millions (1980–2004)**

Period	Bolivia	Colombia	Ecuador	Perú	Venezuela	Andean Pact
1980–89	39.40	434.78	85.10	28.89	22.70	610.87
1990–99	398.30	1,803.00	470.80	1,573.10	2,067.00	6,312.20
2000–04	454.54	2,060.88	1,220.06	1,360.40	2,511.20	7,607.08

Source: Author's elaboration from ECLAC data.

foreign investors, as PDVSA approved the operation by two US firms (Chevron and Texaco) and one Norwegian firm (the state-owned Statoil) of two offshore blocks close to the border with Trinidad and Tobago. In the natural-gas industry, the government launched a bidding process in April 2005 over exploration rights for six offshore blocks in the Gulf of Venezuela and in the northeast region of the country. A total of 29 companies from 15 different countries participated and the PDVSA ultimately awarded 6 licenses (PDVSA 2005). Contracts are expected to last for a 25-year period. The government may have a share of up to 35 percent through PDVSA, and the gas produced will be mainly devoted to the internal market (exports are allowed only after meeting domestic demand).

In the case of Bolivia, new FDI is expected after the revival of the Argentinean export market following the natural gas shortage. Bolivia has signed a new agreement with Argentina, fixing an initial price of US$5 per MBTU. Investment will be directed not only at the development of gas fields (US$ 3 billion) but also at the construction of the pipeline necessary for export (over US$ 4 billion). Notably, private companies will invest only in gas field development, not the pipeline project.

Finally, in the case of Ecuador, FDI inflows have continued to grow in the present decade, making it the region's top FDI recipient in 2003, with U$S 1,55 billion.[19] From the latest data available, as of 2005 it appears that FDI inflows to Ecuador have continued to increase (ECLAC 2006).

Governments' Policy Options and Investors' Strategies

The latest policy decisions in these countries represent a reversal of the liberalization trend initiated in the 1980s and deepened in the 1990s. What is more, in the oil-and-gas sector, the regulatory change was undertaken against an industry always characterized by strong bargaining power.[20] In view of the Argentinean experience, one might expect foreign investors to insist on the a priori rules and to unleash a massive dispute response. However, if their sunk FDI and future stakes in the countries under study are large enough, investors may well have incentives to avoid disputes. From this perspective, investors may use litigation mainly as a signaling device and a threat when facing renegotiation with host countries, as a closer look at the Argentinean experience has also highlighted (Stanley 2004).

On November 13, 2001, under the enabling law authorized by the National Assembly, President Chavez signed the new Hydrocarbons Law, which came into effect in January 2002. The new law replaced the Hydrocarbons Law of 1943 and the Nationalization Law of 1975. Among other things, the 2001 law declared all oil production and distribution activities to be the domain of the Venezuelan state, with the exception of the joint ventures targeting extra-heavy crude oil production. Under the new law, private investors cannot hold a majority stake in an exploration project. Furthermore, PDVSA will have a majority stake plus operational control over the fields. In addition, by virtue of the new rules, royalties were increased from one percent to 30 percent (later raised to 33.3 percent), and taxes raised from 34 percent to 50 percent. The Venezuelan government gave foreign investors short notice to sign new contracts in compliance with the new conditions.

In late 2005 the government started to apply the 2001 Hydrocarbon Law more strictly, forcing oil companies to accept a new mixed-ownership contractual scheme. To this end, the government revised 32 operational agreements signed during the 1990s, which it argued were disguised concessions, a contractual form illegal under 1975 Organic Law. According to the government, the previous arrangements had also allowed tax havens, paving the way for tax-evasion operations in the millions of dollars.[21] Finally, in January 2007 the Venezuelan government moved further toward nationalization (*"Transition is over"*), announcing that foreign oil companies operating in the Orinoco belt would have to give the state company a majority stake in the oilfields (though not the refineries) (*The Economist* 2007).[22] The main foreign companies operating in the Orinoco are from the US (Conoco-Phillips, Chevron, Exxon Mobil), France (Total), Italy (ENI) and Norway (Statoil).

In Ecuador, institutional changes were introduced even before Correa took office. In April 2004 the Congress passed a law raising oil taxes to 50 percent whenever oil prices exceeded a fixed level (Ley 2006-42 Reformatoria a la Ley de Hidrocarburos). The Ecuadorian government gave foreign oil firms 45 days to submit new contractual terms conforming to the modified Hydrocarbon Law. It also took over Block 15, previously run by the US firm Occidental Petroleum (Oxy), outright.[23] PETROECUADOR began to operate this field in May 2006. The introduction of a windfall tax by President Palacio was seen by foreign investors as cause for arbitration claims against the Ecuadorian government, but few companies dared defy the government.

On May 1, 2006 Evo Morales announced the nationalization of Bolivia's oil-and-gas industry. By virtue of Decree 28,701, the government took "ownership, possession and total and absolute control" of the country oil and gas reserves (Article 1). Further, the decree empowered the Bolivian government to manage the marketing of all oil and gas produced in the country, to establish the volume, prices, terms and conditions for the sale of Bolivian gas (Article 2), and to control transport, refinement, storage and distribution of gas within the country (Article 5). The government gave foreign companies a 180-day deadline to enter into new contracts with YPFB. Rent reallocation was substantial: Until May 2005, 82 percent of natural gas revenue went to multinational companies; one year later, the government claimed the lion's share.[24] However, final terms ended up less draconian for the foreign companies than the nationalization decree had initially suggested.[25] The Bolivian government also initiated a renegotiation process with Brazil in order to modify contract prices (i.e., natural gas export prices).

As mentioned above, the drastic changes introduced might have triggered a wave of foreign investors' claims before international tribunals. Considering foreign investors' enhanced rights under bilateral investment treaties, we would expect to see these countries facing numerous claims in international tribunals. The following table shows the number of pending cases that these

Table 9.6. **ICSID Pending Cases**

Country	Case	Firm	Sector
Bolivia	ARB/06/2	Química e Industrial del Borax Ltd.	Mining concession
Ecuador	ARB/03/6	MCI Power Group and New Turbine INC	Power generation project
	ARB/04/19	Duke Energy Electroquil Partners	Power generation facilities
	ARB/05/9	Empresa eléctrica del Ecuador (EMELEC)	Electricity enterprise
	ARB/05/12	Noble Energy INC and Machala Power Co.	Electricity enterprise
	ARB/06/11	Occidental Petroleum Co.	Hydrocarbon concession
	ARB/06/17	Técnicas Reunidas	Oil refinery expansion
	ARB/06/21	City Oriente Limited	Hydrocarbon concession
Venezuela	ARB (AF)/04/6	Vannessa Ventures Ltd.	Gold and mining project
	ARB/05/4	I&I Beheer B.V.	Debt Instruments
	ARB/06/4	Vestey Group Ltd.	Farming enterprises
	ARB/07/4	ENI Dación B.V.	Hydrocarbon rights

Source: Author's elaboration based on data at ICSID Webpage.

three countries have at the International Centre for Settlement of Investment Disputes (ICSID) of the World Bank.

In spite of the outstanding legal and contractual changes, Bolivia and Venezuela have few pending cases at international tribunals. Venezuela faces only one case before ICSID, brought by the Italian-owned ENI after Caracas terminated its contract at the Dación field in April 2006, while Bolivia is not facing a single oil-sector-related suit. Ecuador, by contrast, faces several claims,[26] including two in the oil sector. In addition to the Oxy case (mentioned previously), the Ecuadorian government is facing another claim, filed after the introduction of the "windfall tax" on oil profits, by City Oriente Ltd. This was the first and, up to now, the only, company to take Ecuador to arbitration for that reason.

The above evidence should not lead to the conclusion that foreign investors accepted the new contracts passively. However, it suggests that investors were open to renegotiating contracts, and to accepting new conditions as long as the new rules still allowed them to make profits. In other words, contract breaching does not always mean foreign investors will bring disputes before international tribunals.

From a strategic point of view, foreign investors' first reactions were to intimidate host countries with the threat of claims before ICSID or other international tribunals, as they did in both Bolivia and Venezuela.

In the former case, foreign firms made some moves toward suing the host country (e.g., filing so-called triggering letters), basically aimed at intimidating the government. This strategy was pursued by many foreign investors, including some of the most prominent ones. However, on October 28, just before the deadline, all energy firms signed the new contracts.[27] Similarly, Brazil reached agreement with Bolivia over a new gas price (US$ 4.20 per MBTU).

In this case, it should be mentioned that natural gas enhances host country leverage (as the recent Russian example illustrated). By virtue of this, the host government's threats become more plausible. Once investments are sunk, Bolivia's leverage surpasses that of Brazil, which, in the language of game theory, becomes a "hostage."

A similar pattern of acceptance of the new rules was followed by foreign investors in Venezuela. After reacting aggressively to the introduction of new taxes, foreign firms pledged to comply with Venezuelan income tax and hydrocarbons laws and SENIAT regulation.[28] By the time the negotiation process ended on December 31, 2005, however, 32 multinational companies had agreed to a new legal status as PDVSA partners,[29] with the state-owned firm having a majority stake of 60 percent in the new mixed companies.[30] From the firms' perspective, the deal was not too bad. As *The Economist* reported, "with oil selling for almost US$ 50 a barrel—up to five times the price when the original contracts were signed—and access to the world's remaining reserves at a premium, the companies can probably live with the consequences" (*The Economist* 2005). Paradoxically, an independent oil-and-gas company from Texas (Harvest Natural Resources) became one of the first foreign companies to accept the new joint-venture arrangement, becoming PDVSA's partner after the National Assembly approved the formation of the new mixed company PETRODELTA S.A.[31]

For the oil companies, the present situation is not as bad as they first imagined. First, because of the increase in oil prices, the economic and financial equation may still be positive even after the introduction of the new taxes. Second, the government's interest in taxing the Ricardian rent is a worldwide phenomenon and investors might be better off in the Andes than in other regions (*The Economist* 2006; *The Economist* 2007).[32] Third, those companies that have entered the market during the last decade have already recouped their initial investments, as indicated by Stiglitz (2006) in the case of Bolivia.[33] These factors offer some clues as to why foreign investors, although initially tempted to sue host countries, finally ended up accepting renegotiation. However, this might not always be the case. For instance, investors' stances might have been different had oil prices been lower. Furthermore, foreign investors might also avoid new investments in a particular country if the business environment deteriorates further or if the country's demands are too ambitious.

In the case of Venezuela, with the exception of ConocoPhillips and Exxon Mobil, all companies accepted a change in the contractual terms as a result of the Orinoco belt renegotiation. They now participate in a profit-sharing arrangement. Although the deal is similar to the previous one (a joint-venture agreement with a majority stake for PDVSA), some factors differentiate this case from earlier ones. First, a renegotiation process was launched by mid-2006, but no agreement was reached. Second, firms' investments were huge, as were expected revenues. The departure of U.S. inverstors did not translate into a reduction of FDI but a change both in terms of the origin of the FDI as well as the type of firm arriving in the country. Since then, numerous firms have gone to Venezuela to participate in exploration activities. Among others, the following are worth mentioning: Petopass (Iran), Lukoil and Gazprom (Russia), Belorusneft (Belarus), Petronas (Malaysia), ENARSA (Argentina), ANCAP (Uruguay), YPFB (Bolivia), China National Petroleum Co (China), CUPET (Cuba), PetroEcuador (Ecuador) y ONGC Videsh Ltd. (India). The change in the rules of the game clearly represented a change in actors. Most of the new investors are state-owned companies. However, it also represented continuity in terms of the interest of foreign firms in the oil sector, a fact that highlights the strategic nature of the sector.

The case of Ecuador is slightly different. Only one out of seven pending cases at ICSID relates to the regulatory change introduced in the oil industry by the previous administration. This suggests that claims have not been the main business response to regulatory change. But renegotiation has not been initiated by the government yet (La Nacion 2007), so this case remains open.

Conclusions

Until recently, FDI inflows were the most important factor for the development of the hydrocarbon sector in all three Andean countries considered in this chapter. In most cases, foreign investment contributed to the expansion of proven reserves and total production, as the aggregate numbers reflect. With the increased public-sector role in strategic decision-making, investment and resource ownership, this no longer appears to be the case.

These three countries, after experiencing a severe economic crisis, are now going through a vast political transformation in which the key role of foreign investment is being contested. Bolivia's most dramatic crisis took place in the eighties, when hyperinflation severely hurt the economy. After a period of deep political turmoil that brought down three presidents, the country is now moving toward a new political model. In the case of Ecuador, the economic crisis exploded in 1999 with a bank collapse, general strikes and political paralysis, all of which contributed to dollarization. But even as this policy allowed for some growth and stabilization, political uncertainty remained. Local hopes are that the election of Correa will end the political crisis. Finally, in the case of Venezuela, the 1980s were "a terrible decade for Venezuelan development" (Hausmann 1995), and during the 1990s the crisis moved to the political system. In other words, in all three countries, economic crisis led to political transformation, as well as to a new vision of FDI's benefits and costs, especially in the strategic oil-and-gas sector. The explanation may well go beyond economic and institutional factors. Because of the importance of these sectors as engines of growth and development, they affect politics directly through the mood and expectations of ordinary people.

During periods of political tension, the energy sector has come under stress. Debate about the structure of this sector and the role of foreign investment in it is not new. All three countries discussed in this chapter have nationalized oil companies in the past, and all have later called back foreign companies to play an important role in further development of oil and gas.

At the global level, a political race over energy security is under way. This is not new either. The US international energy policy changed in response to energy-security concerns early in the 1980s, and the US government has become aware, once again, of the need for a new strategy (Valenzuela

2006).[34] Furthermore, the increase in fuel demand for the transport sector worldwide and the continuing strong economic growth of India and China are intensifying the race for access to energy supplies.[35]

Aiming to expand world energy markets, developed countries (basically, the US introduced BITs and other special legal frameworks to make the world "safer" for energy-related FDI. In contractual terms, where the 1990s saw a return to pre-nationalization-era contracts and to private-firm rights over energy resources, the present legal U-turn and contract renegotiation has been interpreted as a return to the 1970s (nationalization) experience. A similar tale of swinging mood could be told when observing the treatment granted to foreign investors. The institutions that received investors' favor (and guaranteed their rights) during the nineties may seem pretty useless nowadays. Perhaps it is time for these three countries to look for a political and legal framework working beyond boom and bust, aimed at attracting foreign investment in a way that can contribute to the countries' sustainable development. Strong rules and hard commitments, like those drawn in bilateral treaties, are not essential to this aim. It may be time for the international community to renew debate over a *multilateral* scheme to guarantee FDI contribution to sustainable development.

This chapter looked for explanations for the puzzling fact that firms largely chose to renegotiate their status under new terms imposed by the governments instead of trying to defend their rights under previous contracts. This was analyzed giving special attention to the investors' incentives for renegotiation. In this sense, the discussion may suggest the relative irrelevance of BITs in driving FDI: Foreign investors are attracted by economic rather than institutional factors. At the very least, that seems to be the case of hydrocarbon-related FDI, where foreign investors accepted the new terms, apparently because operations in these countries continued to be profitable. The high oil prices of the current period may have played an important role. If the price cycle changes and rents dissipate, investors might be tempted to change their strategy and bring claims before international courts. This could represent a serious risk for pending contracts (e.g., in the case of Ecuador). Foreign investors' moods might also prevent new investments, keeping host countries from exploiting new opportunities.

These three Andean countries should take into account that their present leverage for negotiation could be short-lived if oil prices decrease below a certain threshold or if new reserves are discovered. This suggests that these countries need a longer-term strategy in their relationship with foreign investment, which is essential in view of all three countries' capital and technology shortages. From this perspective, recent regulatory changes in the oil-and-gas sectors of these countries seem more like a correction of the balance of power in the investor-biased BITs, rather than the optimal policy. Continuing the reduction of companies' profits and rights could hardly be the best long-term option.

To conclude with a general thought on BITs and renegotiation, it is worth noting that, in principle, these countries may pursue the same strategic behavior observed in the oil-and gas-industry, and renegotiate the treaties as a whole. However, the newest bilateral treaties appear to be more ambitious, including new guarantees for foreign investors (e.g., on intellectual property). Therefore, although these countries may enjoy high leverage to renegotiate contracts in the oil-and-gas sector, their bargaining power might be much lower in a broad-based negotiation (in terms of investments in general). Bolivia recently announced its intention to revise BITs, focusing on three areas: definition of investment, performance requirements and dispute resolution (Peterson 2007).[36] An alternative could be to suspend those bilateral treaties seen as prejudicial by the host country. This solution was recently suggested by the Ecuadorian government, when it announced its intention to decline a renewal of the BIT signed with the US (Peterson 2007).

It is too soon to guess what the final decision regarding BITs and renegotiation will be in these countries, even if BIT renegotiation or nonrenewal seems to fit with some recent political decisions (e.g., nationalization).

Chapter Ten

BEYOND POLLUTION HALOES: THE ENVIRONMENTAL EFFECTS OF FDI IN THE PULP AND PAPER AND PETROCHEMICALS SECTORS IN BRAZIL

Luciana Togeiro de Almeida and Sueila dos Santos Rocha

Abstract

Among the most environmentally sensitive sectors are pulp-and-paper and petrochemicals. In a historical perspective, FDI played an important role in the establishment of the petrochemicals industry in Brazil in the 1970's, when it was driven by strategic state policies to develop the domestic intermediate goods industry. In the pulp-and-paper sector, FDI became prominent just after the year 2000, and it has been exclusively driven by market forces. This chapter presents a comparative analysis of the environmental issues related to FDI in these two sectors in Brazil and extensively focuses on the importance of the international context in fostering domestic environmental commitments. One conclusion is that, in general, domestic firms in these sectors are just as environmentally friendly as foreign firms. What would explain such convergence? First, the stringency of the domestic environmental regulations has pushed for higher environmental standards in both sectors; second, and specifically in the case of the pulp-and-paper sector, international market environmental requirements also contributed to this trend. Last, but not least, the technological competencies accumulated by the domestic firms in both sectors, which are closely related to the strategic state industrial policies applied to them, strengthened their capability to enter into an environmental-technological path. One policy lesson drawn from these case studies is that attracting FDI is not a guarantee of a higher level of sectoral environmental control, while an integrated policy approach to environmental, technological and industry capacity to enhance national environmental control at the industry level is highly recommended.

Introduction

Two conflicting views stand out in the literature on the environmental effects of FDI. On the one hand, it is widely emphasized that transnational corporations (TNCs), the major players in FDI, are supposed to have positive environmental effects on the host countries by means of transferring environmentally friendly technologies and advanced environmental management systems, pushing for higher environmental standards and being ahead of domestic firms' environmental performance. On the other hand, it is pointed out that TNCs can strategically locate their FDI in countries where they face less stringent environmental regulations, i.e., they can search for "pollution havens" in developing countries. Aiming to protect the environment, the policy approach to TNCs is radically distinct, depending on which of these views prevails. According to the first one, the more liberalized the economy is to FDI, the better for the environment, while according to the second view, regulating the environmental performance of TNCs is crucial.

Beyond these two extreme conflicting views, considering that the effects of FDI in host economies are very varied, case-specific and sectoral case studies are recommended as an adequate methodology to assess their environmental impacts (Zarsky 1999; UNCTAD 2004; Araya 2005).

Departing from the questions addressed in the literature on the environmental effects of FDI and the previously recommended methodological approach, this chapter brings a comparative analysis of the effects of FDI in Brazil's pulp-and-paper and petrochemicals sectors, aiming to draw out some policy lessons. The main reasons for addressing these sectors are: their potential for environmental impacts, the worldwide importance of FDI in these sectors and their contribution to the Brazilian economy (high share of national production and exports).

The Context: a Historical Perspective of the FDI in Pulp-and-Paper and Petrochemicals Sectors in Brazil

It is worth noticing that, in a historical perspective, there is a sharp contrast between the two sectors concerning the share of FDI.

The establishment of the petrochemicals industry in Brazil can be traced back to the beginning of 1970's, when a governmental initiative adopted the "tripartite model" for joint ventures: One-third of the capital belonged to a state-owned firm under the control of Petroquisa (the petrochemical holding of Petrobras), which was the supplier of the raw material (naphtha) and basic petrochemicals; one-third belonged to a Brazilian partner; and the remaining third belonged to a foreign partner, usually the supplier of the technology. This means that the establishment of the petrochemicals industry in Brazil was marked by strong State and FDI participation.

In the nineties, under the liberalizing economic reforms implemented by the Brazilian government, the structure of the Brazilian petrochemical industry changed deeply due to privatizations and several mergers and acquisitions, coinciding with a worldwide concentration process in this sector. According to Miranda and Martins (2000), 76 percent out of the total value of assets negotiated for the privatization of the petrochemicals sector from 1991 to 1997 were acquired by domestic firms or consortia with very little engagement of foreign companies. Following the international trend, foreign companies initiated a process of concentrating their investments in higher-aggregated-value chemicals, leaving basic chemicals for the domestic companies (Mercado and Antunes 1998). Consequently, the number of TNCs in Brazilian petrochemicals was substantially reduced.[1]

The establishment of the pulp-and-paper sector in Brazil was also strongly supported by government incentives, initiated at the end of the 1950's, but exclusively towards national private companies.

Until recently, the presence of TNCs in the Brazilian pulp-and-paper sector had not been significant, but since the year 2001 this sector has been receiving increasing influx of FDI. Foreign investment in this sector increased from US$ 8.1 million per year between 1995 and 2000 to US$ 440.4 million on average per year between 2001 and 2006.[2] This recent trend of FDI into the Brazilian pulp-and-paper sector is probably connected to the general international trend for substituting long- for short-fiber pulp that has been observed in the world pulp industry. The international producers are searching for new mixtures of the two fibers aiming to increase the content of short-fiber pulp, which is the cheaper one. Consequently a huge increase in the international demand for short-fiber pulp is expected. This trend implies that Brazil has become a preferential destination for the big pulp-and-paper TNCs investments, because this is a water-and-land-resources-abundant country and, above all, because it is highly competitive in the production of short-fiber pulp, controlling eucalyptus-production technology and paper-production technology based on short-fiber pulp.

Table 10.1. **FDI to the Brazilian Pulp-and-Paper Industry, (1980 to 2006)**

Year	FDI, *Thousands of Dollars*
1980	0.37
1981	0.44
1982	0.46
1983	0.45
1984	0.49
1985	0.55
1986	0.56
1987	0.6
1988	0.61
1989	0.74
1990	0.76
1991	0.78
1992	0.74
1993	0.75
1994	0.76
1995	3.92
1996	21.94
1997	0
1998	0
1999	12.5
2000	10.31
2001	150.01
2002	10.77
2003	348.3
2004	177.32
2005	158.62
2006	1,797.38

Source: Brazilian Central Bank.

The Research Approach: Questions Addressed

Besides secondary research sources, both case studies were based on field research on different periods[3]—1999–2000 for the petrochemicals sector and 2005–2006 for the pulp-and-paper sector—marked by increasing rates of growth of domestic production in both sectors, restructuring including privatization in the case of the petrochemicals sectors. and an increasing influx of FDI in the pulp-and-paper sector.

The pulp-and-paper sector case study involved a sample of nine companies (see Table 10.2), including five national and four foreign firms, seven

Table 10.2. **Pulp and Paper Companies Sample: Production Profile**

Companies	Main Products	Production Capacity, 2005 Ton/Year		Number of Plants, 2005	Export, Average for 2002–2004 Percent of Yearly Production	
		Pulp	Paper		Pulp	Paper
National						
Aracruz	pulp	3,000,000	40,000	3	97	–
Klabin	pulp, eucalyptus and pinus logs, improved seeds of eucalyptus and pinus, packaging paper, corrugated box, boards, craft paper for sacks and envelops, sacks	1,200,000	1,500,000	18	–	55.7
Ripasa	pulp, industrial base paper, cut size, coated and uncoated paper and paperboard	570,000	380,000	4	–	46.7
Suzano Bahia Sul	pulp, cut size, coated and uncoated paper and paperboard	1,290,000	1,350,000	3	36.1	40
Votorantim	pulp, cut size, coated and uncoated paper and chemical papers	1,300,000	635,000	4	44.3	28.7
Total 1	–	**7,360,000**	**3,905,000**	**32**	–	–
Foreign						
Cenibra	pulp	940,000	–	1	95	–
International Paper	pulp, eucalyptus and pinus chips, improved wood of pinus, coated and uncoated paper.	450,000	600,000	2	[a]	[a]
Norske Skog	newsprint paper	170,000	185,000	1	[a]	1.33
Rigesa	packaging paper and corrugated paperboard packages	220,000	320,000	9	[a]	[a]
Total 2	–	**1,780,000**	**1,105,000**	**13**	–	–
Total 1+ 2	–	**9,140,000**	**5,101,000**	**45**	–	–

Source: (dos Santos Rocha and Togeiro de Almeida 2007).
[a] Data is not available.

branches of pulp-and-paper-sector labor unions and six regional offices of the environmental control agency of the state of Sao Paulo (CETESB). In 2004 these nine companies were responsible for 81.4 percent and 52.3 percent of pulp-and-paper production in Brazil, respectively. The four TNC subsidiaries in the sample represented 98.4 percent of the pulp production and 46.2 percent of paper production by foreign firms in Brazil in 2004 (BRACELPA 2005).[4]

The pulp-and-paper production has high potential for environmental impacts because it is an energy-and-natural resources-intensive activity, consuming high levels of timber and water, generating toxic chemical substances that can pollute water and cause a characteristic unpleasant smell. These are reasons why this sector has been constantly supervised by government authorities, environmental NGOs and consumers (Dalcomuni 1997). Since evidences of dioxins wastes that are cancerous substances were found in paper packages in the 1980s, the pulp-and-paper sector has been under increasing environmental pressure (Corazza 1996).

The comparison of the environmental performance between domestic and foreign companies in the pulp-and-paper sector took into account the specifics of their production processes. Most of the sampled firms have integrated plants, i.e., plants that produce paper and pulp (see Table 10.2). The exceptions are Aracruz (Brazilian) and Cenibra (TNC) that produce only eucalyptus short-fiber pulp and so they were compared to each other. The firms with integrated plants were grouped by similar production processes as follows: (1) Votorantim, Suzano Bahia Sul and Ripasa (Brazilian firms) and International Paper (TNC), integrated producers of pulp and writing and printing paper; (2) Klabin (Brazilian) and Rigesa (TNC) producers of pulp and mainly packaging papers and corrugated paperboard packaging; (3) Norske Skog stands alone since it is the only manufacturer of newsprint paper in Brazil, besides having its own pulp production.

The pulp-and-paper sample encompassed companies with plants located in several Brazilian states, and concentrated in the Southeastern states, mostly in Sao Paulo and Santa Catarina (see Figure 10.1).

The petrochemicals sector case study was based on a sample of 17 companies, including 13 Brazilian firms, 3 foreign firms and one shared-owned (half foreign, half national capital) (see Table 10.3). These companies encompassed 33 out of 57 plants concentrated in the three major petrochemicals complexes located in Camaçari, Capuava, and Triunfo (in the states of Bahia, São Paulo, and Rio Grande do Sul, respectively; see Figure 10.2), with their respective large-size cracking facilities (Copene, PQU-Petroquímica União, and Copesul).

The petrochemicals sector is one of the most-addressed by environmental regulations due to its high potential for environmental impacts, since it is also

Figure 10.1. Pulp and Paper Industry: Sample Geographical Distribution

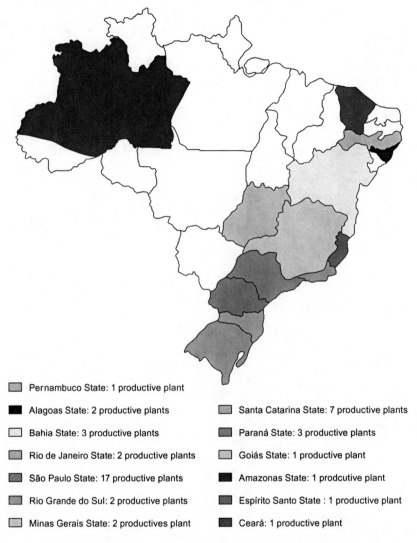

Pernambuco State: 1 productive plant

Alagoas State: 2 productive plants · Santa Catarina State: 7 productive plants

Bahia State: 3 productive plants · Paraná State: 3 productive plants

Rio de Janeiro State: 2 productive plants · Goiás State: 1 productive plant

São Paulo State: 17 productive plants · Amazonas State: 1 prodcutive plant

Rio Grande do Sul: 2 productive plants · Espírito Santo State : 1 productive plant

Minas Gerais State: 2 productives plant · Ceará: 1 productive plant

Source: Authors' elaboration based on (dos Santos Rocha and Togeiro de Almeida 2007).

a natural-resources-intensive activity, making use of high levels of nonrenewable fossil resources (oil and natural gas) and water, resulting in a high potential for pollution. Moreover, the environmental control in this sector is crucial because the petrochemicals products are used as intermediate goods by a great variety of final manufacturers, presenting a huge potential for spillover effects of environmental impacts.

Table 10.3. **Petrochemical Companies Sample: Production Profile**

Companies	Main Products	Production Capacity, 2000 Ton/Year	Number of Plants, 2000	Export, Average for 1999–2000 Percent of Yearly Production
National				
Acrinor	acrylonitrile	88,000	1	49
Copene	ethene, benzene and propene	1,200,000[a]	1	8.6
Copesul	ethene, benzene and propene	1,135,000[a]	1	11
Deten	alkilbenzenes	170,000	1	nd
Metacril	ammonium sulfate and methyl methacrylate	45,000[b]	1	19.3
OPP-Triken	resins, polypropylene, low-density polyethylene, high-density polyethylene, linear low-density polyethylene, ethylene vinyl acetate copolymer, vinyl polychloride, chlorine and sodium hydroxide	1,390,000	9	51
Oxiteno	ethene oxide, polyethyleneglycol and fatty acids ethoxylated	302,000[c]	5	25.1
Petroflex	polybutadiene and styrene-butadiene rubber	275,800[d]	3	4.2
Petroquímica Triunfo	*ethylene copolymer, vinyl acetate and low-density polyethylene*	150,000[e]	1	66.7
Petroquímica União	ethene, benzene and propene	500,000[a]	1	8.7
Polibrasil	polypropylene	430,000	3	15.3
Policarbonatos	polycarbonate	13,500	1	24.3
Unipar	cumene and isodecanol	183,000[f]	1	17.5
Total 1		**5,882,300**	**29**	
Foreign				
Bayer	acrylonitrile	88,000	1	11.6
Columbian	carbon black	173,000	1	5
DSM	EPM/EPDM rubber	25,000	1	50
Total 2		**286,000**	**3**	
National/Foreign				
Carbocloro	chorine and sodium hydroxide	253,000[g]	1	6
Total 3		**253,000**	**1**	
Total 1+ 2 +3		**6,421,300**	**33**	–

Source: Author's elaboration based on (Togeiro de Almeida 2001).
[a] Production capacity of ethene. [b] Production capacity of ammonium sulfate. [c] Production capacity of ethene oxide. [d] Production capacity of styrene-butadiene rubber. [e] Production capacity of low-density polyethylene. [f] Production capacity of cumene. [g] Production capacity of chlorine. [h] For the year 1997. [i] Average for 1998–99.

Figure 10.2. Petrochemical Industry: Sample Geographical Distribution

Pernambuco State: 1 productive plant

Alagoas State: 2 productive plants

Bahia State: 9 productive plants

Rio de Janeiro State: 2 productive plants

São Paulo State: 12 productive plants

Rio Grande do Sul: 7 productive plants

Source: Authors' elaboration base on (Togeiro de Almeida 2001).

The environmental impacts of petrochemicals production depend on the technical specifics of each petrochemicals complex configuration, each firm and plant and obviously, on the local environmental-absorption capacity. In any case, it is possible to identify the main environmental problems potentially generated by petrochemicals production as atmospheric emissions, liquid effluents and solid wastes. Of special concern are hazardous wastes for which specific disposal treatment is required, as they can cause soil and water contamination with serious consequences for the environment and public health.

The sampled petrochemicals firms operated in different segments of the petrochemicals production—basics, intermediate and final goods (see their products in Table 10.2)—and had plants in different locations (see Figure 10.2). So, considering all specifics involved, the analysis of the empirical findings of this case study were carefully contextualized.

Besides the information provided by the companies themselves and by the Brazilian Chemical Industry Association, this case study was also based on reports from the main offices of the environmental control agencies in the three states where these petrochemicals complexes are located (Sao Paulo, Bahia and Rio Grande do Sul).

It must be pointed out that the petrochemicals case study was originally conducted as an illustrative case for a doctoral thesis that was not exclusively focused on comparing environmental performance of domestic and foreign companies, but generally focused on the importance of the international context to foster domestic environmental commitments.[5] This is one of the reasons for the reduced number of foreign companies in this sample. The other reason is that, as mentioned above, the petrochemicals case study was developed in the context of the privatization-and-concentration process in this sector that resulted in a reduced number of foreign firms in the Brazilian petrochemicals industry.

The main questions addressed in the study cases on pulp-and-paper and petrochemicals sectors in Brazil were:

1. What was the level of the environmental control system in these sectors? Was there any evidence of falling behind international standards in the sense of the "pollution havens" hypothesis?
2. What was the profile of the leading companies in environmental management systems? Were they big, exporters, foreign companies?
3. What were the driving forces in firms' commitments towards environmental improvements? Were they most related to international environmental requirements or domestic environmental regulations?

The assessment of the environmental control system in both sectors was based on emission indicators provided by the companies or the state environmental control agencies[6] and several quantitative and qualitative indicators referred to the firm's environmental management system such as[7]: if the environmental department was well integrated to other firm's departments; if the company had clearly established objectives and goals to environmental control, under ISO 14001 certificate or not; which environmental-related initiatives had been already introduced; the percentage of environmental investments out of total investments; and which were the firm's procedures to get updates on environmental regulations (through written notifications by the state environmental control agency, through online database on environmental regulations etc.).

Taking into account all the indicators—quantitative and qualitative—it was possible to assess each firm's environmental control system, whether it followed a preventive or corrective approach to environmental impacts, and how it could be classified according to the following three levels:

1. *Initial level* (★): environmental management focused mainly on pollution control through 'end-of-pipe' treatment technologies, which is a curative rather than preventive approach.
2. *Intermediary level* (★★): includes efforts to prevent pollution; the firm is continuously making efforts to upgrade its environmental performance, reducing or eliminating wastes and effluents, introducing systems to reuse wastes and effluents to save water, energy, raw material, and so on.
3. *Advanced level* (★★★): besides the introduction of management systems for controlling the environmental impacts of the production process, it includes all the impacts at any point of the product life cycle as well. The environmental impacts are controlled by the selection of raw materials, up to and through the distribution and the final disposal of the product by consumers. The purpose is to recover, reuse and recycle the materials used in the production process and the product after its consumption.

Some firms could also be at a *transitional level*, presenting characteristics of more than one level at the same time, i.e., transitioning from the initial to the intermediary level or from that to the advanced level.

Empirical Findings

Concerning the first question addressed—if the environmental control systems in these sectors were falling behind international standards—the evidences were against this hypothesis.

In the case of the pulp-and-paper sector, the indicator of environmental management systems showed that all companies were at least at the intermediary level (see Table 10.4). Precisely, among the nine sampled firms, five were at the intermediary level and four at the advanced level. All the sampled companies had at least one plant certified with ISO 14001; seven counted their environmental investments between 2002–2004, showing that they were taking initiatives to control their environmental impacts. Considering emissions indicators for the most important environmental problems of the industrial phase of the pulp-and-paper sector—such as, high demand for

Table 10.4. **Environmental Management System in the Pulp-and-Paper Sector**

Companies	Certification		Environmental Investments, Average for 2002–2004[a] Percent of Yearly Total Investments	Environmental Management Level
	ISO 14001	Certified Plants		
National				
Aracruz	yes	2 from 2	1.38	II —> III
Klabin	yes	4 from 18	11.73	II —> III
Ripasa	yes	1 from 4	4	II
Suzano Bahia Sul	yes	1 from 3	7.18	II —> III
Votorantim	yes	2 from 4	9.77	II
Foreign				
Cenibra	yes	1 from 1	2.79	II —> III
Internacional Paper	yes	1 from 2	34	II
Norske Skog	yes	1 from 1	–	II
Rigesa	yes	1 from 9	–	II

Source: (dos Santos Rocha and Togeiro de Almeida 2007).
[a] Klabin and Aracruz presented data for years 2003, 2004 and 2005; Cenibra had data only for 2005.

water and energy, generation of toxic effluents and malodorous smell—all firms were complying with emissions regulations or even presenting a better environmental performance.[8]

The assessment of the environmental control system of the Brazilian petrochemicals sector also did not corroborate the hypothesis of "pollution havens." Considering all the evidence, 12 out of 17 firms (71 percent of the sample) had already exceeded the initial level of environmental management system (see Table 10.5). Precisely, among the sampled firms: five (30 percent) were still at the first environmental management level; seven (41 percent) were transitioning to the intermediary level; one firm (6 percent) was at the intermediary level and four (23.5 percent) were approaching the advanced level. The sampled petrochemicals companies were predicting a regulatory context of more stringent environmental requirements and so they were compelled to catch up with international environmental standards. This trend was evidenced by the following indicators: (1) the firms presented significant percentage of environmental investments out of total investments (around 10 percent), (2) 65 percent of the firms were subscribers of the Corporate Environmental Program of the chemical industry (Responsible Care Program) for five or more years, and (3) 41 percent were certified with ISO 14001.[9]

Table 10.5. **Environmental Management System in the Petrochemical Sector**

Companies	Certification		Environmental Investments, Average for 1997–1999	Environmental Management Level
	ISO 14001	Certified Plants	Percent of Yearly Total Investments	
National				
Acrinor	–	–	17,5[a]	I
Copene	–	–	0,4	I—>II
Copesul	yes	1 from 1	–	II—>III
Deten	yes	1 from 1	–	I—>II
Metacril	–	–	5,3	I
OPP-Triken	yes	9 from 9	50,4[b]	II—>III
Oxiteno	–	–	4,5	I—>II
Petroflex	yes	3 from 3	3,0	I—>II
Petroquímica Triunfo	–	–	–	I—>II
Petroquímica União	–	–	0,2[c]	I—>II
Polibrasil	yes	3 from 3	2,1	II
Policarbonatos	–	–	5,1[c]	I
Unipar	–	–	9,2	I
Foreign				
Bayer	–	–	21,9[a]	I —> II
Columbian	–	–	–	I
DSM	yes	1 from 1	–	II —> III
National/Foreign				
Carbocloro	yes	1 from 1	0,3[c]	II —> III

Source: Authors' elaboration based on (*Togeiro de Almeida 2001*).
[a] Available data just for 1998 and 1999.
[b] It also includes the investments in health and work security.
[c] Environmental investment/net revenue in 1998 and 1999.

With respect to the second question addressed in the two case studies, about the profile of the leading companies in environmental performance, one common finding to both cases is that the TNC companies were not always ahead of the domestic ones. In the case of the pulp-and-paper sector, the findings were quite the opposite, i.e., in general, the national firms were leading this process. Considering emissions indicators for the most important environmental problems of the industrial phase of the pulp-and-paper sector, the sampled national firms presented an average of emissions lower than the TNCs in most of the cases, taking into account the specifics of each production segment.

The national firms were also ahead in terms of environmental management systems in the pulp-and-paper sector (see Table 10.5). Among the five local firms, three were moving to the advanced level of environmental management systems, while among the four foreign firms, only one was moving to this level.

In the petrochemicals case study, among the domestic firms, 69 percent had already exceeded the initial level of environmental management, including one large-size cracker (Copesul) that was implementing higher environmental commitments.[10] The shared-owned national-foreign firm was transitioning to the advanced environmental management level. Among the three sampled foreign firms, one was in transition to the advanced environmental management level, one was in transition from the first to the intermediate level and one was still at the first level. The two foreign firms that were lagging behind were relatively recent cases of acquisitions of national firms by foreign ones, which could explain why they were not yet aligned with the environmental management system at their respective matrix. Therefore, based on the data provided by the petrochemical case study, it is neither possible to state that TNCs companies were ahead the domestic firms in terms of environmental management system nor that they were deliberately falling behind the domestic firms. It is also important to remember that the presence of TNCs in the Brazilian petrochemicals industry decreased in the nineties and the sample of firms in this case study reflected this trend.

With respect to the size of the leading companies in environmental management, big firms were leading in pro-environmental commitments and small- and medium-size ones in both sectors were lagging behind. Nevertheless, the case studies found different evidence concerning the importance of the international markets to push for environmental commitments of the big companies. While in the pulp-and-paper sector, exporter firms were evidently the leaders, among the firms that were leading the environmental management in the petrochemicals sector, small exporters and large exporters at the initial level of environmental management were found (see Tables 10.2 and 10.3 for the firms' export performance). So, contradicting the pulp-and-paper case, the petrochemicals case study did not corroborate the hypothesis, widely emphasized in the literature, that exporter firms are the leaders in environmental management.

Still, on the profile of the leading firms, a common finding in both case studies was that the leaders in environmental management were also ahead in terms of quality management. From the petrochemicals sample, only two firms had not yet been certified by ISO 9000 and, coincidentally, they were not subscribers to the Responsible Care Program certified by ISO 14001 either, and they were at the first level of environmental management. In the pulp-and-paper sector, the leading companies in environmental management were exactly those ahead in technological innovations.

Summing up, based on data provided by the pulp-and-paper and petrochemicals case studies, the profile of the leading firms in environmental management included large-size firms, national rather than foreign ones (in the petrochemicals, this was probably due to the case study context), with advanced quality management systems and varied export performance.

Finally, concerning the third question addressed in the pulp-and-paper and petrochemicals case studies—about the driving forces in firms' commitments towards environmental improvements—the importance of domestic environmental regulations was highly emphasized by the companies from both sectors. Moreover, and particularly in the case of the pulp-and-paper sector, environmental requirements arising from international markets were also pushing for higher environmental commitments. In this sector, and especially in the pulp segment, national producers are big exporters and, since the end of 1980s, they had been facing increasing competitive pressure related to environmental requirements. So, to preserve their market shares, they started to invest in forest and industrial certification systems, to introduce updated technologies for controlling and preventing pollution and to implement measures to reduce resources consumption.

In the petrochemicals sector, contradictory evidence was found, with big exporters lagging behind in environmental issues, but leading companies with varied export performance, in environmental management systems (see Table 10.3). It means that the petrochemicals firms' environmental commitments were not correlated to environmental requirements arising from international markets, i.e., their environmental commitments were regulatory-driven rather than market-driven. Although petrochemicals firms were usually induced by domestic environmental regulations to introduce environmental innovations in their methods and production processes, they were also

Table 10.6. **Environmental Control: Comparing Petrochemicals and Pulp-and-Paper Sectors**

Environmental Control	Petrochemicals	Pulp and Paper
Level	Intermediary, against "pollution haven" hypothesis	Intermediary to advanced, against "pollution haven" hypothesis
Leading Firms	National and foreign, large sized, varied export performance	Most national, large sized, exporter
Driving Forces	Regulatory-driven	Market-driven

envisaging economic opportunities of cost-reduction as a consequence of such compliance. Additionally, the sampled petrochemicals firms seemed to be concerned about their external image in the sense that potential investors would not be attracted if they perceived any risk of hidden environmental costs associated with their investments.

A summary of the empirical findings for the three main questions addressed in these two case studies is presented in the Table 10.6.

Final Remarks

In neither case is there evidence to support the thesis that TNCs' environmental performance is ahead of domestic firms' performance, or that TNCs are using Brazil as a "pollution haven." It means that, in general, domestic firms in these sectors are just as environmentally friendly as foreign firms.

Several factors can explain this general trend of convergence in environmental performance between domestic and foreign firms, starting with the stringency of domestic environmental regulations towards sectors characterized by high pollution and natural-resource consumption potential. Firms in such sectors are compelled to establish and operate effective and efficient environmental management systems to comply with regulations under the continuous supervision of local environmental control agencies, customers, and the environmental movement in general. Additionally, and particularly in the pulp-and-paper sector, demand-driven environmental requirements arising from international markets can also explain such convergence.

Nevertheless, one factor seems to be especially important for policy considerations: Both sectors are historically characterized by domestic firms with high level of technological capacity, meaning that there is not a significant technological gap between the TNC affiliates and the local firms. Although technological knowledge is not a guarantee of a high level of environmental performance, it seems to be a necessary condition for this. For instance, in both case studies, a high correlation was found between the existence of quality-management systems, technological innovations and environmental management systems. Furthermore, it is well-known that the technological capacity accumulated by domestic firms in these sectors is closely related to the state industrial policies historically applied to them, through incentives to the private firms, especially in the petrochemicals sector where Petrobras played an important role via technological spillover effects.

Drawing on the case studies briefly reported here, attracting FDI is not a guarantee of a higher level of sectoral environmental control, while an integrated policy approach to environmental, technological and industry capacity to strengthen national environmental control at the industry level is highly recommended.

Chapter Eleven

MISSING LINKS, DASHED HOPES: FDI SPILLOVERS AND SUSTAINABLE INDUSTRIAL DEVELOPMENT IN MEXICO'S SILICON VALLEY

Lyuba Zarsky and Kevin Gallagher

Introduction

Foreign direct investment has been studied for its impacts on development and its impacts on environment, but rarely for both at the same time. Despite an occasional nod to the environment, development scholarship as a whole tends to focus on economic goals—growth, industry upgrading or poverty alleviation. Environmental analysts, on the other hand, often take the economic benefits (or costs) of foreign direct investment (FDI) as a given and seek to uncover evidence of negative or positive externalities for the natural environment.

Using a case study methodology, this paper examines the impacts of FDI on sustainable industrial development—an integrated concept combining economic, environmental and social outcomes. We define sustainable industrial development as evolution along a three-dimensional path delineated by: (1) upgrading of the productive capacities of domestic firms; (2) employment creation, and (3) reduction of the ecological and health impacts of industrial growth and transformation.

For FDI to promote sustainable industrial development, transnational corporations (TNCs) must be linked to local firms, workers and consumers. In particular, they must generate—and host-country firms must absorb—two kinds of knowledge spillovers: technology and skills relevant to domestic industry upgrading and technology and management practices that reduce the ecological footprint of industry. A widespread and dynamic process of industry upgrading, in turn, generates high employment. Without spillovers, especially to local small- and medium-size firms (SMEs), the benefits of FDI tend to be narrowly concentrated in a few, usually urban, enclaves.

Our case study focuses on FDI inflows from US firms into the information technology (IT) sector in Guadalajara, Mexico. Dubbed "Silicon Valley South," Guadalajara attracted a host of IT firms from the US after the signing of NAFTA in 1994. Expectations were raised that Mexico's second largest city would become a knowledge-intensive, high value-added, high-employment cluster for the global information technology industry. Positive environmental externalities—cutting-edge environmental technology, best-practice environmental management, less toxic and chemical waste—were expected as part of the equation.

This paper examines whether FDI in the IT industry in Guadalajara generated spillovers for industry upgrading and the environment. Based on extensive interviews with company managers and government officials, as well as NGOs, we found that spillovers were meager to nonexistent. The primary reason was that, rather than build local linkages, MNCs relied on foreign firms for manufacturing, which in turn sourced inputs from their global supply chains. Rather than upgrading, Mexican SME's went out of business, virtually obliterating Guadalajara's fledgling domestic IT manufacturing capacity. Lacking local linkages, many MNCs shifted production from Guadalajara to China during the industry crisis in 2001, especially after China joined the WTO. Rather than a knowledge-intensive cluster, Guadalajara today is a low-value assembly and subassembly platform for computers and other electronics exported to the United States that is largely divorced from the domestic economy.

Few local business linkages limited the potential for environmental spillovers to local supply firms. Moreover, targeted at US markets, Mexican-based manufacturing has generally not been retooled to meet higher European (and Mexican) environmental standards for the IT industry. Some employment potential remains, but it is low compared to what a high-value cluster would have been able to generate and still has not recovered to precrisis levels.

This chapter is in four sections. The first section presents, defines and evaluates evidence that FDI generates spillovers in developing countries that promote industry upgrading and better environmental management. The second section analyzes the particular challenges for sustainable industrial development posed by the global information technology (IT) industry. The third section presents a case study of FDI spillovers in the IT sector in Guadalajara. In conclusion, the fourth section makes policy recommendations to increase FDI spillovers for sustainable industrial development in developing countries.

FDI Spillovers: Theory and Evidence

MNCs are considered to possess a "bundle of assets"—technology, technical and management expertise, links to global markets—that makes FDI more productive and more environmentally sustainable than domestic investment in developing countries. Because many of these special assets are a source of rents, MNCs work to keep them tightly in-house. Nonetheless, some knowledge "spills over" outside the firm.

Host-country knowledge spillovers from FDI can potentially be captured by:

1. MNC subsidiaries
2. Other firms in the same industry as the MNC (horizontal spillovers)
3. Downstream suppliers to the MNC (vertical spillovers)
4. Firms in upstream market and other industries

Except for MNC subsidiaries, whose access to knowledge is directly determined by their corporate parents, knowledge spillovers may occur in five ways:

1. *Human capital*: MNCs hire and train workers who can apply their technical and management knowledge in starting their own firms or in working for domestic firms in the same industry.
2. *Demonstration effects*: Domestic firms may adopt and produce technologies introduced by MNCs through imitation or reverse engineering. They may also adopt productivity-enhancing standards in relation to inputs, product quality and environmntal and labor management.
3. *Backward linkages*: Domestic suppliers to MNCs may receive technical training to meet product specifications and global quality and environmental standards. If MNCs purchase a substantial volume of inputs locally, and/or if they help their local suppliers find additional export markets, local suppliers may also capture economies of scale, thus increasing productivity and potentially "crowding in" domestic investment.
4. *Forward linkages*: MNC-produced goods and services may enter into and increase the labor and resource efficiency of production processes of firms in upstream and other industries.

While the hope is that developing countries attract "quality" FDI that generates a "virtuous circle" of higher productivity, increasing skills, industry upgrading and better environmental management, it is possible that MNCs will instead transfer out-of-date technologies and inefficient management practices which lock developing countries into dead-end, dirty, nonglobally competitive growth paths. In addition, FDI may have *negative* spillovers—driving local firms out of business—leading to de-skilling, de-industrialization and loss of local jobs and livelihoods.

Spillovers for industry upgrading

Over the past thirty years, a large literature has emerged to determine empirically whether, and in what circumstances, FDI generates knowledge spillovers for industry upgrading (see, for example, Aitken and Harrison 1999; Blomstrom, Globerman et al. 1999; Amsden and Chu 2003; Lall and Urata 2003; Moran, Graham et al. 2005) . Most statistical studies focus on *horizontal spillovers*—improved performance of domestic firms in the same industry as the MNCs. Using cross-sectional, industry-level data in a single year, early studies found that industries with a higher concentration of FDI were more productive (Caves 1974; Blomstrom 1983; Blomstrom and Wolff 1994).

Later studies, using both industry- and firm-level data, found far less optimistic results (Kokko 1996; Aitken and Harrison 1999; Keller 2003; Smarzynska 2003). In a review of 40 studies spanning both developed and developing countries, a World Bank paper found that only six of the 40 studies found evidence of positive spillovers (Görg and Greenaway 2004). *None* were in developing countries. Moreover, six of the 28 studies of developing and transition economies found evidence of *negative* spillovers.

Case studies present a more optimistic, though still mixed, assessment. Amsden and Chu (2003) found that partnerships with MNCs in the 1960s and 1970s helped build globally competitive electronics firms in Taiwan. But Barclay (2003) found that substantial inflows of FDI in the 1990s failed to stimulate domestic development in the natural gas industry in Trinidad and Tobago (Barclay 2003). Ernst (2003, 4) found that, despite large MNC investment in its electronics sector, "Malaysia has failed to develop a sufficiently diversified and deep industrial structure, to induce a critical mass of corporate investment in specialized skills and innovative capabilities."

Given that MNCs seek to prevent knowledge leakages to competitors, but want and need to transfer it to local suppliers, spillovers are more likely to be vertical than horizontal (Saagi 2002). A study of FDI in Lithuania, for example, found evidence of positive vertical spillovers in the manufacturing sector (Smarzynska 2003). Case studies, too, provide some support for vertical spillovers. In Mexico, FDI by the "big three" US car companies in the 1980s worked to upgrade technology and global competitiveness of auto supply firms (Moran 1998). Singapore heavily depended on MNC investment to successfully develop a dense network of local supply firms in its electronics sector in the 1970s and 1980s (Moran 1998; Wong 2003).

Other case studies, however, have found that MNCs generate few backward linkages or spillovers to local firms. In northern Mexico, one study found that despite twenty-five years of FDI, Mexican material inputs accounted for less than 2 per cent of value added in *maquiladora* plants. Based on surveys with plant managers and corporate purchasing agents, the study found that MNC purchasing strategies favored imports over domestic firms (Brannon, James et al. 1994).

Generally, Latin American governments have adopted a passive policy approach to FDI, with the result that MNCs have few linkages with local firms. One recent study concluded (Ernst 2005: 11):

Economic opening in Argentina, Brazil and Mexico did not lead to export dynamism and had a disappointing impact on employment... only Mexico experienced an export surge in manufacturing production and employment during the second half of the 1990s, mainly due to the booming maquiladora sector. However, the maquiladora industry did not develop significant links with the rest of the economy. There was no upgrading of production even for the more sophisticated exports, since the import content of exports also rose significantly. Moreover, the maquiladora industry has declined significantly since 2000 thus reducing drastically formal job creation in Mexico.

The performance of FDI in Asia has been more mixed. Wong (2003) documents the positive role of FDI in the development of globally competitive high-tech industries in Singapore. "About three-quarters of Singapore's manufacturing output in recent years came from MNC's...technology transfer was the major source of technological upgrading in Singapore, not indigenous research and development" (Wong 2003: 194).

Unlike Latin American countries, Singapore adopted a proactive approach that integrated FDI into an overall development strategy with aggressive support for R&D, education, infrastructure investment and science and technology policies. MNCs have also helped to promote industry upgrading in the IT sector in China and the automotive components sector in India (Dussel Peters 2005; Tewari 2005). In both cases, government was highly proactive toward both FDI and domestic SMEs.

As a whole, the evidence suggests that there is no assurance that FDI generates spillovers for industry upgrading. Central to the capture of spillovers is proactive, coherent government industry policy.

Environmental spillovers: Theory and evidence

FDI potentially delivers three types of environmental spillovers for sustainable industrial development:

1. *Clean technology transfer*: Transfer to MNC affiliates of production technologies which are less polluting and more input-efficient production than those used by domestic firms.
2. *Technology leapfrogging*: Transfers of state-of-the-art production and pollution-control technologies.
3. *Pollution halo*: Diffusion of best-practice environmental management techniques to domestic firms, including suppliers.

Empirical studies have found a "mixed bag" in all three areas. A detailed case study of FDI in Chile's mining sector in the 1970s and 1980s found that the two foreign-owned companies performed (far) better than domestic companies, largely due to cleaner technology (Lagos 1999). Using survey methodology, a study of MNCs in India's manufacturing sector likewise found that foreign firms were less polluting than domestic firms (Ruud 2002). Using energy use per unit of output as a proxy for energy emissions, one World Bank study found that foreign ownership was associated with cleaner and lower levels of energy use in Mexico, Venezuela and Cote d'Ivoire (Eskeland 1997).

Another group of World Bank researchers, however, found that foreign firms and plants performed no better than domestic companies in developing countries. Based on firm-level data in Mexico (manufacturing) and Asia (pulp and paper), the New Ideas in Pollution Regulation group found firm environmental performance to depend not on foreign ownnership, but on (1) the scale of the plant (bigger is better), and (2) the strength of local regulation, both government and "informal" (Hettige 1996; Dasgupta, Hettige et al. 1997). In addition, a study of the manufacturing sector in Korea found that domestic firms performed *better* than foreign-owned firms, a result the authors attributed to the sensitivity of Korean *chaebol* to public criticism (Aden 1999).

The Global IT Industry: Challenges to Sustainable Industrial Development

Foreign direct investment in the IT industry is very attractive to developing countries. Beyond benefits common to all FDI, such as jobs and foreign exchange, high-tech FDI offers the promise of industry upgrading: new technology, new skills and a link with the world's fastest-growing industry. Moreover, IT promises a "clean and green" alternative compared to traditional smokestack industries. There are formidable barriers, however, to upgrading industry in the IT sector, and significant health and environmental hazards to address.

Challenges for domestic industry upgrading

The global IT industry is structured in three layers which function as a global production network. At the top are the global "flagships"—companies like HP, Dell, IBM—who bring brand name, global marketing and design capacities to the network and who earn the highest profits. Next are the contract manufacturers (CMs)—large firms like Flextronics, Jabil Circuit, and SCI-Sanmina—who assemble components into a variety of electronic products under contract to global flagships and who increasingly are also undertaking design functions.[1] The CMs purchase inputs from components suppliers, themselves ranging from large firms with substantial manufacturing capacities to small SMEs and mom-and-pop outfits. CMs and suppliers operate on low to razor-thin margins.

The global IT industry is highly concentrated, creating barriers to entry for would-be flagships, CMs, and even higher-level suppliers. Nurtured by highly proactive industry policies, only a handful of developing countries—China, Taiwan, Korea, India—have emerged as major players, "The domination of the United States and Asia in electronics," argues Amsden, "makes it very difficult for newcomers to enter this field" (Amsden 2004). Even in East Asia, it is not clear that important producers like Malaysia and Singapore will be able to meet the challenge of continuous upgrading in the face of the intense competitive dynamics of the industry itself, as well as new competition from China and India (Ernst 2003; Wong 2003).

The primary route for developing countries trying to build a local IT industry is to attract FDI in low-wage export platforms for low- and semi-skilled manufacturing and assembly operations. The plants are owned and operated by foreign CMs and higher-tier suppliers and, in the main, products are exported to markets in US, Europe or Japan. Production is highly standardized but the hope is that knowledge spillovers and MNC procurements will nurture the emergence of a local supply base.[2]

While the promise is palpable, there are four pitfalls. First, competition for IT investment is intense, both among developing (and developed) countries and municipalities. Many developing countries simply do not have the requisite infrastructure, skills and large domestic markets to successfully attract high-tech FDI in the first place. Trying can impose opportunity costs.

Second, intense cost pressures inside the industry undermine the sustainability of low-wage assembly work. CMs tend to rapidly relocate operations to lower-cost locations when global conditions change. Even China, which successfully leverages its cheap labor and domestic market access to build a burgeoning CM industry, is vulnerable. Asked by one of the authors how much of his company's southern China operations would relocate if land and infrastructure subsidies were withdrawn, the head of Asia operations for Flextronics responded, "about 50 percent." Where to? Vietnam.

A third pitfall is that there is little skill acquisition and hence few human-capital spillovers in assembly work. Because an initial level of training is required, assembly workers have been called "semi-skilled." But there is no chance to get further training and little opportunity for workers to innovate on-the-job. Organized into work groups, workers undertake highly standardized and repetitive tasks. Indeed, global standardization and uniformity of work procedures is a defining feature of CMs, who "offer a uniform interface for flagships seeking global one-stop-shopping for manufacturing services" (Luthje 2003: 9).

Fourth, FDI by foreign IT firms may not generate sufficient knowledge spillovers to promote technological upgrading of local firms seeking to become suppliers. Unlike licensing arrangements with MNCs, FDI does not necessarily or directly transfer technology. Besides human capital, spillovers are indirectly captured through backward and forward linkages. But CMs draw inputs from a global supply chain and may have few backward linkages to local firms. Moreover, a neoliberal "hands off" policy framework inhibits governments from helping local firms develop capacities to become suppliers.

A substantial level of infrastructure, manufacturing and innovation capabilities is required to garner MNC interest in sourcing from domestic suppliers. Few developing countries have such "absorptive capacities." Indeed, the focus of the UNIDO report quoted above is precisely "to determine why many developing countries are unable to use new industrial technologies efficiently" (UNIDO 2002: 10). The answer, in a nutshell, is the lack of institutions to nurture local skill acquisition and manufacturing capabilities.

Spillovers will also be scarce if forward linkages are weak. But a single-minded focus on production-for-export inhibits the growth of a domestic market for IT goods and the benefits of IT domestic diffusion, including the spur to product innovation. The lack of a strong domestic market, in turn, makes it more likely that flagships and CMs will be footloose—and less likely that they will be willing to partner with local governments and firms to transfer technology and know-how.

Environmental challenges

Given its "clean and green" image, the IT sector is often a low priority for regulation or monitoring in developing countries. Regulation, however, is important on two counts: (1) there are significant health and environmental problems associated with IT manufacturing and assembly and (2) global environmental standards for IT products are rising rapidly.

The IT industry poses risks to occupational and community health stemming from the highly toxic chemicals used in production and assembly. At the center of all IT products is a microchip—a highly manufactured silicon wafer on which hundreds or even thousands of transistors have been etched. Beyond water and energy, microchip fabrication requires an intensive use of a wide variety of solvents, acid solutions and alcohol. A survey by the US Environmental Protection Agency (EPA) in 1995 listed thirty-one categories of chemicals used in photolithography alone, one of the last stages of manufacturing (Mazurek 1999: 52).

While somewhat less chemical-intensive, the component manufacturing and assembly parts of the IT global production network expose workers to some of the same hazardous substances, including solvents. Moreover, they pose new occupational health risks in the form of exposure to lead and formaldehyde. Assembly involves plating copper and soldering components to the plates with lead and tin. The copper plating process emits formaldehyde while the soldering process produces lead "solder drass" that is highly contaminating, especially if its ends up in local waterways (Kuehr 2003).

A newer but possibly even greater hazard is the widespread use of brominated flame-retardants, such as the compound polybrominated diphenyl ether (PBDE). Workers routinely add brominated flame-retardants to a wide variety of IT goods, including circuit boards and plastics in computer cabinets, to reduce flammability. The compounds are bioaccumulative and are rapidly rising in human breast milk in North America. While toxicology studies are still being undertaken, there is evidence that exposure is linked to thyroid hormone disruption, neurodevelopmental deficits, and possibly cancer (Kuehr 2003).

A second environmental challenge of the IT industry is end-of-life product management. When consumers have finished with a computer—often replacing it with a newer, faster version—a computer becomes waste. In landfills, chemicals and other hazardous substances inside a computer—lead, arsenic, selenium, brominated flame-retardants, antimony trioxide, cadmium, chromium, cobalt, mercury—leach into land and water. In the US, about 70 percent of the heavy metals found in landfills, including mercury and cadmium, comes from electronic products. In 2001 California and Massachusetts banned CRTs from municipal landfills, BAN (Basel Action Network) and SVTC (Silicon Valley Toxics Coalition) 2002).

In an effort to reduce landfill hazards, the EPA and municipal governments have promoted computer recycling. A vibrant e-recycling industry has sprung up in the US. About 11 percent of US e-waste is recycled. However, about

80 percent of the e-waste sent to recyclers is exported to Asia, nine-tenths of it to China, where computers are pulled apart by hand, useful components sold, and the rest thrown into landfills, waste dumps or just the nearest piece of empty land (BAN (Basel Action Network) and SVTC (Silicon Valley Toxics Coalition) 2002).[3]

With its witches brew of lead, heavy metals and toxic chemicals, the production and disposal of IT products pose hazards to workers and the environment wherever they occur. But there are extra hazards in developing countries stemming from lack of waste-management infrastructure and regulatory oversight. The scarce resources of environment ministries prioritize "dirtier" industries, leaving IT firms to self-regulate.

Occupational health standards in particular tend to be sketchy or nonexistent in developing countries. In Thailand in the early 1990s, for example, four workers at a Seagate disk drive facility died after a pattern of fatigue and fainting. A study by the country's most prominent occupational health doctor found that some 200 plant employees had blood levels that suggested chronic lead poisoning, perhaps aggravated by exposure to solvents (Foran 2001).

Even a relatively well-off industrializing country like Taiwan has suffered the effects of toxic chemical use. In a study of the Hsinchu Science-Based Industrial Park, the heart of Taiwan's high-tech industry, the Taiwan Environmental Action Network found a shocking pattern of neglect of risks to human health and the environment, starting from the 1960s and continuing through to 2001. The legacy of Taiwan's spectacularly successful high-tech development is a cohort of former employees with a high rate of rare cancers, and a severe and widespread problem of freshwater and coastal chemical pollution (Shang 2003).

Rising EU standards: Globalization or bifurcation?

Environmental regulation is important not only to protect workers and the public but as part of industry policy. With public concern mounting, national and municipal authorities in Europe, Japan and the United States, as well as companies themselves, are undertaking a wide range of regulatory and voluntary initiatives to reduce chemical hazards and electronic waste and to improve energy and resource efficiency.

The European Union, however, has gone the farthest towards "raising the bar" in terms of environmental regulation of the IT industry, as well as hazardous chemicals in general. A signatory to Annex One of the Basel Convention, which prohibits the export of hazardous waste from developed countries, EU regulation is focused on reducing the amount of waste entering, produced, and stored in Europe.

Along with new sweeping regulation of chemicals, two EU directives have changed the rules for IT market access in Europe:

1. **Restriction on Hazardous Substances** (RoHS). The RoHS Directive, which went into effect on July 1, 2006, bans the placing on the EU market of new electrical and electronic equipment containing more than agreed levels of lead, cadmium, mercury, hexavalent chromium, and the flame-retardants polybrominated biphenyl (PBB) and polybrominated diphenyl ether (PBDE).
2. **Directive on Waste from Electrical and Electronic Equipment** (WEEE). Adopted in the Spring of 2003, WEEE sets criteria for the collection, treatment, recycling and recovery of waste electrical and electronic equipment and makes producers responsible for financing most of these activities (producer responsibility).

Other large electronic markets, notably the United States and Japan, have not adopted such laws, at least not yet, giving rise to the possibility that global standards will bifurcate by end market. While there is mounting concern about landfill contamination from e-waste, the United States is not a signatory to Annex One of the Basel Convention. Indeed, the EPA views the export of e-waste to Asia as part of its industrial waste management strategy (BAN (Basel Action Network) and SVTC (Silicon Valley Toxics Coalition 2002).

On the other hand, MNCs may find it too costly to design products and processes around multiple standards, suggesting that globally harmonized standards might be in the making. The state of California, for example, has enacted its own version of RoHS, and the EPA is working with chemical manufacturers to phase out the most toxic of the brominated flame-retardants (Pohl 2004).

Full global harmonization may be in the cards in the future. In the short to medium term, however, IT markets will bifurcate along the lines of higher EU versus lower US environmental and health standards. Japan, which was the first country to pass a law requiring recycling of domestic e-products, is likely to be in between. Developing countries—and the MNCs that invest in them—will need to strategically align their environmental management policies with their export markets. If they choose markets with lower standards, they may be at risk of being squeezed out if and when standards are globally harmonized.

Mexico's Silicon Valley: Missing Spillovers, Missed Opportunity

Fuelled by liberalization, Guadalajara's small but promising IT industry boomed after the signing of NAFTA. Between 1994 and 2000, FDI in the

Figure 11.1. Guadalajara Electronics Exports and FDI

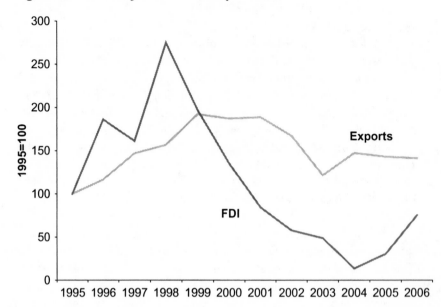
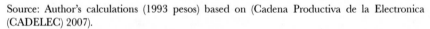

Source: Author's calculations (1993 pesos) based on (Cadena Productiva de la Electronica (CADELEC) 2007).

electronics sector grew by five times (reaching $742 million) and the value of exports quadrupled to $20 billion (though not as robustly in real terms, as shown in Figure 11.1). An influx of global flagships expanded or newly located in Guadalajara, including Hewlett Packard, IBM, Intel, Lucent Technologies and NEC. They were soon followed by CMs, including Flextronics, Solectron, Jabil Circuit and SCI-Sanmina. "High-Tech Jobs Transfer to Mexico with Surprising Speed," proclaimed the *Wall Street Journal* in an article dated April 9, 1998. To the Journal's surprise, Guadalajara had become home to a booming IT assembly industry that exported $7.7 billion worth of IT products in 1998 and seemed poised to become the IT manufacturing hub of North America.

It was a short-lived triumph. Between 2000 and 2003, the global flagships shut down all but sales and service operations of computers and perhipherals in Guadalajara, relocating to China or elsewhere in East Asia. Exports dropped by 60 percent, FDI fell by 123 percent, and 60,000 jobs were lost. By 2000 the cover of *MexicoNow*, a leading Mexican business magazine, bemoaned "Rescuing Mexico's Electronics Industry." The global firms have indeed recouped since 2003 through fairly impressive industrial upgrading from "hard" to "soft" tooling that entails greater worker skill, but such upgrading operates in a virtually complete enclave that has few connections to the domestic economy.

What happened to the promise of "Silicon South"? While fingers can be pointed toward a variety of government and market failures, the central problem can be summed up as the failure to capture FDI spillovers.

Enclave economy

Linked to MNCs, firms in Guadalajara built up substantial electronics manufacturing capacities under Mexico's import substitution industrialization (ISI) policies from the 1940s to the 1980s. By the early 1990s, close to fifty local firms were involved in electronics manufacturing, including CM assemblers, suggesting great promise for the emergence of an industry cluster with strong local linkages between MNCs and local suppliers (Shaiken 1990; Wilson 1992). According to Wilson (Wilson 1992: 120), it was just a matter of the government playing a nurturing role in capturing MNC spillovers:The Mexican government can increase the local linkages not only of the locally owned *maquiladoras* but also of some of the foreign-owned *maquiladoras*. In Guadalajara, the sector of locally owned producers and the sector of foreign owned electronics producers show particular potential.

In the event, government support did not materialize. Under the liberalization regime, the old ISI-type industry policies were rapidly dismantled. Little in the way of contemporary industry policy, which seeks to correct market failures, was put in its place. New approaches to industry policy aim squarely to help

Table 11.1. **IT Plant Closings—Wholly- or Partly-Owned Mexican Firms**

Firm	Ownership (percent)	Activity
Cumex Electronics	50/50 Mex-US	CM of PCBs
Mitel	51/49 Mex-Canada	Telephone Components
Phoenix International	50/50 Mex-US	Plastic Injection
Encitel	100 Mex	CM of PCBs
Info Spacio	100 Mex	CM of printers
Logix Computers	100 Mex	Design and manufacturer of PCs
Mexel	100 Mex	CM of PCBs
Unisys	100 Mex	CM of computers and peripherals
Electron	100 Mex	Design and manufacturer of PCs
Scale Computers	100 Mex	Design and manufacturer of PCs
Advanced Electronics	100 Mex	Design and Manufacturer of PCBs
Compuworld	100 Mex	CM of hard drives
Microtron	100 Mex	Buffers and Carton Packages

Source: Woo (2001); Rivera Vargas (2002); Author interviews.

build local firm capacities, including integrating into global MNC value chains. Policies include technical and business management training programs for local firms and workers, support for R&D to develop local niche markets, promotion of MNC-university partnerships to expand value-added, the creation of science and technology parks and the provision of credit to domestic firms.

Moreover, Mexican trade and monetary policies actively undermined MNC spillovers to local firms. The PITEX program allows companies to import inputs duty-free as long as more than 65 percent of the finished product is exported (Dussel Peters 2003). Not only does PITEX encourage MNCs to source from foreign suppliers, thus cutting off the potential for backward linkages, but in its tilt towards exports, it reduces the scope for forward linkages through sales in domestic markets (Dussel Peters, Paliza et al. 2003; Dussel Peters and Palacios 2004).

The capacity for Mexican firms to absorb spillovers was also constricted by macroeconomic policies—high interest rates and an overvalued peso—to support NAFTA and keep inflation at bay. The overvalued peso provided an additional incentive for CMs to source components globally rather than locally. High interests not only contributed to peso overvaluation but also choked off domestic investment. Foreign firms, including those in the IT sector, had access to internal company sources of finance and global capital markets. Domestic firms did not (Dussel Peters, Paliza et al. 2003; Dussel Peters and Palacios 2004).

The unsupportive policy environment for SMEs in Mexico was exacerbated by restructuring processes within the global IT industry. In the late 1980s, the global flagships began to outsource manufacturing functions, a trend that accelerated in the 1990s. Increasingly, they turned towards the "top five" CMs—Solectron, Flextronics, Sanmina-SCI, Celestica, and Jabil Circuit. Between 1995 and 2004, the "top five"—all US firms—grew by a roaring compound annual growth rate CAGR) of 24 percent and in 2004, accounted for just over half of world production by the top 100 CMs (Sturgeon 2006). In June 2007 Flextronics, now based in Singapore, bought its California-based rival, Solectron, creating a company that operates in 35 countries with a combined workforce of 200,000 and expected annual net revenues of $30 billion (Taylor 2007).

In the mid-1990s there was a small window of opportunity for Mexican CMs to take advantage of the flagships' shift to outsourcing, in the same way that firms in Taiwan had upgraded domestic industry by contracting with global flagships two decades earlier. Many Taiwanese firms are now among the leading global CMs, while others have grown into global flagships (Amsden and Chu 2003).

To seize the opportunity, Guadalajara-based firms would have had to expand their production scale significantly, which entails large sunk costs.

But SMEs had no access to credit. Between 1994 and 2003 total domestic credit as a percentage of Mexican GDP fell by 66 percent, the result of high interest rates and a dysfunctional financial system. Even more dramatically, credit to firms nosedived by almost 84 percent. In a survey of Mexican firms, the Bank of Mexico learned that an astonishing 82 percent were not able to access credit between 1998 and 2003. The majority were squeezed out by high interest rates, while the rest were simply rejected (UNIDO 2005). With access to internal sources of finance, as well as global capital markets, MNCs were exempted from the credit squeeze (Gallagher and Zarsky 2007).

Rather than explore the potential to contract with and help build capacities of Mexican CMs, the global flagships invited the "top five" to co-locate in Guadalajara. By the mid-1990s, US-based CM giants Jabil Circuit, Sanmina-SCI, Flextronics, and Solectron (along with NatSteel from Singapore) had established plants in Guadalajara and conducted virtually all of the manufacturing for HP and IBM and the other flagships (Sturgeon 2002).

Mexican CMs like Unisys had relied on local suppliers for up to 18 percent of their inputs. The "top five" CMs, on the other hand, have extensive global supply networks. Today, local firms supply a very limited range of CM inputs—cardboard boxes and shipping labels, cables and wires and disposal services. Over 95 percent of components used in CM assembly are imported (Gallagher and Zarsky 2007).

The result of the "double whammy"—changes in global industry strategy and Mexican policy—was the virtual wipeout of the local IT industry, including manufacturers, assemblers and suppliers. Between 1985 and 1997 the number of indigenous electronics firms in Guadalajara declined by 71 percent (Rivera Vargas 2002). And 13 of the 25 indigenous electronics firms that were still in existence at the end of 1997 had been closed by 2005 (Gallagher and Zarsky 2007). Thirteen of the twenty-five domestic firms still in existence at the end of 1997 had gone out of business by 2004. As one study (Rivera Vargas 2002: 171) concluded:

In the case of Guadalajara, what foreign investment has done is, first, to sweep away entrepreneurial capacity by pushing the endogenous electronics and computer industry out of the market. Second, foreign investment may limit the process of building scientific and technological capacities in the host country by demanding major emphasis in operational and manufacturing capabilities in detriment to the electronic design orientation.

From 2000–2002 the global flagships abandoned Guadalajara, relocating to China and other East Asian locations. There were two driving forces.

First, the industry suffered a crisis of overcapacity and stock prices fell dramatically. Second, China acceded to the WTO. Mexico had based its competitive advantage on the combination of geographical proximity to US markets and low wages relative to the US. But manufacturing wages in Mexico averaged $2.40 per hour in 2005, compared to 95 cents in China. Moreover, China offered both a well-developed local supplier base and a large and growing domestic IT market.

What remains in Guadalajara today is an IT enclave dominated by foreign CMs using imported inputs to assemble products for export to the US. There is still some employment potential: about 41,000 were employed in seven assembly plants in Guadalajara in June 2006, compared to 47,000 before the crisis (Sturgeon, 2006). Indeed, the foreign CMs have recovered to become the "just in time" assembly floor favorites for communication switches, internet firewalls and other more sophisticated and labor-intensive products headed for the United States. However, the dynamism that infused hopes of a high-growth, knowledge-intensive IT industry cluster that included spillovers to the domestic economy had evaporated. Without a significant change either in market conditions or government policies—or both—it is unlikely that Mexico will recapture it.

Environmental spillovers: Missing links, missing waste

As in most developing countries, Mexico's capacities for the regulation of industry are thin and the IT industry is not a high priority. On the contrary, the Mexican government had expectations of positive environmental spillovers from FDI. With the exception of broad rules applicable to all industries, such as the requirement to dispose of hazardous wastes and sulfur dioxide emissions off-site, the IT industry in Guadalajara blossomed in the 1990s largely in a regulatory void.

How did the IT industry fare in terms of delivering the three types of environmental spillovers identified above, viz., clean technology transfer, technology leapfrogging, and pollution halo?

Clean technology and best practice

Circuit board assembly operations based in Guadalajara use a considerable amount of lead in attaching components to copper plates. Moreover, the copper plating process emits formaldehyde and brominated flame-retardants. The on-site handling and storage of lead and the transport and "disposal" of hazardous wastes are important environmental and health management issues not only for workers, but also for local communities (Kuehr 2003).

An industry-wide regulation requires firms taking part in the *maquiladora* and PITEX programs to return toxic waste of production processes to their countries of origin. Since US companies dominate in the high-tech sector, this means shipping toxic waste across the border. IT production generates liquid wastes and scrap, comprised of solid waste and hazardous waste. The Mexican environmental agency Procuraduría Federal de Protección al Ambiente (PROFEPA) certified one firm, Environmental Electronics Recycling, to take and separate the scrap from IT manufacturing sites. The solid waste is sent to Japan, while the hazardous waste is sent to a treatment plant in Nuevo Leon or to the United States. Permits are needed for every transaction along the chain. Despite its limited monitoring capacity, PROFEPA uncovered a significant amount of fraud, including forged permits by unauthorized waste haulers (PROFEPA 2003).

How much of the hazardous electronic waste actually makes it to Nueva Leon or the United States? Separate data for the electronics industry are not available. One study found that, of the 60,000 tons of reported waste generated in 1996 that required special handling, 60 percent was returned to country of origin and 12 percent was kept in known locations in Mexico. However, the whereabouts of 26 percent of the waste was unknown (ECLAC 2003). Moreover, many firms do not report hazardous waste generation.

All five of the global flagships we interviewed in Guadalajara said that, during the period when they were conducting manufacturing or assembly operations in Guadalajara, they sent waste back to the US through certified waste handlers. However, none filed notices of hazardous waste return with Mexican authorities (TCPS 2004). All had in place an environmental management system (EMS) and environmental professionals on staff. All were ISO 14001 certified and some went beyond ISO to create their own EMS.

Facility-level data are not available. However, given different corporate cultures and policies, it is likely that environmental performance varied. HP, for example, is a recognized leader in global corporate social responsibility (CSR), while IBM, which has been sued by US workers claiming occupation-related illness, has a more mixed reputation. Lucent Technologies built a state-of-the-art facility in Guadalajara which employed 12,000 workers at its peak and was the first facility in Mexico designed to have zero effluents. They also installed an innovative wave soldering process, which replaced manual soldering and facilitated capture and recycling of solder dross. Unfortunately, Lucent's state-of-the-art facility went bust—a victim of the technology stock crash in the early 2000s (Gallagher and Zarsky 2007).

Like the flagships, few hard data are available about the environmental performance of CMs in Guadalajara, either in the period under study or today. All generate significant amounts of solder dross, lead and tin. All have an EMS and an environmental health and safety (EHS) unit, one has applied for Responsible Care certification and another is certified to ISO 18000. Like the flagships, CMs claim they sent hazardous waste back to the US through certified disposal services. However, only one—SCI-Sanmina—filed notices of hazardous waste return to Mexican authorities (TCPS 2004).

In addition to EMS, the majority of the plants—both flagships and CMs from the US—use relatively less energy and water. This is due to the plant vintage of the firms. Virtually all of the plants were constructed since 1994. Energy and water use are so very much part of the core production processes of IT firms that newer plants by nature are cleaner than older ones. However, when pollution is a function of end-of-pipe technologies it is not clear that a new plant will automatically be relatively less pollution intensive (Gallagher 2007). Guadalajara IT firms use formaldehyde, solder dross, and polybrominated diphenyl ether (PBDE)—end-of-pipe process pollutants which are less regulated and hardly inspected in Mexico. Based on our interviews with workers and representative groups, these pollutants are rife in Guadalajara (Partida 2006).

Given the difficulty in wielding the "stick" of inspections and fines, PROFEPA devised an innovative, facility-based, voluntary "carrot"-based certification approach to improve environmental performance in manufacturing industries— the Industria Limpia (clean industry) program. To obtain certification, firms must sign up, undergo an environmental audit and negotiate an action plan with PROFEPA. To stay in the program, firms must quantifiably demonstrate every three months that they remain in compliance with their plan goals. All firms must register on-site hazardous wastes with PROFEPA. The only IT firms that signed up, however, are SCI-Sanmina, IBM, HP and Motorola. Only SCI-Sanmina completed the process all the way to certification.

One shortcoming of the Industria Limpia certification is in the area of occupational health and safety. In May 2004 there was a toxic explosion at SCI-Sanmina just a few months after it was certified. The 400 people working on the shift were evacuated for an hour and 39 employees were taken to the hospital for respiratory or nervous system problems. Another shortcoming is that it doesn't exactly fit into the plans of the MNCs. The "prize" of Industria Limpia is what amounts to an eco-label so your products can be sought after by green consumers in Mexico. Given that the majority of IT (virtually all) of production is sent to the United States, there is little incentive to go for the prize.

Occupational heath and safety lags in all Mexican CMs. In one plant visited by the authors, the smell of solvents on the assembly floor was so overpowering that we had to leave after a few minutes. All CMs conduct blood tests for lead and urine tests for solvents at least twice a year. One firm uses the American Conference of Government Industrial Hygienists (ACGIH) standards that establish threshold limit values based on permissible exposure standards based on exposures of eight hrs/day, 40 hours/week and 20 years of working.

Given that CMs favor temporary, usually six-month contracts, benchmarking to such standards means that the companies simply avoid, rather than grapple with, the issue of worker health risk due to chemical exposure. For example, according to interviews with workers carried out by the UK-based Catholic Agency for Overseas Development CAFOD), women workers are subjected to regular and intrusive questioning to determine if they are pregnant. If they are pregnant, they are subject to immediate job termination. The short-term contracts disqualify them from maternity benefits (CAFOD 2004).

Generally, the picture that emerges is that MNC environmental performance was uneven. Some, like Lucent, clearly transferred clean technology and best practice. In the main, however, there is little evidence of environmental spillovers generated by clean technology transfer or best-practice management.

Pollution halo

Beyond the transfer of clean technology and good management to their own affiliates, MNCs can generate environmental spillovers to domestic firms through demonstration effects and requirements on local suppliers. Given the absence of local competitors, the primary channel for environmental spillovers in Guadalajara is the supply chain.

HP currently has a strong supply chain policy. Established in 2002, its Supply Chain Social and Environmental Responsibility (SER) Policy commits the company to "[working] with suppliers to ensure they operate in a socially and environmentally responsible manner." In 2004, in conjunction with Dell and IBM, HP took the lead in bringing together a coalition of eight flagship and CM firms that created and launched an Electronics Industry Code of Conduct. The Code outlines broad management standards for the electronics supply chain in the areas of labor rights, health and safety, and environment.

The implementation of HP's policy, however, may have missed Guadalajara. An EHS manager for HP in Guadalajara told us that their theory is to keep costs down and thus do not make demands on suppliers. One SME supplier confirmed that none of their flagship clients, including HP, had ever imposed any environmental requirements. However, HP Mexico was part of a small business group formed in 1993 to promote best practice, including ISO 14001, among manufacturing firms in Guadalajara.

Lucent created an industry association of flagships to develop local suppliers and improve their environmental performance. Lucent also participated in and contributed funds towards a World Bank project in 1997 and 1998 that aimed to train SMEs in environmental management. However, the project's success was mixed. In some cases, the mentoring foreign firms themselves did not have an EMS, reducing their capacity to positively influence and work with their suppliers (World Bank 1998).

The policies and good will of at least some of the flagships suggest that "pollution halo" environmental spillovers, at least theoretically, were on offer in Guadalajara. In the event, the lack of local business linkages mitigated against their capture. The flagships contracted with the CMs, who sourced almost nothing locally. Even if the CMs had imposed environmental requirements on suppliers—which they did not in the early 2000s—there would have been few spillovers to SMEs in Guadalajara.

Technology upgrading

In the face of rising EU standards, the key question for all IT production sites throughout the world is whether MNCs and domestic firms are upgrading technological and management capacities to serve high-standard EU markets or the lower-standard US market. Mexican IT assembly is geared overwhelmingly to the US market.

MNCs involved in electronics assembly in Mexico—at least along the northern border—have generally been slow to introduce innovations that reduce the toxic substances used in production and embodied in products. The problem is that there are no incentives to upgrade. On one hand, there are no national environmental standards for the IT industry in Mexico. On the other hand, Mexico-based MNCs export overwhelmingly to the US market.

In Guadalajara, we found little evidence that IT firms are retrofitting their production operations in anticipation of the new European laws. Of all the firms we interviewed, only Solectron is working towards compliance with the EU's Restriction on Hazardous Substances (ROHS). The explanation given was that the vast majority of exports from the Jalisco plants are headed for the US, which is showing no signs of creating such a law. Some firms noted that their subsidiaries in Ireland and Hungary are already ROHS compliant because those branches of their operations export into the European market.

In the absence of national or global regulatory pressures, MNCs can—and apparently do—tailor their environmental technology and performance to particular markets. The lack of environmental upgrading in Guadalajara suggests that the IT sector will remain locked into the US market—and locked out of higher-standard markets like the EU.

There is little data and few studies on the environmental performance of MNCs in Mexico's IT Sector. A World Bank study that analyzed the determinants of environmental compliance in Mexican manufacturing as a whole found that foreign firms were no more likely to be in compliance than domestic firms (Dasgupta 2000). In 2002 the UN Economic Commission for Latin America and the Caribbean conducted a survey of 298 electronics firms on Mexico's northern border with the US. The study found some signs that environmental compliance was improving. About two-thirds of the companies in their large sample—over three-quarters of which were foreign—had an environmental unit. Over half said they had raised the level of environmental protection in the preceding three years.

However, the report identified what it calls a foreign firm "double standard" by showing that the country source of FDI had no influence on the environmental policy or performance of the plant. Only half of the companies had an "active" environmental policy, defined as environmental management measures complemented by technologies to mitigate contaminant emissions from the plants. Moreover, only half had even limited supervision of applicable Mexican environmental laws, which are much lower than norms in other countries with electronic assembly industries, such as the Philippines.

The report cautioned that this low level of performance would create barriers for Mexican products in markets with high environmental requirements, such as the European Union. Comparing Mexico with the Philippines, it concluded that, overall, the Mexican electronics industry is being left behind in the speed and scope of environmental policy, especially in terms of production processes and product life cycle (ECLAC 2003).

Capturing FDI Spillovers: Lessons for Policy

FDI in the high-tech sector in Guadalajara offered initial promise of spillovers for sustainable industrial development. Some of the world's best companies in terms of environmental performance invested in Guadalajara. One built a state-of-the-art plant that met the world's highest standards at the time. A number banded together to develop both the supply capabilities and environmental management skills of local firms.

But the capture of significant spillovers was stymied by three factors. First was the Mexican government's failure to match FDI inflows with adequate environmental regulatory infrastructure. As a result, there was no local incentive to eco-innovate—and a significant amount of unaccounted-for hazardous IT waste is likely buried somewhere in the Mexican countryside.

The second obstacle was the evolution of the IT sector into an enclave economy, the result of both government and market failures. With no domestic competitors, there were no direct demonstration effects on local firms. With a bias towards foreign contract manufacturers and few local suppliers, there were few spillovers via backward linkages either for industry upgrading or environmental management.

The third obstacle was the lock-in of IT production for export to the US market. With its lagging environmental standards, the US offered no incentive for Guadalajara-based firms to leapfrog to the global technology frontier. While being in the US backyard keeps assembly operations viable, it provides little incentive to move up the value chain.

The experience of Guadalajara offers four policy lessons about how governments may increase the benefits of FDI for sustainable industrial development:

1. *Capturing spillovers requires explicit linkage policies which integrate FDI in an overarching development strategy.*
   The literature demonstrates unambiguously that positive FDI spillovers are not automatic and that, in developing countries, FDI is as likely to deliver negative spillovers—the hollowing and crowding out of domestic firms—as positive ones. Moreover, in the instances when FDI has generated positive spillovers, it has been the result of deliberate public policies geared toward encouraging MNCs to supply them and increasing the capacities of domestic firms to absorb them. Put another away, the literature shows that it is not the quantity of FDI, but the integration of FDI into a coherent, strategic set of development policies that matters. Ignoring this insight, Mexico's leaders in the 1990s adopted a passive approach in which the overarching objective was to increase the quantity of FDI inflows. Treating FDI as an end rather than as a means grew out of what we call the "maquila mindset"—a perception of Mexico's role as simply a low-wage, low-tax-and-tariff, export-oriented manufacturing base for North American MNCs. The strategy permeated the entire manufacturing sector. In the IT industry, there was little vision or investment in building local knowledge assets or upgrading local industrial capabilities. Without significant local knowledge assets, MNCs tend to transfer their low-skill, low-technology operations and rely on global suppliers than help to develop a local supply base. Mexico's experience shows clearly that treating FDI as an end in itself rather than as part of an overarching development strategy is more likely to generate enclaves than broad-based growth.

2. *Relying on low wages alone to attract FDI leaves developing countries vulnerable to pullout by MNCs.*
   Mexico's primary objective in attracting FDI inflows was to increase employment and income, as well as to help balance the capital account. Low wages were central to achieving this goal. Given that FDI inflows increased dramatically, the strategy may appear to have been successful. However, MNCs pulled out rapidly when demand contracted in the US and when China joined the WTO. The lesson is clear: an FDI enclave built around low

wages rather than local knowledge assets and domestic markets is vulnerable to the emergence of even lower-cost producers. Only geographical proximity to the US and NAFTA preferences sustain Guadalajara's assembly operations.

3. *Garnering environmental spillovers requires explicit attention to environmental policy.* Mexico, like other developing countries, considered IT investment to be "clean and green" and made environmental oversight a low priority. But significant environmental and occupational health problems are associated with IT production, problems the MNCs are still struggling to address. Moreover, the expectation that MNCs will transfer "best practice" was not borne out in Mexico. As a result, Mexican-based firms are not equipped to meet the new, high environmental standards of the European Union and will be locked out of that market. The lesson is that, like knowledge spillovers, there is nothing automatic about environmental spillovers from FDI. Proactive government policy is needed to generate and to capture environmental spillovers.

4. *The benefits of FDI in IT manufacturing are limited for late-industrializing countries.* Barriers to entry in the global IT industry, even at the level of third-tier suppliers, suggest that it will be very difficult for developing countries to gain a foothold in the global IT industry in the absence of strong government policy and simultaneous changes in MNC strategic interests. Without such policies, large MNC firms are bound to crowd out domestic firms with global supply chains and generate few knowledge spillovers to the local economy.

Even with proactive industry policies, however, it may not be possible for late-industrializing countries with relatively small domestic markets to enter the global IT industry except as assembly and semiskilled manufacturing platforms for CMs. Without significant local knowledge assets, MNCs are unlikely to transfer proprietary technology. Rather, technology and skills transfer will be low-end and, as argued above, vulnerable to relocation to cheaper production sites.

In the short term, the employment potential of FDI in the IT sector might be substantial, though again, in the medium to long term, low-wage producers are vulnerable to footloose MNCs. Revenue potential, however, will be limited because of fierce global wage competition and the tax breaks developing countries offer to attract MNCs.

Taken together, these factors suggest that the benefits of attracting IT investment may be limited in developing countries. To promote sustainable industrial development, governments should look to industries that better suit local productive assets and capacities, domestic market potential and development objectives.

NOTES

Foreword

1 Of course, the only socialist economy of the region, Cuba, had expropriated foreign investors in the 1960s, and processes of that sort took place in Cuba and Nicaragua later on.

2 José Antonio Ocampo and Juan Martín (coordinators), *Globalization and Development: A Latin American and Caribbean Perspective*, Palo Alto: Stanford University Press, ECLAC and World Bank, 2003, Table 3.2.

3 Thus, according to CEPAL estimates based on the sales of the largest thousand firms operating in the region, the share of foreign firms increased constantly through the 1990s, from 29.9 percent in 1990–1992 to 41.6 percent in 1998–2000. The share of domestic private firms increased from 37.7 percent to 42.7 percent during the first half of the decade, but then fell to 41.3 percent. That of public-sector firms fell continuously and strongly, from 32.5 percent to 17.1 percent.

4 This is the interpretation offered in José Antonio Ocampo, "Latin America's Growth and Equity Frustrations During Structural Reforms," *Journal of Economic Perspectives*, Vol. 18, No. 2, Spring 2004.

5 United Nations, *World Economic and Social Survey 2006: Diverging Growth and Development*, New York: United Nations, 2006.

Chaper 2: Is Foreign Investment Always Good for Development?

1 Of course, such foreign investments may be desirable for other reasons, such as introducing competition into stagnant or backward sectors. However, what we are concerned about here is the impact on domestic investment and entrepreneurship. Given the enormous superiority of MNEs over domestic firms in most developing countries, the competition is likely to be one-sided.

2 Of course, we are dealing with matters of degree. Investment regimes have become pretty liberal throughout the developing world as a consequence of a profound reassessment of the benefits and costs of FDI.

Chapter 3: Islands of Possibility: MNCs and Economic Development in Brazil

1 See, for example, Mendonça de Barros and Goldenstein (1997), Franco (1999), and Moreira (1999).

2 About 30,000 companies.

Chapter 4: Foreign Investment and the Polarization of the Mexican Economy

1 I am very thankful to Roberto Porzecanski for the translation.

2 For further analysis on this issue, see: Bengoa y Sánchez-Robles (2003); Blomström, Lipsey y Zejan (1994); Culem (1988); de Mello (1997, 1999); Dussel Peters, Galindo y Loría (2003); Görg y Greenaway (2001); Lall y Narula (2006); Mortimore y Vergara (2003).

3 Lester and Piore (2004) highlight the importance of inter-firm linkages (the mesoeconomic level)—in contrast with processes based on single-firm efficiency, competition and the market—on the "interpretive process" that generates creativity in the economy. In terms of economic policy, the authors lean towards the creation of protected spaces such as educational institutions that contribute to innovation in management and engineering.

4 This implies a territorial perspective on competitiveness at the municipal and city level, the state or province level, the country level, and the group-of-countries (world region) level. Commercial, industrial and business policies should begin with a territorial perspective, taking into account the specific characteristics of these territories and their integration into specific segments of global commodity chainsthat in turn determine the specific socioeconomic characteristics of these territories according to their particular products and processes, the size and type of companies involved, their specific financing, technological, training, R&D needs, their orientation to the domestic or foreign market, their potential for upgrading, etc.

5 Rodrik (2006ª) highlights the fact that countries like China and Vietnam have implemented market policies and have massively expanded to the world market, but without abandoning massive public incentives and the methods of a planned economy; they have opened to foreign trade through special economic zones in a generally protectionist environment.

6 The capacity to attract and promote FDI, from this perspective, is a critical element in the growth experiences of Asian countries.

7 This research proposal (Dunning 2006) is similar to that proposed by students of "systemic competitiveness" and the "meso" analytical level.

8 The 1993 Foreign Investment Law actually allows for the evaluation of FDI petitions on the basis of criteria like employment, technology, environment and competitiveness.

9 For more on this issue, see Dussel Peters, Galindo, Loría y Mortimore (2007).

10 Executed FDI—*inversión extranjera directa realizada*—refers to real FDI, in contrast to expected FDI, recorded in official statistics before 1994. It includes only new investments, not reinvestment of profits or intrafirm transfers of capital.

11 The tendency is strongly linked to service sector companies like Wal-Mart.

12 For an analysis of the specific methodology used to select these companies, see Dussel Peters, Galindo, Loría y Mortimore (2007).

13 The industry-level information obtained by INEGI and Ministry of the Economy allows for a comparison between industries on employment, wages, sales, production, exports, imports, etc. However, when cross-referencing the information from both databases we could not obtain the characteristics of eight industries (which could be found in only one of the two databases). As a result, we analyze 197 manufacturing industries out of 205. The data do not include the exports and imports for the "*maquila* industry for export," and in most of the cases for the period until 2003, since this is the last year where INEGI published this information.

Chapter 5: A Missed Opportunity: Foreign Investment and Sustainable Development in Argentina

1 Industrial promotion policies granted generous fiscal and credit subsidies as well as duty-free imports of capital goods.

2 Market-seeking investments are aimed at exploiting the host country's market—and, eventually, neighboring countries' markets (Dunning 1993).

3 Law 21382 guaranteed equal treatment of foreign and domestic investors and the free remittance of profits and principals.

4 Perry and Servén (2002) estimated the real effective exchange rate with respect to its "equilibrium value," at 35 percent in 1999 and 55 percent in 2001.

5 In contrast, portfolio investment reacted more quickly to the crisis and began a rapid and steady decline in 1998.

6 These figures were substantially higher than their counterparts during the ISI period. Between 1959 and 1963, FDI inflows to Argentina averaged US$ 464 million annually (measured in constant 2001 dollars). In the 1990s the same figure was over US$ 6,760 million. While in the first period FDI inflows amounted to around 0.3 percent of GDP, in the 1990s they were above two percent of GDP almost every year.

7 The oil industry, together with the mining sector, attracted mainly resource-seeking investments; resource-seeking FDI is motivated by the availability and/or cost of natural and human resources (Dunning, 1993).

8 Comparisons with the trading performance of MNCs during the ISI period are only available for US affiliates. According to data from surveys undertaken by the US Bureau of Economic Analysis, export/sales ratios for US affiliates in the manufacturing industry increased from an average of 12 percent in 1983 to 21 percent in 1999. Although it is clear that US affiliates are much more export-oriented than in the past, it is also true that their export propensity is lower than in other regions (all US affiliates in the world exported, on average, 41 percent of their sales in 1999).

9 Investments made by MNC affiliates aimed at increasing the efficiency of their activities by integrating assets, production and markets to better exploit economies of scale and scope are called "efficiency-seeking" investments (Dunning 1993).

10 Patent applications in Argentina increased by 128 percent between 1990 and 2002. However, almost the entire increase was due to applications by foreign companies aiming to get protection for products already patented in other countries.

11 As for payments for technology transfer, while in 1992 the contracts registered amounted to a total of US$ 74 million, the respective figure in 1996 was US$ 632 million and in 1999 it had climbed to US$1.45 billion (Rodríguez, 2004). While the remarkable growth in technology payments may have been due to a real increase in the amount of expertise transferred from abroad in the context of economic restructuring, it may also have been related to the strong presence of affiliates of MNCs in Argentina.

12 The regime consisted of a combination of import quotas, investment and balanced trade requirements for established manufacturers, minimum content rules for locally produced vehicles and preferential import tariffs for domestic producers. The program aimed at promoting specialization and fostering competitiveness among established car manufacturers in order to take advantage of the rapid increase in domestic demand that followed stabilization.

13 MERCOSUR's role in FDI attraction was higher in some specific sectors such as automobiles.

14 29.3 percent of the population was below the poverty line in Greater Buenos Aires in 2000, a figure that escalated to a historic peak of 52 percent in 2002 (Household Permanent Survey). In turn, the Gini coefficient in Greater Buenos Aires increased from 47.4 percent in 1999 to 49.1 percent in 2000 and 50.7 percent in 2002.

15 Portfolio investment turned negative in 2001–2002 (more than US$ 5 billion each year) and after recording small positive inflows in 2003–2004, became negative again in 2005.

16 By June 2005 Argentina was the country with more suits in the ICSID (40 out of a total of 183).

17 While the large increase in "other regions" share could suggest that Asian investors were active after the crisis, this only explains a part of the increase, since official sources explain that part of the FDI included in other regions correspond to unidentified operations.

18 Difference-in-difference methods compare a treatment and a comparison group (first difference) before and after the intervention (second difference).

19 The authors distinguish three categories of environmental management activities: (a) the "end-of-pipe" approach, which focuses on treating pollution once it has been created; (b) "simple" clean production activities, such as water, energy, and input savings; (c) "complex" clean production activities, generally involving greater investments, longer lead times, and higher technological complexity and uncertainty, such as the development of new cleaner technologies. It is assumed that the larger the role of complex clean production activities, the higher the "quality" of environmental management.

Chapter 6: Foreign Investment and Economic Development in Costa Rica: The Unrealized Potential

1 In an empirical study, Noorbakhsh, F., A. Paloni, et al. (2001). "Human Capital and FDI Inflows to Developing Countries: New Empirical Evidence." *World Development* 29, no. 9 shows that human capital is a statistically significant determinant of FDI, that it is one of the most important determinants of FDI, and that its relevance has increased over time. Miyamoto, K. (2003). Human capital formation and foreign direct investment in developing countries, OECD Development Centre. Argues that human capital becomes especially important when FDI is efficiency-seeking, rather than market-seeking.

2 Cordero, J. A. (2000). El Crecimiento Económico y La Inversion: El Caso de Costa Rica. *Empleo, crecimiento y equidad. los retos de las reformas económicas de finales del siglo XX en Costa Rica.* A. U. Quiros, San José, Editorial de la Universidad de Costa Rica: 199–282, raises the same concern, even though his econometric work shows a statistically significant negative relationship between FDI and national investment.

3 Computations based on Central Bank data.

4 Calculated based on data from Intel, Central Bank of Costa Rica, and PROCOMER.

5 Taking into account profit repatriation, Paus, E. (2005). *Foreign Investment, Development, and Globalization. Can Costa Rica Become Ireland?* New York, Palgrave Macmillan. Paus (2005, 147) estimates that the Special Export Regimes generated nearly $ 5 billion in net foreign exchange between 1991 and 2003.

6 Data on the tax burden in OECD countries are from the OECD web site: *http://stats.oecd.org*

7 Leiton, P. (2007). Auge económico de Guanacaste no se refleja en los impuestos. *La Nacion.* Leiton argues that taxes on real estate activities are very low, and the ones that exist can be evaded easily.

8 Villasuso, J. M. (2007). Una crónica de apagones anunciados. *Tribuna Democrática*. Villasuso provides a historical account of how government budget regulations have hampered the ability of ICE to undertake the needed investments in new capacity. The way in which general guidelines on the budget deficit have caused severe delays in ICE's investments had been documented in Cordero, J. A. (2000). El Crecimiento Económico y La Inversión: El Caso de Costa Rica. *Empleo, crecimiento y equidad. los retos de las reformas económicas de finales del siglo XX en Costa Rica.* A. U. Quiros. San José, Editorial de la Universidad de Costa Rica: 199–282. Cordero (2000).

9 The same trend is found if we use ratios of national expenditures to exports.

10 Roberto Calvo from Costa Rica Provee kindly provided the data regarding CRP.

11 Data from the Compendio Estadístico, XII Informe Estado de la Nación, Programa Estado de la Nación (2006).

12 Website at the Instituto Costarricense de Turismo, <http://www.visitcostarica.com/ict/paginas/ictnotaict.asp?idnota=341>, accessed May 23, 2007.

13 Law number 6990, July 1985 and amendments in 1992 and 2001.

14 Programa Estado de la Nacion (2006). XII Informe del Estado de la Nación en Desarrollo Humano Sostenible. San José, Programa Estado de la Nación.

Chapter 7: Investment Rules and Sustainable Development: Preliminary Lessons from the Uruguayan Pulp Mills Case

1 The most relevant to cite are: the Administrative Commission of the Uruguay River (CARU); the Foreign Offices of the two countries and the High Level Technical Task Force constituted by them; the consultative process involved in the environmental impact assessment requirements of the World Bank and the International Financial Corporation; the International Court of Justice—two cases were presented by Argentina and one by Uruguay—and the Finnish focal point for the OECD Guidelines for International Enterprises (who received a complaint from an Argentinian NGO).

2 As a result of the acquisition phase initiated in the 1990s, most Argentinean production of market pulp is carried out by a Chilean company (notably Celulosa Arauco/Celulosa Constitución), while the largest share of integrated pulp-and-paper production is in the hands of local companies (Papel del Tucumán, Papel Misionero, Papel Prensa, Massuh, etc.).

3 All production and export figures taken from FAOSTAT (2006 update), available on <http://www.fao.org>.

4 As a matter of fact, in Chile, two local groups (Celulosa Arauco/Celulosa Constitución and CMPC) account for 100 percent of pulp production market, while in Brazil local companies hold the majority stake in all (seven) large pulp-and-paper firms. In some cases, atomistic foreign investors hold a large—but not controlling—stake in the companies (e.g., Aracruz, Klabin, Votorantim (VCP), and Suzano). In one case (CENIBRA) a Japanese company was the cofounder, and controls the company jointly with a Brazilian group (CVRD). Other examples of Brazilian groups operating in this sector are Jari and LWART.

5 The former, dating from 1974 was amended in the 1990s, to extend tax-reduction benefits to FDI and to a wider range of sectors. The latter, also involving tax reliefs for new investments, was issued in 1987.

6 It is also important to note that no explicit requirement is made regarding cost-benefit analysis neither in each country's regulations (that only require EIAs) nor at the regional level (in the framework of the Uruguay River Statute or MERCOSUR).

Chapter 8: Foreigners in the Forests: Saviors or Invaders?

1 For a more detailed description of this framework and the analytical aspects see, for example, UNEP (1999) or OECD (1995).
2 This section concentrates on FDI in the Brazilian forestry sector in tropical timber and the pulp-and paper-industries.
3 In the mid-nineties, the share of timber from native forest used as a component of the forest industry peaked at nearly 5 percent, diminishing its share to close to 2 percent since the late nineties.
4 These advantages are the availability of land apt for forestation and the ecological characteristics which allow planted species to grow much more rapidly than has been registered in traditional timber-producing countries of the northern hemisphere.
5 Current estimates show that nearly two million hectares of barren land, owned by around 100,000 property owners, could qualify for benefits under this law.
6 See, for example, Richards et al. (2003).
7 Aldo Cerda, Fundación Chile and María Teresa Arana, CORMA.
8 Both projects have gone through several years of environmental impact assessment and court suits on environmental grounds. Trillium was initially approved in 1998 and Forestal Cascada in 1999. However, Forestal Cascada withdrew its investment in 2001, and Trillium withdrew in the late 1990s, both having been severely environmentally conditioned by the authorities. The Trillium project involved a total amount of investment of US$ 250 million and consisted of the exploitation of 75,000 hectares of lenga forests, one of the native forests in the south of Chile. Environmental groups argued that the project area was a very isolated and sparsely populated region, making enforcement an enormously difficult task. The project Cascada involved a total amount of investment of US$ 180 million and consisted in an industrial complex for the production of strand boards and chips, as well as a port for the shipment of the products. Production was estimated at 925,000 cubic meters of wood annually. The reaction of environmentalists referred, basically, to the magnitude of the operations, their effect on the native forest, and the lack of policies and enforcement capacity related to management plans of the native forest. For both of these initiatives, especially Trillium, the challenges for environmental regulation went far beyond existing Chilean environmental legislation.
9 Eladio Susaeta, INECON; Fernando Raga, CORMA; Maria Teresa Arana, CORMA, personal communications.
10 CertforChile was constituted as a legal independent corporation, to manage the forest certification standards in Chile. Its founding associates include Fundación Chile, CIPMA, the Chilean Wood Corporation CORMA, the Department of Agriculture, CONAMA, and the Association of Registered Professional Foresters. According to CERTFOR's website, the objective of Certfor is to develop an internationally recognized National Forest Management Certification Standard for radiata pine and eucalyptus plantations, natural forests of Lenga and second-growth forest.
11 Whereas ISO 14001 is a certification related basically to environmental management in industry, the Forest Stewardship Council and CERTFOR are certification schemes referring to the sustainability of forest management.

12 See EIA studies for the different forestry projects - <www.conama.cl/seia>.

13 For references on substitution see, for example, Dourojeanni (2000), or Borregaard and Bradley (1999).

14 INFOR (2005a) reports that nearly 85 percent of the total land substituted for plantations between 1962 and 1990, was either agricultural lands, brush lands, or cut forests.

15 See for example Radio Cooperativa, December 21, 2004: "Pulp Plant of Celulosa Arauco was fined US$ 70,000,- for bad odours."

16 See, for example, Resolución Exenta 182, Comisión Regional de Medio Ambiente, Región de Los Lagos .

17 The Brazilian Aracruz in the largest pulp producer but is not vertically integrated.

18 However, the authors argue it is difficult to compare its performance, as the company is the only one producing newsprint paper.

19 In the case of domestic investment, Forestal Arauco developed a new chlorine-free bleaching process. In the case of foreign investment, Shell, when owning Santa Fé, embarked on the introduction of Totally Chlorine Free (TFC) production, a line of production that has later been discarded by almost all producers.

20 The Clean Development Mechanism is a system for financing emissions-reducing or emissions-avoiding projects in developing nations as defined by the Kyoto Protocol. This international agreement, which builds on the United Nations Framework Convention on Climate Change, sets legally binding targets and timetables for cutting the greenhouse-gas emissions of industrialized countries.

21 In order to build experience and "learn by doing," the first United Nations Conference of the Parties in 1995 launched a pilot phase of activities implemented jointly (AIJ) under which projects could be implemented that reduce emissions of greenhouse gases or enhance their removals through sinks. AIJs were undertaken on a voluntary basis and were to bring about climate change mitigation benefits that would not otherwise occur.

22 The first register is from June 2000; a forest preservation initiative, the Río Cóndor Carbon Sequestration Project, is reducing carbon emissions from a 272,880-hectare forest management project in Tierra del Fuego, Chile. The land is owned and managed by Forestal Savia Ltda., a Chilean company. CFix, LLC, a Washington State Limited Liability Company, is managing the carbon-offset opportunity in partnership with Fundación Chile, a Chilean nonprofit organization focused on technology transfer, new business development and sustainable development in Chile. The second register is an afforestation project from June 2001, the SIF Carbon Sequestration Project that seeks to bring about the afforestation and sustainable management of approximately 7,000 hectares in regions VII and VIII of Chile. The Project consortium includes the Sociedad Inversora Forestal, a private Chilean company, Cfix LLC, two Chilean forestry companies (Forestal Mininco and Forestal Millalemu, the latter associated with Terranova), and a Netherlands-based certification company.

23 This situation was confirmed in personal communication with Fernando Raga, Environmental Manager of the Chilean Forestry Association, CORMA.

24 For lists with the companies and operations that have been certified, see <www.icefi.cl>.

25 For lists with the companies and operations that have been certified, see <www.certfor.cl>.

26 Authors: Dubois et al (1995). Experts interviewed: Aldo Cerda, Fundación Chile; María Teresa Arana, CORMA; María Inés Miranda, CERTFORCHILE; and Hernán Verschure, CODEFF.

27 Forestal Monte Aguila, at that time owned by Shell; Millalemu, at that time owned by the Swiss Schmidheiny Group; and Forestal Los Lagos, at that time owned by the Swiss-based mining complex Xstrata.

28 Quoted in Johnson Annic 1996 "Asian logers latest threat to Brasil rainforest" World Wide Fund for Nature, September.
29 See, for example, Ambiente & Desarrollo, Vol. XII, No. 4, 1996 or Vol. XV, No. 3, 1999.
30 Richards M., Palmer C., Frickmann Young C., and Obidzinski K. (2003), "Higher international standards or rent-seeking race to the bottom? The impacts of forest product trade liberalisation on forest governance." A Background paper for the Global Project: Impact Assessment of Forest Products Trade in Promotion of Sustainable Forest Management GCP/INT/775/JPN, Food and Agriculture Organization (FAO) of the United Nations.
31 From Richards et al. (2003).
32 Borregaard, N. y Annie Dufey (2001). "Environmental effects of foreign investment versus domestic investment in the mining sector in Latin-America." World Resources Institute and CIPMA.

Chapter 9: Bucking the Trend: The Political Economy of Natural Resources in Three Andean Countries

1 Venezuela gained MERCOSUR full-member status in 2006, and Bolivia is seeking membership.
2 However, most of them come from local gasoline taxes. When looking at revenues arising from NG exports, the figure for that period is only 6 precent.
3 *UKOOA Response to Budget 2006 – Current Press Releases.* March 22, 2006 (available at <*http://www.ukooa.co.uk/media/view-press.cfm/386*)>.
4 The 1956 Hydrocarbon Decree (also called Davenport code), granted important advantages to oil companies. Paradoxically, this decree also established royalties at 18 percent, but Gulf's payments were fixed at 11 percent (Source: *La Prensa*, La Paz, Bolivia. May 2, 2006).
5 During the 1930–1970 periods, tin accounted for more than 60 precent of exports. Tin remained as the main export until the nineties when become surpassed by natural gas exports.
6 Talks with Brazil began in 1974, after the subscription of the "Cooperation and Industrial Complementation Agreement," aimed at the export of 6.8 MMC/day.
7 Whereas oil is usually traded internationally and prices are more or less fixed at market rates, natural gas is different: trade takes place at bi-national level, where prices and conditions are fixed in contractual terms under some kind of "take or pay" clause. Another characteristic feature of this industry relates to delivery: a pipeline must be constructed or should be available.
8 Two main discoveries were TOTAL's discovery in Campo Itaú, Tarija and PETROBRAS's confirmation of natural gas reserves in San Alberto and Sábalo.
9 In July 2002 some of the industry main players (Repsol-YPF; BG and BP) created a consortium in order to produce LNG (Liquid Natural Gas) to be exported to the US market. The project included a 688 km pipeline to be built between the Margarita gas field in southern Bolivia and some Pacific port (either Ilo in Peru or Mejillones in Chile).
10 This company's concession in the Block 15 site was withdrawn in May 2006, and since then the field is operated by PETROECUADOR. Therefore, state share over total oil production increased significantly but is showing lower productivity than the former private operator (BCE 2006).

11 Pérez Alfonso is known as the father of the OPEC.

12 Actually, this state-owned company ranks first among Trans-Latin corporations, totaling annual sales of US$ 63,200 billion and operations in three continents (ECLAC 2006).

13 In order to initiate the exploration and exploitation process, the government divided the area (54,000 km^2) into four sub-regions: Cerro Negro, Machete, Hamaca and Zuata. The benefits introduced by the original contract embarked oil companies in a process of drilling and, recently, in upgrading the Orinoco crude oil into a lighter, marketable product. Production in this area amounts to 600,000 barrels a day.

14 The most important are: Resolutions 1803/62 and 3171/73 on permanent sovereignty over Natural Resources, Resolution 3201 on New Economic Order, and Resolution 3281/74 adopting the Charter of Economic Rights and Duties.

15 In the 1970s, most of the countries in the region introduced some type of operational or service contracts, a contractual form from Middle East countries. Under such a scheme, foreign companies undertake exploration and exploitation risks, and are compensated by the host country in cash or oil. Certainly, under such a legal scheme oil belongs to the state.

16 These are examples of the main legal frameworks adopted during the nineties. However, in the case of Ecuador, a wide range of agreements was introduced: service contracts; participation agreements; marginal fields, operational alliances; strategic alliances; and specific services contracts (UNDP/WB ESMAP, 2005).

17 The state-owned company (YPFB) was divided up into three independent parts: Chaco, Andina and Transredes.

18 However, the traditional literature dealing with MNCs, always stress economic motivations. In principle, most of the FDI directed at some specific country is either attracted by lower wages at comparable skill levels, or by the availability of natural resources (i.e., vertical FDI) or because of transport costs, tariffs and non-tariffs-barriers (i.e., horizontal FDI).

19 Recently, companies from China and Japan entered the market. CNPC from China acquired Rompetrol in late 2003 (Block 11), whereas Teikoku Oil from Japan bought Ecuadorean block stakes in early 2005, and joined in developments controlled by PETROBRAS (a 40% share in Blocks 18 and 31).

20 According to Fortune, seven oil companies rank among the top 25 world corporations in 2006 (Exxon Mobil, Royal Dutch/Shell Group, BP, Chevron Texaco, Conoco Phillips, Total, and Sinopec).

21 For example, production costs declared by oil firms reached values up to US$ 20 per barrel, much above the US$ 4 cost for PDVSA (PDVSA Newsletter, 2005 and 2006).

22 The plan not only touched companies working in the energy sector, but it also included nationalizations in the telecommunications and electricity industries.

23 Since it arrived in Ecuador in 1999, the company invested US$ 1 billion. Before its departure, Oxy was producing almost a fifth of total oil output (around 100,000 barrels of petrol per day). The Ecuadorian government accused Oxy of having breached its contract, by failing to register its sale of a stake in another field. For the company, this was nothing but expropriation, and it consequently filed an arbitration case with ICSID Tribunals.

24 This was a two-step movement. By virtue of the new legislation passed by president Mesa (Hydrocarbon Law No. 3058 of May 17 of 2005), royalties increased up to 50 percent of production. The remaining increase was introduced by President Morales after the sanction of Supreme Decree 28701 of May, 2006.

25 That was the case for the two main gas fields under Petrobras's concession, which finally agreed to pay royalties and taxes of 50 percent (*The Economist* 2006).

26 From a total of seven cases pending until ICSID, five of them relate to procurement contracts or regulatory activity.

27 Contracts were finally approved and signed on May 2, 2007 (Andean Information Network, Friday May 4, 2007).

28 The Venezuelan government introduced a retroactive tax package for unpaid taxes over the period 2001–2004. According to Venezuela's tax agency, related revenues might sum up to US$ 891 million. Among the 22 companies included, Royal Dutch Shell became the first to receive a retroactive tax bill (Peterson, 2006a and 2006b).

29 The negotiations were closed with small groups of firms over time. First, with Spanish Repsol, Chinese CNPC, and some Venezuelan oil firms. Second, Petrobras Brazil signed the new agreement on September 28; three days later was the turn of Tecpetrol and other small firms. Finally, during December it was the turn of French Total, British Petroleum and Chevron.

30 Even in its dispute with ENI, the Venezuelan government is confident it will settle the oilfield dispute and resolve the issue (Settlement with ENI Possible - BNAmericas, 5/25/2007).

31 "Venezuelan Assembly Okays Harvest's Mixed Company Conversion" (Harvest Natural Resources, INC. 6/18/2007, from <http://www.rigzone.com/news/article.asp?a_id=46557)>.

32 Furthermore, in the same article it is argued that Ecuador even outperforms the US market, when looking at profits made "even after the windfall tax introduced last year" (*The Economist* 2007b).

33 Seems to be the case for PETROBRAS, according to Mr. Gabrielli (company CEO) (*The Economist* 2006).

34 The author quotes a report by the International Energy Agency (IEA), analyzing the consequences entailed in the US energy forecast: as internal production is expected to stagnate in the near future, thus highlighting the role of oil imports (Valenzuela 2006).

35 In contrast with the 1970s, when high prices responded to supply-side policies, the current price increase might be better explained by demand pressure (Sánchez-Albavera and Vargas 2005).

36 At the same time, the Bolivian government announced its decision to withdraw from the ICSID Convention. If such a move is pursued formally, Bolivia will become the first country to do that. This issue deserves a separate analysis, which is beyond the scope of the present chapter.

Chapter 10: Beyond Pollution Haloes: The Environmental Effects of FDI in the Pulp-and-Paper and Petrochemicals Sectors in Brazil

1 There are no statistically comparable available data on the amount of FDI to the Brazilian petrochemical sector for the period from the 1970s to the present, but aggregate data for the whole chemicals sector are available.

2 In 2006 a single North American company—International Paper—was responsible for US$ 1.2 billion of the FDI in the Brazilian pulp-and-paper sector (UNCTAD, 2007, p.58).

3 de ALMEIDA, L. T. (2001). Harmonização Internacional das Regulações Ambientais. Um Estudo da Petroquímica Brasileira. Doutorado em Economia. Instituto de Economia da Universidade Estadual de Campinas, Campinas, Brasil; ROCHA,

S. dos S., ALMEIDA, L. T. de (2007). "Does Foreign Direct Investment Work for Sustainable Development? A case study of the Brazilian pulp and paper industry." Discussion Paper Number 8. Working Group on Development and Environment in the Americas, GDAE-Tufts University.

4 For more information on the significance of this sample see Rocha & Almeida (2006).

5 This thesis is entitled "International Harmonization of Environmental Regulations: A case study of the Brazilian petrochemicals industry" (Almeida 2001).

6 Emissions indicators per company were not available for the petrochemicals sector, but are available for most companies in the pulp-and-paper sector.

7 The assessment of the environmental control system in the pulp-and-paper sector here refers just to the industrial phase, i.e., the forest phase is not included in this study.

8 According to the Environmental Control Agency from the state of Sao Paulo (CETESB).

9 The Responsible Care Program was created in 1985 by the Canadian Chemical Producers Association and adopted by the US Chemicals Manufacturers Association in 1989 in a context of declining public opinion about the chemical industry. After being recommended by the International Council of Chemical Associations, Responsible Care was rapidly spread worldwide as the Environmental Corporate Program of the chemicals industry (Roberts 1998).

10 This cracker is located in the state of Rio Grande do Sul (in southern Brazil) where there is a very active environmental social movement that is reflected in this state environmental regulations, supposedly more stringent than in other Brazilian states, at least concerning the environmental regulations applied to the petrochemicals sector.

Chapter 11: Missing Links, Dashed Hopes: FDI Spillovers and Sustainable Industrial Development in Mexico's Silicon Valley

1 Also called Electronic Manufacturing Services (EMS) companies.

2 A domestically based IT industry can also help to locally diffuse IT products, with large benefits for productivity and poverty alleviation UNDP 2001. *Human Development Report.* Oxford, Oxford University Press.

3 Production of micro-chips is also energy-intensive. See Mazurek 1999.

REFERENCES

Abugattas, L. and E. Paus (2006). Policy Space for a Capability-Centered Development Strategy for Latin America. *Paper presented at the Conference Responding to Globalization in the Americas: The Political Economy of Hemispheric Integration.* London School of Economics, London.

Acuña, V. and I. Molina (1991). *Historia económica y social de Costa Rica (1750–1950).* San José, Editorial Porvenir.

Aden, J., Kyu-Hong, A., and Rock, M. (1999). What is Driving Pollution Abatement Expenditure Behavior of Manufacturing Plants in Korea? *World Development* **27**(7): 1203–1214.

Agnani, B. and A. Iza (2005). Growth in an oil abundant economy: The case of Venezuela. Working papers from university of the Basque Country - Department of Foundations of Economic Analysis II. September 22.

Agosín, M., R. Machado, P. Nazal (eds). (2004). Pequeñas economías, grandes desafíos: Políticas Económicas para el desarrollo de Centroamérica. Washington, DC: Inter-American Development Bank.

Agosin, M. R. (1996). El retorno de la inversión extranjera a América Latina. In Inversión extranjera directa en América Latina: su contribución al desarrollo. M. R. Agosin (ed). Santiago: Fondo de Cultura Económica.

―――. (2001). Korea and Taiwan in the financial crisis. In Financial crises in "successful" emerging economies. R. Ffrench-Davis (ed). Washington, DC: Brookings Institution Press and United Nations Economic Commission for Latin America and the Caribbean.

Agosin, M. R. and R. Machado (2006). Openness and the International Allocation of Foreign Direct Investment. *Economic and Sector Study Series.* Washington DC: Inter-American Development Bank.

―――. (2006). *Openness and the International Allocation of Foreign Direct Investment.* Washington DC: Inter-American Development Bank.

―――. (2007). Openness and the international allocation of foreign direct investment. *Journal of Development Studies* **Forthcoming**.

Aguilar, C. and H. Vallejo (2002). Regional Integration and Foreign Direct Investment: The Case of Latin America. CEDE working paper No. 2002–13.

Aitken, B. and A. Harrison (1999). Do Domestic Firms Benefit from Foreign Direct Investment? *American Economic Review* **89**(3): 605–18.

Amsden, A. (2004). Import substitution in high-tech industries: Prebisch lives in Asia! *CEPAL Review* **82**(April).

Amsden, A. and W. Chu (2003). Beyond Late Development: Taiwan's Upgrading Policies. Cambridge: MIT Press.

Amsden, A. H. (1989). Asia's next giant – South Korea and late industrialization. New York: Oxford University Press.

Andario, P. and N. D'Avila (1999). A margem da lei. Greenpeace.

Andersen, L. and M. Messa (2001). The natural gas sector in Bolivia: An overview. Instituto de Investigaciones Socio-Económicas. Universidad Católica Boliviana, Andean Competitiveness Project.

Angel, J. and G. Treviño (1993). Flujos de capital: el caso de México. *Serie Financiamiento del Desarrollo* **27**.

Araújo, R. (2004). Desempenho inovador e comportamento tecnológico das firmas domésticas e transnacionais no final da década de 90. Diss. *Instituto de Economia* Unicamp.

Araya, M. (2005). FDI and the environment: what empirical evidence does – and does not – tell us? *International investment for sustainable development:* Balancing Rights and Rewards L. Zarsky (ed). London: Earthscan Publications.

Arbache, J. S. and J. A. D. De Negri (2004). Filiação industrial e diferenciais de salários no Brasil. *Revista Brasileira de Economia* **58**(2):159–184.

Arbelaez, H., J. Daniels, et al. (2002). Market Reform and FDI in Latin America: an Empirical Investigation. *Transnational Corporations* **Vol. 11**(1): pp. 29–47.

Armesto, J. (1999). Impacto Potencial del Proyecto Cascada Chile sobre los Ecosistemas Forestales de la X Región y su Diversidad Biológica. *Ambiente y Desarrollo* **15**(3).

Bahia, L. D. and J. S. Arbache (2005). Diferenciação salarial segundo critérios de desempenho das firmas industriais. *Inovações, padrões tecnológicos e desempenho das firmas industriais brasileiras.* J. A. D. De Negri and M. S. Salerno. Brasília, Ipea.

Bair, J. and E. Dussel Peters (2006). Global Commodity Chains and Endogenous Growth: Export Dynamism and Development in Mexico and Honduras. *World Development* **34**(2): 203–221.

BAN (Basel Action Network) and SVTC (Silicon Valley Toxics Coalition) (2002). Exporting Harm: The High-Tech Trashing of Asia.

Banco Central del Ecuador (BCE) (2006). Análisis del Sector Petrolero, Banco Central del Ecuador – Dirección General de Estudios.

Barbero, M. I. (2003). Impacto de la inversión extranjera directa en la industria argentina en la década de 1920. Estrategias empresariales y sus efectos sobre el sector productivo local. 6ª Conferência Internacional de História de Empresas.

Barclay, L. A. (2003). FDI-facilitated development: the case of the natural gas industry of Trinidad and Tobago. *Institute for New Technologies Discussion Paper.* United Nations University.

Bengoa Calvo, M. and B. Sanchez-Robles (2003). Foreign Direct Investment, Economic Freedom and Growth: New Evidence from Latin America. *European Journal of Political Economy* **19**(3): 529–45.

Bethel, L. (2002). Historia de América Latina: Los países andinos desde 1930. Cambridge University Press.

Bittencourt, G. and R. Domingo (2000). Inversión extranjera directa y empresas transnacionales en Uruguay en los 90: tendencias, determinantes e impactos. Montevideo, Departamento de Economia, Universidad de la República.

Bittencourt, G. and R. Domingo (2004). Los determinantes de la IED y el efecto del MERCOSUR. *El Trimestre Económico* **71**(1):73–128.

Bittencourt, G., R. Domingo and N. Reig. (2006). Efectos de derrame de las ET sobre el comercio exterior de la industria manufacturera uruguaya 1990–2000. In El desarrollo industrial del MERCOSUR: qué impacto han tenido las empresas extranjeras? M. Laplane (ed). Buenos Aires, Siglo Veintiuno Editora Iberoamericana/Red MERCOSUR.

Blackman, A. and X. Wu. (1998). Foreign direct investment in China's power sector: Trends, benefits, and barriers. Washington D.C., Resources for the Future.

Blomstrom, M., S. Globerman, A. Kokko. (1999). The determinants of host country spillovers from foreign direct investment: review and synthesis of the literature. *Working Paper No. 76.* European Institute of Japanese Studies.

Blomstrom, M., R. E. Lipsey, et al. (1994) What explains growth in developing countries? *NBER Discussion Paper 1924* **Volume**, DOI:

Blomstrom, M. and E. N. Wolff (1994). Multinational Corporations and Productivity Convergence in Mexico. In Convergence of productivity: cross-national studies and historical evidence. W. J. Baumol, R. R. Nelson and E. N. Wolff (eds). Oxford University Press.

Blomstrom, M. a. H. P. (1983). Foreign investment and spillover efficiency in an underdeveloped economy: Evidence from the Mexican manufacturing industry. *World Development* **11**: 493–501.

Borregaard, N. and T. Bradley (1999). Análisis de Tres Sectores Exportadores Chilenos. *Ambiente y Desarrollo* **15**(4).

Bouzas, R. and D. Chudnovsky (2004). Foreign Direct Investment and Sustainable Development: The Recent Argentine Experience. Buenos Aires: Universidad de San Andrés.

BRACELPA (2005). Relatório Estatístico 2004/2005. São Paulo: Instituto de Pesquisas e Estudos Florestais.

BRACELPA (2007). Pulp and Paper Sector Brasileira de Celulose e Papel.

Brannon, J. T., D. D. James, et al. (1994). Generating and Sustaining Backward Linkages Between Maquiladoras and Local Suppliers in Northern Mexico. *World Development* **22**(12): 1933–1945.

Bulmer-Thomas, V. (1994). The Economic History of Latin America since Independence. Cambridge University Press.

CADELEC. (2007). From *www.cadelec.com.mx*

CAFOD. (2004). Clean Up Your Computer, Working Conditions in the Electronics Sect. from *http://www.cafod.org.uk*

Caves, R. E. (1974). Multinational firms, competition and productivity in host-country markets. *Economica* **41**(162): 176–93.

CEPAL (1999). La Inversión Extranjera en América Latina y el Caribe. CEPAL.

Chudnovsky, D. and A. Lopez (2000). La Competencia Por Atraer la Inversion Extranjera Directa su Dimension Global y Regional. *Serie Brief.* Buenos Aires: Latin American Trade Network.

———. (2001). La Inversion Extranjera Directa en el Mercosur: un analisis comparativo. El Boom de la Inversion Extranjera Directa en el Mercosur. D. Chudnovsky (ed). Buenos Aires: Siglo Veintiuno de Argentina Editores.

———. (2001). *La Transnacionalización de la Economía Argentina.* Buenos Aires: Eudeba.

———. (2002). The literature on environmental practices of MNCs. *Managing the environment across borders: A study of environmental management practices at affiliates of transnational corporations in China, Malaysia and India.* M. Hansen. Copenhagen Samfundslitteratur.

———. (2002). Policy Competition for FDI: the global and regional dimensions. In *Trade negotiations in Latin America. Problems and Prospects.* D. Tussie (ed). Palgrave Macmillan.

———. (2004). MNCs strategies and regional economic integration: the case of MERCOSUR. *Cambridge Journal of Economics* **28**: 635–652.

Chudnovsky, D., A. Lopez, et al. (2002). *Integracion Regional e Inversion Extranjera Directa: El Caso del Mercosur.* Buenos Aires, BID-INTAL.

Chudnovsky, D., A. López et al. (2007). Impact of Foreign Direct Investment on Employment, Productivity, Trade, Innovation, Wage Inequality and Poverty: A study of Argentina 1992–2001. Global Development Network.

Chudnovsky, D., A. López et al. (1996). La nueva inversión extranjera directa en la Argentina: privatizaciones, mercado interno e integración regional. In *Inversión extranjera directa en América Latina: su contribución al desarrollo.* M. R. Agosin (ed). Santiago: Fondo de Cultura Económica.

Chudnovsky, D., A. López et al. (2006). Derrames de la Inversión Extranjera Directa, políticas públicas y capacidades de absorción de las firmas nacionales del sector manufacturero argentino (1992–2001). In *El desarrollo industrial del MERCOSUR: ¿qué impacto han tenido las empresas extranjeras?* M. Laplane (ed).

Chudnovsky, D. and G. Pupato (2005). Environmental Management and Innovation in the Argentine Industry: Determinants and Policy Implications. International Institute for Sustainable Development.

Cimoli, M. and J. Katz (2003). Structural Reforms, Technological Gaps and Economic Development: A Latin American Perspective. *Industrial and Corporate Change* 12(2): 387–411.

CINDE (2006). Informe de Labores 2006. San José: CINDE.

Corazza, R. I. (1996). Inovação tecnológica e demandas ambientais: notas sobre o caso da indústria brasileira de papel e celulose. Campinas, Instituo de Geociências, Universidade Estadual de Campinas. **PhD**.

Cordero, J. A. (2000). El Crecimiento Económico y La Inversion: El Caso de Costa Rica. In *Empleo, crecimiento y equidad. los retos de las reformas económicas de finales del siglo XX en Costa Rica.* A. U. Quiros (ed). San José, Editorial de la Universidad de Costa Rica: 199–282.

Cordero, J. A. (2004). Política Comercial y Desarrollo Económico: Reflexiones en torno al TLC. In *TLC con Estados Unidos:Contribuciones para el debate. ¿Debe Costa Rica aprobarlo?* M. Florez-Estrada and G. Hernández (eds). San José, Costa Rica, Instituto de Investigaciones Sociales, Editorial Universidad de Costa Rica.

Cordero, J. A. (2006). Direct Foreign Investment and Economic Development in a Small Economy: Costa Rica. XXVI International Congress of LASA (Latin American Studies Association). Puerto Rico.

Cotton, C. and T. Romine (1999). Facing destruction: A Greenpeace briefing on the timber industry in the Brazilian Amazon. Amsterdam: Greenpeace International.

Culem, C. G. (1988). "The location determinants of direct investment among industrialized countries." *European Economic Review* 32: 885–904.

Dalcomuni, S. M. (1997). Dynamics capabilities for cleaner production innovation. The case of the market pulp export industry in Brazil. Brighton: Unidade de Pesquisa em Política Científica, Universidade de Sussex.

Dasgupta, S., H. Hettige, et al. (2000). What Improves Environmental Compliance? Evidence from Mexican Industry. *Journal of Environmental Economics and Management* 38: 39–66.

Dasgupta, S., H. Hettige, et al. (1997). What Improves Environmental Performance? Evidence from Mexican Industry. Washington, DC: Development Research Group, World Bank.

Daude, C., E. Levy Yeyati, et al. (2003). Regional Integration and the Location of FDI. Washington DC: Inter-American Development Bank.

de Mello, L. R. (1997). Foreign direct investment in developing countries and growth: a selective survey. *Journal of Development Studies* 34(1): 1–34.

————. (1999). Foreign direct investment-led growth: evidence from time series and panel data. *Oxford Economic Papers* **51**: 133–151.

De Negri, F. (2004). Desempenho comercial das empresas estrangeiras no Brasil na década de 90. *Prêmio BNDES de Economia* **26**.

Donoso, C. (1999). Proyectos de Manejo de Bosque Nativo en Chile. *Ambiente y Desarrollo* **15**(3).

dos Santos Rocha, S. and L. Togeiro de Almeida (2007). Does Foreign Direct Investment Work For Sustainable Development? A case study of the Brazilian pulp and paper industry. Working Group on Development and Environment in the Americas.

Dunning, J. H. (1993). Multinational Enterprises and the Global Economy. Reading: Addison Wesley.

————. (1998). Changing Geography of Foreign Direct Investment: Explanations and Implications. *Globalization, Foreign Direct Investment and Technology Transfers: Impacts on and Prospects for Developing Countries*. N. Kumar. London and New York, Routledge.

————. (2005). More – yet more – on globalization. *Transnational Corporations* **14**(2): 159–168.

Dunning, J. H. ————. (2006). Towards a new paradigm of development: implications for the determinants of international business. *Transnational Corporations* **15**(1): 173–227.

Dussel Peters, E. (2000). La inversión extranjera en México. *Serie Desarrollo Productivo* **80**.

————. (2003). La industria Electronica en Mexico: Problematica, Perspectivas y Propuestas. Guadalajara, Mexico: Universidad de Guadalajara.

————. (2005). Economic opportunities and challenges posed by China for Mexico and Central America. Bonn; German Development Institute.

Dussel Peters, E., L. M. Galindo Paliza et al. (2007). El origen y destino de la IED y sus condiciones en México. Una perspectiva macro, meso y micro, la Facultad de Economía/ Universidad Nacional Autónoma de México, la Secretaría de Economía. México.

Dussel Peters, E. and J. J. Palacios (2004). Condiciones y retos de la electrónica en México. E. Dussel Peters and J. J. Palacios. México, NYCE.

Dussel Peters, E., L. M. G. Paliza et al. (2003). Condiciones y efectos de la inversión extranjera directa y del proceso de integración regional en México durante los noventa. Una perspectiva macro, meso y micro. México: Facultad de Economía/Universidad Nacional Autónoma de México, Banco Interamericano de Desarrollo-INTAL, Plaza, Valdés.

ECLAC (2003). La industria maquiladora electronica en la frontera norte de Mexico y el medio ambiente, (Economic Commission on Latin America and the Caribbean) LC/MEX/L.585.

————. (2005). Foreign Investment in Latin America and the Caribbean. New York and Santiago: United Nations.

————. (2006). Foreign Investment in Latin America and the Caribbean. New York and Santiago: United Nations.

Egger, P. and M. Pfaffermayr (2004). The Impact of bilateral investment treaties on foreign direct investment. *Journal of Comparative Economics* **32**(4): 788–804.

Ernst, C. (2005). Trade liberalization, export orientation and employment in Argentina, Brazil and Mexico. *Employment Strategy Papers*, Employment Strategy Department.

Ernst, D. (2003). How sustainable are benefits from global production networks? Malaysia's upgrading prospects in the electronics industry. *Working Papers*. East-West Centre.

Eskeland, G. a. H., A (1997). Moving to greener pastures? Multinationals and the pollution-haven hypothesis. World Bank, Public Economics Division, Policy Research Department, January.

Esser, K. (1999). Competencia global y libertad de acción nacional. Nuevo desafío para las empresas, el Estado y la sociedad. Caracas: Nueva Sociedad/Instituto Alemán de Desarrollo.

EurActive.com. (2005). Big economies lose competitiveness race.

Fairlie Reinoso, A. (2005). Integración regional y tratados de libre comercio: algunos escenarios para los Países Andinos. LATN.

FAO (2006). The State of the Forest, Annex, Food and Agriculture Organisation.

FARN (2006). Las plantas de celulosa en el Río Uruguay: El análisis de la normativa para una posible resolución del conflicto. Fundación Ambiente y Recursos Naturales.

Fernández-Arias, E. and R. Hausmann (2000). Is FDI a Safer Form of Financing? The New Wave of Capital Inflows: Sea Change or Just Another Tide? New Orleans, BID.

FIEL (2002). Productividad, competitividad y empresas – Los engranajes del crecimiento. Buenos Aires: FIEL.

Fonseca, E. (1998). Centroamérica: su historia. 2nd edition. San José, FLACSO-EDUCA.

Foran, T. (2001). Corporate social responsibility at nine multinational electronics firms in Thailand. Report to California Global Corporate Accountability Project, Nautilus Institute.

Franco, G. (1999). O desafio brasileiro: ensaios sobre desenvolvimento, globalização e moeda."Editora 34.

Frenkel, R. and M. Damill (2006). El mercado de trabajo argentino en la globalización financiera. Revista de la CEPAL 88.

————. (2007). Toward a theory of innovation and industrial pollution: Evidence from Mexican Manufacturing. Industrial Innovation and Environmental regulations. S. Parto and B. Herbert-Copley (eds). New York: United Nations University Press.

Gallagher, K. and M. B. L. Birch (2005). Do investment agreements attract investment? Evidence from Latin America. Journal of World Investment and Trade, 7(6): 961–974.

Gallagher, K. P. (2004). Free trade and the environment: Mexico, NAFTA and beyond. Palo Alto: Stanford University Press.

Gallagher, K. P. and R. Porzecanski (2007). Economic reform and foreign investment in Latin America: A critical assessment. Progress in Development Studies 7(3): 217–233.

Gallagher, K. P. and L. Zarsky (2007). The enclave economy: Foreign investment and sustainable development in Mexico's Silicon Valley. Cambridge: MIT Press.

Gallagher, K. S. (2006). China Shifts Gears, Automakers, Oil, Pollution and Development. Cambridge: MIT Press.

Garcia-Johnson, R. (2000). Exporting environmentalism: US multinational chemical corporations in Brazil and Mexico. Cambridge: MIT Press.

Gasparini, L., M. Marchionni et al. (2001). La distribución del ingreso en la Argentina. Perspectivas y efectos sobre el bienestar. Buenos Aires: Fundación Arcor.

Gatto, F. and G. Yoguel (1993). Las PyMEs Argentinas en una etapa de transición productiva y tecnológica. El desafío de la competitividad. In La industria Argentina en transformación. B. Kosacoff (ed). Buenos Aires: ECLAC/Alianza.

Gelb, A. (1988). Oil Windfalls: Blessing or Curse? World Bank-Oxford University Press.

Gentry, B. S. (1998). Private capital flows and the environment, Lessons from Latin America. Cheltenham, UK: Edward Elgar Publishing.

Gereffi, G. and M. Korzeniewicz (1994). Commodity Chains and Global Capitalism. Westport, Praeger.

Görg, H. and D. Greenaway (2001). foreign direct investment and intra-industry spillovers: A review of the literature. Research Paper Series, Globalization and Labour Markets Program. The Leverhulme Trust.

_____. (2004). Much ado about nothing? Do domestic firms really benefit from foreign direct investment. *The World Bank Research Observer* **19**(2): 171–197.

Government of Chile (2005). Plan nacional de implementación para la gestión de los Ccontaminantes orgánicos persistentes (COPs) en Chile. Fase I: 2006–2010. CONAMA.

Government of Uruguay (2006). National Implementation Plan, Stockholm Convention on Persistent Organic Pollutants.

Greñas, R. (1985). Costa Rica en la época del Gobernador Don Juan de Ocón y Trillo. San José: Editorial Costa Rica.

Grupo Interinstitucional de Inversión Extranjera Directa (2006). Inversión eextranjera directa en Costa Rica, 2006 (Preliminar). San José: Banco Central de Costa Rica.

Grupo Interinstitucional de Inversión Extranjera Directa (2007). Inversión extranjera directa en Costa Rica, 2006 (Preliminar). San José: Banco Central de Costa Rica.

Guerson, A., J. Parks et al. (2006). Exports structures and growth: a detailed analysis for Argentina. World Bank.

Hallward-Dreimeier, M. (2003). Do Bilateral Investment Treaties Attract FDI? Only a bit... and it might bite. Washington DC: World Bank.

Haltia, O. and K. Keipi (2000). Financiamiento de inversiones forestales en América Latina: el uso de incentivos. In Políticas forestales en América Latina. Washington DC: Banco Interamericano de Desarrollo.

Haskel, J. E., S. C. Pereir, et al. (2002). Does inward foreign direct investment boost the productivity of domestic firms? National Bureau of Economic Research.

Hatfield Consultants (2006). Expert Panel Report (to the Draft Cumulative Impact Study).

Hausmann, R. (1995). Dealing with negative oil shocks: the Venezuelan experience in the eighties. IADB – Office of Chief Economist.

Hausmann, R., J. Hwang et al. (2005). What you export matters, NBER.

Hausmann, R., D. Rodrik et al. (2004). Growth Diagnostics, Harvard University.

Haussmann, R. and D. Rodrik (2003). Economic development as self-discovery. *Journal of Development Economics* **72**(December).

Herbert-Copley, B. (1998). Innovation, regulation, and environmental management in the Chilean and Canadian pulp and paper industries. Diss. Ottawa: Carleton University.

Hettige, H., M. Huq, S. Pargal and David Wheeler (1996). Determinants of pollution abatement in developing countries: Evidence from South and Southeast Asia. *World Development* **24**(12): 1891–1904.

Hiratuka, C. (2006). Internalization of transnational corporations's research and development: analysis of the insertion of Asian and Latin American Affiliates. *Second Annual Conference on Development and Change*. Campos do Jordão: Brazil.

Hiratuka, C. and F. De Negri (2004). Influencia del origin del capital sobre los patrones del comercio exterior brasileño. *Revista de La CEPAL* (82).

Hiratuka, C. and R. Dias (2007). Exportações das firmas domésticas e influência das firmas transnacionais. In As empresas brasileiras e o comércio internacional. J. A. De Negri and B. C. Araújo (eds). Brasilia: IPEA.

Hiratuka, C. and P. Fracalanza (2006). Diferenciais de salários entre empresas domésticas e estrangeiras na indústria brasileira. In Tecnologia, Exportação e Emprego. F. De Negri, J. A. D. De Negri and D. Coelho (eds). Brasília: IPEA.

Hirschman, A. (1958). The Strategy of Economic Development. New Haven: Yale University Press.

Humphrey, J. (2004). Upgrading in global value chains. *IDS Working Paper*. IDS: 1–40.

Ibarra, D. and J. C. Moreno-Brid (2004). La inversión extranjera. México: CEPAL.

IIED (1996). Towards a Sustainable Paper Cycle. London: International Institute for Environment and Development.

INDEC-SECYT-CEPAL (2003). Segunda encuesta nacional de innovación y conducta tecnológica de las empresas Argentinas. *Serie Estudios* **38**.

INDEC-SECYT (1998). Encuesta sobre la conducta tecnológica de las empresas industriales argentinas. *Serie Estudios* **31**.

INFOR (2005). El sector forestal Chileno en una mirada, INFOR.

Jimenez, J. P. and V. Tromben (2006). Política fiscal en países especializados en productos renovables en América Latina. *Serie Macroeconomía del Desarrollo N° 46.*, ECLAC.

Katz, J. (1999). Reformas estructurales y comportamiento tecnológico: Reflexiones en torno a la naturaleza y fuentes del cambio Ttecnológico en América Latina en los años noventa. *ECLAC Economic Reforms Series* **13**.

Katz, J. and E. Ablin (1977). Tecnología y exportaciones industriales: Un análisis microeconómico de la experiencia Argentina reciente. *Desarrollo Económico* **17**(65).

Keller, W. a. S. R. Y. (2003). Multinational enterprises, international trade, and productivity growth: Firm level evidence from the United States. Working Paper 9504. NBER: February.

Kokko, A. (1996). Productivity spillovers from competition between local firms and foreign affiliates. *Journal of International Development* **8**(4): 517–530.

Kokko, A., Ruben Tansini, and Mario C. Zejan, (1996). Local technological capability and productivity spillovers from FDI in the Uruguayan manufacturing sector. *Journal of Development Studies* **32**(4): 602–7.

Konings, J. (2000). The effects of foreign direct investment on domestic firms: Evidence from firm level panel data in emerging economies. London: Centre for Economic Policy Research.

Kosacoff, B. (1999). El caso Argentino. *Las multinacionales Latinoamericanas: Sus estrategias en un mundo Gglobalizado.* D. Chudnovsky, B. Kosacoff and A. López (eds). Buenos Aires: Fondo de Cultura Económica.

Kosacoff, B. and G. Bezchinsky (1993). De la sustitución de Iimportaciones a la globalización. Las empresas transnacionales en la Iindustria Argentina. In El desafío de la competitividad. La industria Argentina en transición. B. Kosacoff. Buenos Aires (eds). ECLAC, Alianza.

Kuehr, R. and E.Williams (Eds). (2003). Computers and the environment: understanding and managing their impacts. Dordrecht: Kluwer Academic Publishers and UnitedmNations University.

La Nacion (2007). Correa reiteró que revisará contratos con las petroleras: son los de las empresas extranjeras. *La Nacion.*

La República (2007). Intel pide educación pero no impuestos. *La República*: 6.

Lagos, G. and P. Velasco. (1999). Environmental policies and practices in Chilean mining. In Mining and the Environment, Case Studies from the Americas. A. W. (ed). Ottawa: International Development Research Centre. **Chapter 3**.

Lall, S. (2003). Reinventing industrial strategy: The role of government policy in building industrial competitiveness. G-24 Discussion Paper Series. Une York: United Nations.

———. (2005). Global value chains and networks: opportunities or challenges. Global Networks: Interdisciplinary Perspectives on Commodity Chains. Yale University.

Lall, S. and S. Urata (2003). Competitiveness, FDI and Technological Activity in East Asia. Cheltenham, UK: Edward Elgar Publishing.

Landell-Mills, N. (1999). Country Profile for Brazil, IIED.

Laplane, M. and F. Sarti (2002). "O investimento direto estrangeiro e a internacionalização da economia brasileira nos anos 90." *Economia e Sociedade* **11**(1 (18)): 129–164.

Laplane, M., F. Sarti et al. (2001). El caso brasileño. In El boom de las inversiones extranjeras directas en el MERCOSUR. D. Chudnovsky (ed). Buenos Aires: Siglo XXI.

Leighton, M., N. Roht-Arriaza and L. Zarsky (2002). Beyond Good Deeds, Case Studies and a New Policy Agenda for Global Corporate Accountability. San Francisco: Natural Heritage Institute.

Leiton, P. (2007). Auge economico de Guanacaste no se refleja en los impuestos. *La Nacion*.

Lester, R. and M. Piore (2004). *Innovation. The missing dimension*. Cambridge: Harvard University Press.

López, A. and E. Orlicki (2005). Regional integration and foreign direct investment: the potential impact of the FTAA and the Eu-Mercosur agreement on FDI flows into Mercosur countries. XL Reunión Anual de la Asociación Argentina de Economía Política, La Plata.

Loza, G. (2002). Bolivia's commodity price shock. *CEPAL Review N° 76*. CEPAL.

Luthje, B. (2003). IT and the changing social division of labor: the case of electronics contract manufacturing. Institute of Social Research, University of Frankfurt, January.

Maia, J. L. and M. Kweitel (2003). Argentina: Sustainable output growth after the collapse. *Dirección Nacional de Políticas Macroeconómicas, Ministry of Economy and Production*. Buenos Aires.

Mann, H. (2001). Private rights, public problems: A guide to NAFTA's controversial chapter on investor rights, IISD/WWF.

Mann, H. (2005). The final decision in Methanex v. United States: Some new wine in Ssome new bottles, IISD.

Mazurek, J. (1999). Making Mmicrochips, policy, globalization and economic restructuring in the semiconductor industry. Cambridge: MIT Press.

McQueen, D., M. Grieg-Gran et al. (2004). Exportando sem crises: a indústria de madeira tropical brasileira e os mercados internacionais. London: International Institute for Environment and Development.

Mendoca, M. (2000). El ccomplejo forestal en Brasil, CEPAL.

Mendonça de Barros, J. and L. Goldenstein (1997). Avaliação do processo de reestruturação industrial brasileiro. *Revista de Economia Política* **17**(2).

Mercado, A. and A. Antunes (1998). Evolução histórica da indústria química brasileira. In A aprendizagem tecnológica no Brasil: a experiência da indústria química e petroquímica. A. Mercado and A. Antunes (eds). Rio de Janeiro: EQ/UFRJ: 33–47.

Mesquita Moreira, M. (1999). Estrangeiros em uma economia aberta: impactos recentes sobre produtividade, concentração e comércio exterior. A Economia Brasileira nos Anos 90. M. Moreira and F. E. M. Giambiagi (eds). Rio de Janeiro: BNDES.

Messner, D. and J. Meyer-Stamer (1994). Systemic competitiveness: Lessons from Latin America and beyond: Perspectives for eastern Europe. *The European Journal of Development Research* **6**(1): 89–107.

Meyer-Stamer, J. (2005). Systemic competitiveness reviseted. Conclusions for technical assistance in private sector development. Duisburg, Mesopartner.

Miranda, J. C. and L. Martins (2000). Fusões e aquisições de empresas no Brasil. *Economia e Sociedade*(14): 67–88.

Miyamoto, K. (2003). Human capital formation and foreign direct investment in developing countries, OECD Development Centre.

Monge Gonzalez, R., J. R. Tijerino et al. (2004). Analisis costo-beneficio del régimen de zonas francas. impactos de la inversión extranjera directa en Costa Rica, Report prepared for PROCOMER (Promotora de Comercio Exterior de Costa Rica).

Moran, T. H. (1998). Foreign Direct Investment and Development: The New Policy Agenda for Developing Countries and Economies in Transition. Washington DC: Institute for International Economics.

Moran, T. H., E. M. Graham et al. (2005). Does Foreign Direct Investment Promote Development? Washington DC: Institute for International Economics and Center for Global Development.

Mortimore, M. and S. Vergara (2003). Nuevas estrategias de empresas transnacionales. México en el contexto global. In Perspectivas y retos de la competitividad en México. E. D. Peters (ed). México City: UNAM and CANACINTRA: 91–133.

Murillo Romo, D. (2001). The sectoral impact of foreign direct investment in the Mexican industry: Spillovers and the development of technological capabilities. Woodrow Wilson School of Public and International Affairs.

Narula, R. and S. Lall (2006). Foreign direct investment and its role in economic development: Do we need a new agenda? In Understanding FDI-Assisted Economic Development. R. Narula and S. Lall (eds). New York: Routledge: 1–18.

Neumayer, E. and L. Spess (2005). Do bilateral investment treaties increase foreign direct investment to developing countries? World Development 33(10): pp. 1567–85.

Noorbakhsh, F., A. Paloni et al. (2001). Human capital and FDI inflows to developing countries: New empirical evidence. World Development 29(9).

Nunnenkamp, P. (2000). The changing pattern of foreign direct investment in Latin America. In The transformation of Latin America: Economic development in the early 1990s. F. Foders and M. Feldsieper (eds). Cheltenham: Edward Elgar Publishing.

Partida, R. (2006). Labor rights and occupational health in Jalisco's electronics industry. In challenging the chip: Labor rights and environmental justice in the global electronics industry. T. Smith, D. Sonnenfeld and D. Pellow (eds). Philadelphia: Temple University Press.

Paus, E. (2005). Foreign investment, development, and globalization. Can Costa Rica become Ireland? New York: Palgrave Macmillan.

Paus, E. and H. Shapiro (2007). Capturing the benefits from offshore outsourcing in developing countries: The case for active policies. In Global capitalism unbound: Winners and losers from offshore outsourcing. E. Paus (ed). New York: Palgrave Macmillana.

PDVSA (2005). 29 companies await to be granted 6 Venezuelan gas licences next September. PDVSA – Newsletter.

PEF (Poder Ejecutivo Federal) (2007). Plan Nacional de Desarrollo 2007–2012. México, PEF.

Perry, G. and L. Serven (2002). La Aanatomía de una crisis múltiple: ¿Qué tenía Argentina de especial y qué podemos aprender de ella? Desarrollo Económico 42(167): 323–375.

Peterson, L. E. (2003). Emerging bilateral investment treaty Arbitration and sustainable development. Winnipeg: International Institute for Sustainable Development.

Peterson, L. E. (2007). Bolivia notifies World Bank of withdrawal from ICSID, purgues BIT revisions. ITN.

Peterson, L. E. (2007). Ecuador announces that it wants out of US investment treaty. ITN.

Pohl, O. (2004). European environmental rules propel change in the US. New York Times.

PROFEPA (2003). Interview with authors. Guadalajara: October 29.

Programa Estado de la Nación (2006). XII Informe del Estado de la Nación en Desarrollo Humano Sostenible. San José: Programa Estado de la Nación.

Rainforest, A. (2000). News from the front: Banana eco-labeling program is world's largest. *The Canopy*. January/February.

Responsibility, B. f. S. (undated). Monitoring of global supply chain practices. Issue Brief.

Richards, M., C. Palmer et al. (2003). Higher international standards or rent-seeking race to the bottom? The impacts of forest product trade liberalization on forest governance, A Background paper for the Global Project: Impact Assessment of Forest Products Trade in Promotion of Sustainable Forest Management FAO.

Rivera Vargas, M. I. (2002). *Technology transfer via the university-industry relationship: The case of foreign high technology electronics industry in Mexico's Silicon Valley*. London: Routledge.

Riveros, F.-D., J. Vatter and M. R. Agosin. (1996). La inversión extranjera directa en Chile, 1987–93: aprovechamiento de ventajas comparativas y conversión de deuda: Inversión extranjera directa en América Latina: su contribución al desarrollo. Santiago: Fondo de Cultura Económica.

Rodriguez-Clare, A. (2001). Costa Rica's development strategy based on human capital and technology: how it got there, the impact of Intel, and lessons for other countries. *Human Development Report, 2001*, UNDP.

Rodríguez, H. M. (2004). Análisis de la balanza de pagos tecnológica Argentina. Buenos Aires: SECYT.

Rodrik, D. (2004). Industrial policy for the twenty-first-century. John F. Kennedy School of Government. Cambridge: Harvard University.

Rodrik, D. (2004). Rethinking growth policies in the developing world. Cambridge: Harvard University.

Rodrik, D. (2006). Goodbye Washington concensus and Hhallo Washington confusion? Cambridge: Harvard University.

Romer, P. (1993). Two strategies for economic development: using ideas and producing ideas. *Proceedings of the World Bank Conference on Development Economics, 1992*. Washington, DC: The World Bank.

Romero, L. A. (2002). A history of Argentina in the Ttwentieth Ccentury. University Park: Pennsylvania State University Press.

Rosenthal, E. (2002). Conflicts over transnational oil and gas development off Sakhalin Island in the Russian Far East: A David and Goliath tale. In Human Rights and the Environment, Conflicts and Norms in a Globalizing World. L. Zarsky (ed). London: Earthscan Press, 96–122.

Ruud, A. (2002). Environmental management of transnational corporations in India: Are TNCs creating islands of environmental excellence in a sea of dirt? *Business Strategy and the Environment* **11**(2): 103–118.

Saagi, K. (2002). Trade, foreign direct investment, and international technology transfer: A survey. Background paper for the World Bank's Microfoundations of International Technology Diffusion project. Department of Economics, Southern Methodist University.

Salacuse, J. W. and N. P. Sullivan (2005). Do BITs really work?: An evaluation of bilateral investment treaties and their grand Bargain. *Harvard International Law Journal* **46**(1).

Sánchez-Ancochea, D. (2004). Leading coalitions and patterns of accumulation and distribution in small countries. Diss. New School University.

Sánchez Albavera, F. (1997). Reformas petroleras: Las opciones en juego. *Revista de la CEPAL 62*, CEPAL.

Shaiken, H. (1990). Mexico in the global economy: High technology and work organization in export industries. San Diego: University of California.

Shang, S., Wen-ling Tu, Wen-chuan Yan and Li-fang Yang (2003). Environmental and social aspects of Taiwanese and US companies in the Hsinchu Science-Based Industrial Park. Report to California Global Corporate Accountability Project, Nautilus Institute.

Sjoeholm, F. (1999). Technology gap, competition and spillovers from direct foreign investment: Evidence from establishment data. *The Journal of Development Studies* **36**(1): 53–73.

Smarzynska, B. K. (2003). Does foreign direct investment increase the productivity of domestic firms? In search of spillovers through backward linkages. William Davidson Working Paper Number 548, University of Michigan Business School, March.

Sojo Garza-Aldape, E. (2005). De la alternancia al desarrollo. Políticas públicas del Gobierno del Cambio. México: FCE.

Solimano, A. (2003). Governance crisis and the Andean region: a political economy analysis. *Macroeconomía del Desarrollo Nº 23*, ECLAC – Economic Development Division.

Sornarajah, M. (2006). A law for need or a low for greed? Restoring the lost law in the international law of foreign investment. *International Environmental Agreements*, 6: 329–357.

Sourrouille, J. V., B. Kosacoff et al. (1985). Transnacionalización y Política Económica en la Argentina. Buenos Aires: CEAL/CET.

Spar, D. (1998). Attracting high technology investment. Intel's Costa Rica plant. Washington, DC: World Bank.

Stanley, L. E. (2004). Acuerdos bilaterales de inversión y demandas ante tribunales internacionales: la experiencia argentina reciente. *Serie Desarrollo Productivo Nº 158*. Santiago: Comisión Económica para América Latina y el Caribe (CEPAL).

Stiglitz, J. E. (2006) Who Own Bolivia? Project Syndicate **Volume**, DOI:

Sturgeon, T. J. (2002). Modular Production Networks: A New American Model of Industrial Organization. *Industrial and Corporate Change* **11**(3): 451–496.

———. (2006). The changing role of the Guadalajara (Jalisco state) Mexico electronics cluster in a modular global value chain.

———. (2006). Services Offshoring Working Group. Final Report. Boston: Industrial Performance Center/MIT.

Taylor, C. (2007) "Flextronics buys rival EMS player Solectron for $3.6B." *Electronic News* **Volume**, DOI:

TCPS. (2004). The generation and management of hazardous wastes and transboundary hazardous waste shipments between México, Canada and the United States since NAFTA: A 2004 Update. from <http://www.texascenter.org/publications/hazwaste04.pdf>.

Tewari, M. (2005). Foreign direct investment and the transformation of Tamil Nadu's automotive supply base. In *Local production systems and global Markets in emerging economies: Brazil, India, Mexico*. F. Yves- André, L. Kennedy and P. Labazée (eds). Paris: IRD/Karthala.

The Economist (2005). Chávez squeezes the oil firms: A forthright abuse of market power that could eventually backfire. *The Economist*.

The Economist (2006). The long goodbye: North Sea oil and gas.

The Economist (2007). Energy and Nationalism: Barking louder, biting less.

The Economist (2007). With Marx, Lenin and Jesus Christ.

Tobin, J. and S. Rose-Ackerman (2004). Foreign Direct Investment and the Business Environment In Developing Countries: The Impact of Bi-lateral Investment Treaties. Yale Center for Law, Economics, and Policy.

Togeiro de Almeida, L. (2001). Harmonização Internacional das Regulações Ambientais. Campinas, Brasil: Instituto de Economia da Universidade Estadual de Campinas.

Trejos, J. D. (2004). Desigualdad y Reforma Fiscal. *La Nación*: 30A.

Tuman, J. P. and C. F. Emmert (2004). The Political Economy of US Foreign Direct Investment in Latin America: A Reappraisal. *Latin American Research Review* 39(3): 9–28.

UNCTAD (1998). Bilateral Investment Treaties in the Mid-1990s. Geneva, UNCTAD.

UNCTAD (1999). Trends in International Investment Agreements: An Overview. *UNCTAD Series on issues in international investment agreements*. New York: United Nations Commission on Trade and Development.

UNCTAD (2002). World Investment Report 2002. New York: United Nations Commission on Trade and Development.

UNCTAD (2004). Making FDI work for sustainable development. Nova York: United Nations Commission on Trade and Development.

UNCTAD (2005). World Investment Report 2005, United Nations Commission on Trade and Development.

UNCTAD (2006). World Investment Report 2006. Ginebra: United Nations Commission on Trade and Development.

UNDP (2001). *Human Development Report*. Oxford: Oxford University Press.

UNDP (2004). Human Development Report. New York: United Nations.

UNDP (2005). Comparative Study on the Distribution of Oil Rents in Bolivia, Colombia, Ecuador and Peru. UNDP/WB Energy Sector Management Assistance Programme (ESMAP).

UNEP (2006). Revised edited draft guidelines on best available techniques and guidance on best environmental practices relevant to Article 5 and Annex C of the Stockholm Convention on Persistent Organic Pollutants. Expert Group on Best Available Techniques and Best Environmental Practices, UNEP.

UNIDO (2002). Industrial Development Report 2002/2003, Competition through Innovation and Learning. Vienna: United Nations Industrial Development Organization.

UNIDO (2005). Monitor de la Manufactura Mexicana. *Monitor de la Manufactura Mexicana*. Mexico City: United Nations Industrial Development Organization. 1.

UNSAM (2006). Acta del Foro Académico sobre Industrialización en Países en Desarrollo y Conservación del Ambiente, 1° encuentro: El caso de las instalación de las plantas de celulosa en la margen izquierda del Río Uruguay. Transcript from the First Meeting of the Academic Forum on Industrialization in Developing Countries and Environmental Protection, Universidad Nacional de San Martín-Escuela de Posgrado (Provincia de Buenos Aires, Argentina).

Valenzuela, A. (2006). The United States and Latin America: Security and Energy. US Policy in Latin America – Seventh Conference. Aspen Institute.

Valor Econômico (2007). Indústria de Celulose e Papel. *Valor Econômico*.

Vargas, A. and F. Sánchez-Albavera (2005). La volatilidad de los precios del petróleo y su impacto en América Latina. *Recursos Naturales e Infraestructura*, No 100, CEPAL.

Vázquez Barquero, A. (2005). Las nuevas fuerzas del desarrollo. Madrid.

Viana, G. (1998). Relatorio Da Comissao: Externa Da Camara Dos Deputados Destinada a Averiguar a Aquisicao de Madeireiras, Serrarias e Extensas Porcoes de Terras Brasileiras por Grupos Asiáticos.

Villasuso, J. M. (2007). Una crónica de apagones anunciados. *Tribuna Democrática*.

Vis-Dunbar, D. (2006). Venezuela signs contentious new contracts with foreign oil companies. *ITN*.

Von Moltke, K. and H. Mann (2004). Towards A Southern Agenda on International Investment: Discussion Paper on the Role of International Investment Agreements. IISD.

Wade, R. (1990). Governing the market: Economic theory and the role of government in East Asian industrialization. Princeton: Princeton University Press.

Williamson, J. (1990). What Washington Means by Policy Reform. In How Much Has Happened? J. Williamson (ed). Washington, DC: Institute for International Economics.

Wilson, P. (1992). Exports and Local Development: Mexico's New Maquiladoras. Austin: University of Texas Press.

Wong, P. K. (2003). From using to creating technology: The evolution of Singapore's national innovation system and the changing role of public policy. In Competitiveness, FDI and Technological Activity in East Asia. S. Lall and S. Urata (eds). Cheltenham: Edward Elgar Publishing: 191–238.

World Bank World Development Indicators.

World Bank (1998). Mexico: The Guadalajara Environmental Management Pilot. Washington, World Bank.

World Bank (2008). World Development Indicators.

Yoguel, G. (1998). El ajuste empresarial frente a la apertura: La heterogeneidad de las respuestas de las PyMEs. *Desarrollo Económico* **38**: 177–198.

Yoguel, G. and R. Rabetino (2002). Algunas Consideraciones Generales sobre la Incorporación de Tecnología en la Industria Manufacturera Argentina. In Apertura e innovación en la Argentina. R. Bisang, G. Lugones and G. Yoguel (eds). Buenos Aires: Editorial Miño y Dávila.

Zarsky, L. (1999). Havens, halos and spaghetti: untangling the evidence about foreign direct investment and the environment. OECD, Conference on Foreign Direct Investment and the Environment. The Hague: Netherlands.

INDEX

Printed in the United States
140531LV00004B/3/P